I0441052

OH SAY,
CAN'T YOU SEE ...

OH SAY, CAN'T YOU SEE ...

How America Got Sidetracked

Joseph Sterling

iUniverse, Inc.
New York Bloomington Shanghai

Oh Say, Can't You See …

How America Got Sidetracked

Copyright © 2008 by PDS Consulting LLC

All rights reserved. No part of this book may be used or reproduced by any means, graphic, electronic, or mechanical, including photocopying, recording, taping or by any information storage retrieval system without the written permission of the publisher except in the case of brief quotations embodied in critical articles and reviews.

iUniverse books may be ordered through booksellers or by contacting:

iUniverse
1663 Liberty Drive
Bloomington, IN 47403
www.iuniverse.com
1-800-Authors (1-800-288-4677)

Because of the dynamic nature of the Internet, any Web addresses or links contained in this book may have changed since publication and may no longer be valid.

The views expressed in this work are solely those of the author and do not necessarily reflect the views of the publisher, and the publisher hereby disclaims any responsibility for them.

ISBN: 978-0-595-52110-4 (pbk)
ISBN: 978-0-595-62174-3 (ebk)

Printed in the United States of America

C ONTENTS

SECTION IV: JUSTICE

Foreword

America is a great country. America's independence was an example for other countries to shed the burden of the feudal system and classes of society. America gave every opportunity to every person willing to work hard and smart. The world's first middle class has its roots in America. America proved that countries with a strong middle class would flourish. America is the most powerful country in the world, economically and militarily. Every other country in the world envies the strongest, and will do everything in their power to replace the strong one. In business many of the strongest companies in their field learned the hard way that there are no guarantees about being the strongest. They learned that it is one thing to become #1 but that it is a whole different story to stay #1. The successful ones constantly re-invent themselves; they cut cost, develop new products with a frantic pace, learn everything about competitors and have superb visions and strategies to stay in their #1 position. Many companies failed to do that and went into obliteration. The state of Rome failed to do that and went into obliteration. They forgot to sacrifice as they indulged in consumerism and slowly decayed until barbarians ran them over.

How do we stack up today? How does America view the world and itself? Are we acting responsibly to secure America's leadership position for our children? We voted for George W. Bush, not once but twice. China is running so fast economically and America is running so slow comparatively, experts predict that China will become the world's most powerful country in the next decades.

America's powerful CEOs and Wall Street enjoy obscene incomes. America's workers have not seen a rise in real income (income adjusted for inflation) for thirty years while they lost job security and pension plans. America's system of justice that began sublimely in the days of our founders has become a joke. Politicians have never before been so polarized in partisan ideology rather than in the spirit of cooperation needed to move America forward. What's wrong with us, America? Most Americans know that something is very wrong; they just don't know what caused it, and therefore don't know how to fix it. We want change; that much is clear but change to what?

This book is about changes and attitudes that have sidetracked America from its path towards a continued future of greatness. Are changes in attitudes to blame for the decay that has already set in? In your author's view, America's decay is a direct result of negative changes in American attitudes that occurred in a short time span of some thirty years, in particular attitudes in certain groups of Americans.

Attitudes change over time, some are good, some are irrelevant to the dynamics of a society and other attitude changes could be devastating to the environment or country. Think about how attitudes changed in the way in which we communicate. In a short ten years, technology has transformed life. The Internet was largely responsible. Was the Internet relevant, irrelevant, positive or negative to the dynamics of our society? Even simple long-standing traditions in life have changed. The tradition of Christmas greetings with fancy "Hallmark" cards is largely replaced by on-line cards or mass emails. At first most people considered this novelty rude and called it bad attitudes, too lazy to write personalized cards. But just a few years later, the under-forty crowd adopted it while even some older ones that keep up with the times got used to it. Our attitudes changed and in this case, it probably did little to change the dynamics.

Today, we know instantly what happened thousands of miles away. In the days of our Founders it would take weeks or months before news reached our leaders, let alone spread throughout the country. Back then nobody knew, let alone cared what happened in Africa or Asia; even thirty-five years ago few did. Because of technology, our attitude towards the world changed in far-reaching ways. President Bush changed America's cautious foreign policy into actively spreading democracy because the revolution in communications technology opened our eyes. A mere ten years ago the Internet was just a toy, and certainly didn't affect our daily lives. Twenty years ago, there were no fax machines or fiber optic cables on the ocean floors. There were no commercial satellites. Thirty years ago we couldn't make direct international phone calls to Europe; we had to go through the international operator first. Rarely would we make international calls. Thirty-five years ago, most news agencies relied on antiquated telex machines with Morse code. Today we use the Internet for international calls, but also for up to date news. Manned with Blackberries we are on top of the world every conscious hour of the day. Changes in technology changed attitudes in a mostly positive way. Globalization was made possible by rapid changes in technology. Globalization changed a lot of attitudes in America and the rest of the world, mostly for the better but not everywhere.

Over the last thirty-five years many good changes happened. In the seventies, a Republican President stopped a senseless war in Vietnam. Violent crime of the seventies and eighties were reduced, especially in the nineties. In the eighties, the Federal Reserve corrected the out-of-control inflation that roared in the seventies. Recent changes showed a significant decline in the number of abortions. The overall wealth of our nation increased. Racism largely disappeared when compared to the level of racism that still existed in the nineteen sixties and seventies. Back then it would have been unthinkable for a black person to run for President without being dismissed as a joke. Many things improved and perhaps a book should be written about that. But this book is about the changes in attitude that began to sidetrack America from its path of greatness. Collectively these negative attitudes have become a serious danger to our American society. They are serious enough to write this book about.

If an individual pursues his fortune legally, though with total disregard for others, well, that could be a bad moral attitude, yet it is pretty much accepted as an American birthright. Attacking that attitude seems to violate the promise of American society to pursue one's individual prosperity and happiness (with or without regard to others). But as a society, should we accept attitudes of powerful groups of Americans that pursue their fortune with total disregard for others? What if their collective actions would tear down the fabric of our society? Should society act?

What if we learn that the nation's wealthiest groups, making in excess of $2 million a year, are only paying 17.5% federal income taxes, per dollar of income, compared to up to 35% payroll taxes that are paid by the middle class? When FICA taxes are included the middle class pays well over 40% in taxes while FICA taxes barely influence the tax rate of the wealthiest group of American. This was a result of an attitude change in American government towards a "fair" tax system. Or what would we think about the hypocrisy of government pretending to care about our dysfunctional school system, while campaigning at the same time for tax cuts that took funds away from education to mainly benefit the rich? After all, we lack the public money to pay teachers a decent salary, let alone to attract good teaching talent.

Thirty-five years ago, all income groups used to participate in the increasing wealth of our society. No longer! Since then, chief executive officers, as a group, have increased take-home pay ten-fold while over the same period real income for the average worker has been stagnant. This attitude change among business leaders drove a nail into the coffin of an unwritten fairness principle that prevailed in our country even a mere twenty years ago. Other attitudes toward a conservative lifestyle changed from prudent savings to excessive consumerism. The rich still save but the average middle class worker who needs to save for retirement is now in debt; their submission to consumerism overpowers the sense of personal responsibility.

Over the last twenty years, certain groups changed the political climate with truly negative attitudes. Thirty years ago, political compromise used to be smart business but today powerful groups consider compromise unprincipled and spineless. What used to be stubbornness is now called principled and strong character. As a result, the country is more polarized than ever. Afraid to upset pundits on talk shows; political leaders are no longer capable of uniting the country. As a result Congress is now a paralyzed institution, not capable of leading America towards continued prosperity. Supporters of either main political party have been ideologically brainwashed by talk shows and special interest groups that use technological advancements in mass media and communications to influence the public. Issues of national interest are demonized. National health insurance (NHI) was branded as socialized or un-American without giving the subject even a chance for serious discussion. Yet, under the current system, the health insurance of many Americans was canceled when they needed healthcare the most. NHI would provide better health care at less cost but most Americans are brainwashed into believing NHI would somehow be bad.

Most Americans sense that "things" in America are seriously wrong. Everybody wants change. But what change? Electing a new person in the White House and Congress is a change but is that enough change? We need to know what to change first before we vote. The true causes of the negative changes in attitudes are quite complex. Therefore, we need to peel off the onion before we attempt to apply fixes. For some people who don't like to peel onions, they believer to have the answers but more than likely they are wrong.

AFL-CIO; chambers of commerce; hunters; fishermen; old conservatives; neo-conservatives; environmentalists; "Wall Street"; liberals. No matter what specific interest groups and disagreements existed a mere thirty years ago; they had one thing in common, they appreciated one another as true Americans. Except for that brief time of McCarthyism in the fifties, these interest groups would not commonly accuse other groups of being unpatriotic, misguided perhaps, but not unpatriotic. That has changed. Currently, the thread that bound us as Americans is unraveled as talk show hosts and politicians treat Americans from opposing parties as the enemy of America, more so than America's real enemies. Ever listened to Rush Limbaugh? Or read a bestselling book by Ann Coulter? Or watched Real Time with Bill Maher? Then you know. (Note: When this book uses the term Rush Limbaugh, it does not mean the man by that name but the group of conservative talk-show hosts that espouse similar results.)

We are a polarized nation. Some predict that America could burst into anarchy. Alan Greenspan, the retired chairman of the Federal Reserve, described a possible "large-scale violence" caused by just one of the group-attitude changes that are discussed in this book, namely the disparity in income between wealthy groups and the middle and lower classes. Large-scale violence? Anarchy in America? Unthinkable, yet possible! Should we wait to find out? Or is it time now for Americans to act and demand specific changes from our elected politicians that will restore the glory of America?

As an immigrant, my personal experience in my new country, America, spans only 35 years, and therefore, my personal observations are restricted to that period. But this period was very relevant to what has changed in America. Some ten years ago I retired as CEO of a public hi-tech company. I was born in Holland where I grew up and started my career. In 1973, at a young age-career wise-I was offered an interesting job. The catch.... my family and I had to move to the United States. The Dutch attitude towards America was very positive and no doubt got a big boost in 1945 when Americans (and Canadians) liberated Holland from Nazi Germany. My feeling towards America was typical of most Dutch, very positive; yet, I had no particular desire to leave Holland. Why leave country, home, parents, family, friends and culture for a job? Bottom-line: I said yes anyway ... and never turned back. Upon my arrival here I discovered something refreshing about America that no one could have told me without experiencing it. Americans had a remarkable "can-do" spirit, an uplifting feel of excitement with a more daring attitude. While individualism in America was more apparent, people still cared a lot about others, even in companies from management on down.

I also liked the fewer regulations in business, compared to Europe. Being a follower of Adam Smith, the father of market capitalism, I appreciated the American philosophy. In Europe, the government had too many fingers in the business pot that tempered the fun. Further, in Europe, a manager had to be addressed as sir (though that has changed today), and socially they were unapproachable. In the U.S., my manager invited me over to his house and we played baseball in the park. Pretty quickly I began to like living in America. Of course, the general American culture took a bit longer to getting used to. But now, America has become my true "home" and I don't want to see it decay any further. My frequent travel for business and in retirement for pleasure to Europe, Japan, and even China gave me the opportunity to further maintain a unique perspective of the world, much broader than most people have a chance to experience. After all, I had spent the first half of my life in Europe in different cultures which gave me the perspective that Americans who grew up here can never attain; that of "looking into America from the outside". This gave me a slight edge to undertake the task of this book.

In general, scholars and pundits who specialize in their field of study write books. Accordingly, these or other experts have written many books about each of the main subjects covered in this book, in depth. To my knowledge, however, there are not enough books that look at the overriding big picture that puts together various disciplines of study as they affect one another. As we will see, many attitude changes do affect different disciplines but who would dare to write a book that covers many different disciplines? Add some world events to it, and things can get really complex.

The reason few would attempt to write big-picture books is simple. No individual could be a scholar or otherwise an expert in all of these subjects. Therefore, if no one is an expert, who is going to feel comfortable, writing about it? Who would read a book that is not written by a recognized expert? Yet, as we know from business, the leader best equipped to lead businesses and make the right observations and decisions are those who see the big picture. Big-picture-leaders, called generalists, know something about everything but not enough about anything to be an expert (except on leadership and perhaps the discipline that started their career). Not knowing enough about specific details of a discipline makes them easy target for experts to rip them apart. Big picture is my expertise. I can see how America is being sidetracked and what causes it. I believe I know enough about each of the various disciplines in this book to touch the surface barely enough to uncover the essence of what needs to be conveyed.

Economy books have alluded to political influences. Political books discuss the state of the economy, or judicial issues. But when books discuss the need to be energy independent, do they address that technology companies (who could contribute to energy independence) often spent less on R&D than on tort lawsuits? When President George W. Bush addressed his foreign policy to bring democracy to the Middle East, did he discuss that this is mere idle talk until we first become energy independent? In other words, to satisfy our needs for oil, we have no choice but to defend the dictators in the Middle East or protect their oil-fields ourselves. When we combat terrorism do we discuss that Islamic fascists will not cease their recruitment of potential terrorists until we stop supporting Islamic dictators or bring home our troops from Islamic land? When we discuss the need to alleviate world poverty, do we address that our push for ethanol from corn contributed to the 2007 doubling of world food prices, starving those we intended to help? Everything is intertwined. Addressing the right solutions is not possible until we study and unlock the interlocking elements.

The purpose of this book is three-fold: To discuss the current trends in economics, politics and justice, compared with history. To expose how changes in group attitudes have negatively affected those disciplines. And to propose solutions that would bring America back on the right track.

In no way does this book attempt to be critical of America. Its only ambition is to save America from taking a wrong path to misery. Anyone, who loves this country and sees self-interests pursuing their agenda while destroying America's greatness, must speak up. I chose to speak up.

SECTION I:
ATTITUDES

In this section we look at some of the changes in the last 35 years that are of great concern. These attitudes are observed in the fields of economics, politics, and justice.

CHAPTER 1

▼

THE ECONOMY

According to the Society of Government Economists, growth in income between 1947 and 1973 was relatively uniformly distributed throughout the classes of ranks of all employees including CEOs. Family income growth during this period almost doubled. CEOs on average earned 40 to 50 times the average factory worker.

In contrast, according to a recent report of the Plebian Policy Study Group, in the last thirty years, family income for the bottom 40% of families remained essentially flat (as adjusted for inflation). Yet, CEOs pay increased to an average of $9.3 Million, which took the ratio of CEO pay to the average worker totally out of proportion. What is so disturbing, the report cited, is that historically, workers saw a strong surge in wage growth during an economic recovery. As Corporations reported record earnings in the last years and, as CEO incomes went through the roof, workers hardly saw any growth in their wages (after adjustment for inflation). A report in "Who rules America" by Professor Domhoff at the University of California showed the ratios of CEO pay compared to factory workers:

> The ratio of CEO pay to factory worker rose to 531:1 in 2000 when CEOs cashed in on big stock options. This ratio was 411:1 in 2005 (when stock-option gains were lower). By way of comparison, the same rate in Europe is 25:1.

The bewildering difference between European and American pay ratios beg the question: Are American CEOs today so much smarter than their counterparts in Europe or are workers in Europe so much smarter than in America? Likely not. The only correct answer is that American CEO pay-packages have lost any sense of proportion, decency and social responsibility.

Under Republican President Eisenhower in the 1950s, the rich paid a 91% marginal federal income tax. Democratic President Kennedy reduced these marginal rates to 70% that stayed in effect until the early nineteen eighties. These high marginal rates are not to be confused with the effective tax rate that individuals pay (due to tax progression, deductions and loopholes). For example, during Eisenhower's midterm in 1957, the super rich, those who made over $5.3 Million in 2007 dollars, paid 51.6% federal income taxes on their total income. When taking a snapshot of this in 2007, the change is drastic, beyond belief. According to Pulitzer Price-winning tax analyst David Cay Johnston, the nation's wealthiest households are now paying in federal income taxes a mere 17.5% after exploiting all loopholes. Middle class family incomes are easily charged 35% or more in Federal and Social Security taxes.

Not surprisingly, Edward Wolff, professor of economics at New York University, reported that the income gap and wealth gap between the rich and poor have increased significantly in America. This is extraordinary because in developed countries as wealth increases, the income and wealth gap would normally narrow; on the other hand in less developed countries, the income gap and wealth gap are comparatively wide. The widening income and wealth gap in the U.S. is getting close to those of less developed countries. Something has gone very wrong in the United States of America.

USA TODAY reported on 8/30/2007 that the top 30 hedge fund and private equity fund managers made on average, in 2006, the nice sum of $657.5 million dollars each, yes, each, per person. According to the Institute for Policy Studies this is 22,255 times the average pay of U.S. workers. (If the average worker earned $15/hour, these fund managers earned $334,000/hour.) Adding insult to injury, these top twenty managers are paying fewer taxes for each dollar of income than most American workers do. Because their income of fees is under a loophole of capital gains, they pay for their income of work 15% capital gain taxes while normal income from work, especially the middle class, is taxed up to 35% and more when including social security taxes.

The numbers describe vividly the degree of astonishing change in our country, exhibited by a growing apathy toward fairness by the powers in the economic and political arena. This process began to take root in the nineteen eighties.

When I immigrated in 1973, my European friends and business advisors warned me about the American Culture. It was, they said, dominated by a harsh individualistic materialism over family, friendship and kindness. To my pleasant surprise, I found that it wasn't that simple. The individualistic materialism was there all right but it had a refreshing depth. Most people worked hard, had little fear and enjoyed the outdoors, playing hard. Americans had a sense of responsibility. They saved for their retirement. Debts were relatively low. Lawsuits were uncommon. Besides the usual grumbles, people were by and large happy. People didn't stick their noses into other people's lives; at least not to the degree they did in Europe. When asked they offered help but left you otherwise alone. Americans were individualistic, yet united. And they were proud to be American. My European friends were wrong, at least back then.

As I became integrated in American life in the seventies, I found that all income groups participated in the increasing wealth of America, not necessarily proportionally mind you-but sharing nonetheless. It wasn't just that unions demanded real wage raises. Even in non-union shops, labor received real wage increases because management backed those from a conviction of social responsibility. It wasn't just market demand. In my personal experiences with upper management; they seemed to adhere to an unwritten fairness that dictated a social responsibility. Most large companies provided workers with the comfort of a pension that allowed members of labor the security of retiring in a dignified manner. Perhaps this unwritten social responsibility was an outgrowth of Andrew Carnegie's The Gospel of Wealth in which he declared that the rich have a moral obligation to the less fortunate. Or, perhaps it was an outgrowth of President Franklin Roosevelt's Social Security Act of 1935 that provided the elderly a modest amount for retirement; before 1935 the elderly were dependent on their children. In any event, social responsibility was alive and well among most Americans in all circles of society, in the nineteen seventies.

While a fabric of social responsibility existed, this doesn't mean that everything in the seventies was great. The Vietnam War debacle stirred many emotions with pro- and anti-war protesters. A near hyperinflation began under President Nixon, escalating under President Carter. Violent crime was high. America began to feel the threat of Japan's rising economic power, while Iran kept over fifty Americans hostage.

America was ready for a more confident and optimistic President. Ronald Reagan proved to be that President. On the day of his inauguration on January 20, 1981, Iran released the hostages. Reagan slashed the marginal tax rates in half and placed emphasis on deregulating the markets. With the emergence of the microprocessor, technology companies sprouted everywhere. All together, America roared back in confidence and economic power. Yet, along with this new adrenaline, many devastating attitudes began to develop, as explained in Section 2 of this book, and that eventually destroyed social responsibility and fairness for the lives of most Americans.

Was it a mistake for Reagan to slash the marginal tax rates as deeply as he did? Would a slashing from 70% to a 50% marginal tax rate have been as effective without the many negative side effects that developed? Far right Conservatives have long argued that low tax rates for the rich stimulate the economy while high tax rates on the rich reduce the personal incentive to invest in capital that is needed for economic growth. They back their argument up with selective statistics although they never show statistics that prove the opposite. Despite the very high marginal rates on the rich (over 90% in the nineteen forties and nineteen fifties, and 70% since the nineteen sixties through the nineteen seventies), America thrived. American companies brought America unbelievable prosperity. Yet, our income gap between the rich and the poor was quite acceptable and in line with comparable developed countries. The high marginal tax rates did not temper the interests of America's business leaders to lead major companies that ruled their field in the world, and collectively made America the richest country on earth. Statistics are numbers, and numbers don't lie. However, certain interpretations do. The fact is that America's prosperity outgrew the world in periods with both low as well as high marginal tax rates. With low marginal rates, we saw strong economic growth in the 1920s as well as in the 1990s though neither period was known for generous employee benefits. With very high marginal tax rates we saw unbelievable economic progress between the 1940s and 1970s-along with generous employee benefits. It was in this period that America truly began to dominate the world economically and militarily. However, with the low marginal tax rates today, the prospect for America's economic growth in 2008 and 2009 is at best mediocre. These conclusions make the statistical interpretations from the ideological conservative wing (that high marginal taxes are bad for America) a complete myth. Perhaps the right theory is to correct an out-of-balance situation when we see it, and we are seeing it today.

We are making the observation, further substantiated in section 2, that there is an apparent correlation between taxes and social responsibility. Charge the rich high marginal taxes and they resign themselves to being a major contributor to the country's well-being. That contribution to our well being fostered a sense of social responsibility, and as a result the top economic leaders consciously kept increases of their pay package in line with their workers. Charge the rich extraordinarily low tax rates and their awareness of being a major contributor to the nation's well-being fades and along with that their consciousness and sense of social responsibility. That fading opened the gates for excessive greed, removed all constraints of responsibility, and made them indifferent to their workers.

Marginal tax rates are a significant regulator to the factor of fairness in American's system of market capitalism. The proof is in the numbers.

> *When the government charges the rich too low of a tax rate, it destroys the fabric of social responsibility towards those who helped them build their wealth.*

A similar conclusion pointing to a loss of social responsibility can be derived from the observation by AmericanProgress.org; citing the General Accounting Office, that "an astonishing 94% of corporations reported tax liability of less than 5% of their total income during the same time period [2003]." They charged that the policies of the Bush Administration have exacerbated the problem by furthering the culture of tax avoidance by big corporations. Once the sense of social responsibility disappeared, CEOs lost their obligation to America to have their corporation pay their fair share in taxes. Yet, candidates for President are tripping over themselves to further reduce corporate tax rates.

Labor lost its position as a valuable partner in the economic process, reducing its position to not much more than a disposable tool. When tools are discarded, there is no need to take care of them. The same goes true for labor today. Thirty years ago it was common for workers to work a lifetime for one employer, enjoying job security, health plans and a pension to retire comfortably. Labor today can get discarded easily without pension or health plans. Today labor is frustrated and angry. It sees the tremendous wealth build-up by their CEOs but also by many youngsters who made it big in financial derivatives or dot coms. While the standard of living of most Americans declined per hour worked, the sight of all that luxurious spending displayed by the more fortunate Americans and as advertised everywhere, turned Americans from a saving nation into a nation of consumerism. It seemed that the widening of income and wealth gap should have had the opposite effect. The phenomenon of consumerism has put most Americans' up to their necks in debt. Their future can only become bleaker.

The dynamics of the widening gap in income inequality caught the attention of Maestro Alan Greenspan. The former Chairman of the Federal Reserve wrote in The Age of Turbulence,

> "… unless … we begin to reverse a quarter century of increases in income inequality, the cultural ties that bind our society could become undone. Dis-

affection, breakdowns of authority, even large-scale violence could ensue, jeopardizing the civility on which growing economies depend."

Does it really make sense that Jessica Zimmermann, Secret Service Officer who helps keep America safe, makes $48,400 a year, while John Paulson, hedge fund manager, makes $3.5 billion (and gets to keep most of that)? (Source: Parade of the Los Angeles Times). How long before Americans will no longer accept the out-of-control pay packages on the top? God forbid that we would have to face large-scale violence in America. It is not too late to avoid that but it will take the collective efforts of middle class Americans to prevent a catastrophe.

In summary, the slashing of tax rates on the rich have contributed to significant attitude changes by the top leaders of America's economic powers. It removed their sense of social responsibility and fairness; both were essential complements to the American system of capitalism in order for market capitalism to benefit the nation as a whole.

▼

POLITICS

Americans have lost confidence. According to the third annual Center for Public Leadership/U.S. News poll, conducted in the fall of 2007, nearly 80% of America feels that the country will decline while 51% believes that we are already falling behind other nations. About two thirds say that today's leaders pale in comparison with those twenty years ago.

Americans feel intuitively that something is very wrong with America today. They feel it in their paycheck. They see it in their political leaders. When leaders pale in comparison with twenty years ago, we could easily substitute that for fifty or sixty years ago when strong leaders with charisma, such as Franklin Roosevelt and John Kennedy, called on the nation to sacrifice for a higher purpose, the well-being of America. Today, few politicians have the courage to call for tough decisions to move America forward, because the tough decisions might involve sacrifice, or, god-forbid, compromise. Most politicians do not call for sacrifice, believing that would kill their bid for election.

One of our greatest founders, the second President of the United States, John Adams, mused about history in his writings. He wrote that when nations

"have reached the summit of grandeur, some minute and unexpected cause commonly affects their ruin, and the empire of the world is transferred to some other place" (from John Adams by David McCullough)

Many seemingly minute and unexpected causes are aggregating towards America's path to ruin. They are prohibiting progress in America. Other countries have never before worked so furiously to unseat us while using an American-type system of market capitalism. We on the other hand are paralyzed facing a deep abyss called political polarization that has excluded compromise from our vocabulary.

America's founders had disagreements too. But in the end they worked things out for the common cause of liberty, equality and the pursuit of happiness. They compromised and used common sense. As humans, we all think differently. Therefore, nothing will ever be achieved unless we compromise. In today's politics, it seems as if compromise has become a dirty word. Common sense is lost in harsh ideology and partisanship. The latter is particularly obvious in the subject of taxes. Nobody likes to pay taxes; even liberals don't like taxes. But if our elected representatives approve government spending, and particularly Republicans approved plenty of them during the terms of the Bush Administration, then taxes need to be raised to pay for them. Yet, the Republican Party's anti-tax sentiment isolates the word taxes as if taxes are the villain. Taxes are not, spending is. Republicans fought hard for huge tax cuts, and they got it, while at the same time increasing federal spending. To spend more with reduced income just doesn't cut it in common sense. Republicans point at President Reagan as their inspiration but they forget that Mr. Reagan still had common sense that is void today from the Republican Party. As Bill Stahl, a contributing editor to the Los Angeles Times, pointed out: "Ronald Reagan, as Governor of California, was responsible for the largest tax hike in state history (adjusted for inflation), approving a one billion dollar hike on a six billion dollar budget. And it made California healthier.

The disappearance of compromise, sacrifice and common sense in politics as well as the disappearance of social responsibility and fairness are collectively Adam's "minute and unexpected causes" that will affect "our ruin".

America demonstrated great sacrifice during World War II. In his seven episodes rich documentary The War, Ken Burns told us the story about our fathers and grandfathers who fought in World War II, demonstrating the richness of shared sacrifice of our entire nation and the cohesiveness that it created in this great country. In Burn's own words this shared sacrifice created community and made us spiritually richer, which we are so lacking today. We aren't asked to give up anything anymore. We are narcissistic free agents.

Lynn Cheney, the wife of America's Vice President, wrote with nostalgia in her new book Blue Skies, No Fences: a Memoir of Childhood and Family. She recalled the 1950s as an era of innocence. America had triumphed in World War

II, and people walked with heads high with confidence in their country and in themselves. Cynicism wasn't part of our world, she revealed in an interview with Ronald Kessler in Newsmax, a conservative magazine in print and on the web. Today, cynicism runs high as demonstrated by the poll of the Center for Public Leadership/U.S. News. No wonder when we peel the onion and see the changed attitudes since Cheney's youth in our economic and political leaders.

In World War II, President Franklin Roosevelt united America, a result of his considerable leadership talents and charisma. He demanded sacrifice from everybody in the nation, not just from the troops he sent to war in Europe and Asia to fight with their lives. He didn't allow those who stayed behind at home to squander in luxury. Franklin Roosevelt made it a war for every American; the richer you were, the more you paid; everybody sacrificed to his ability. As a result, the country felt united. If a war is essential, everyone in the nation that isn't serving in the military should shoulder the cost. Besides paying for the war, it demonstrates and proves solidarity with our young men and women on the front lines. This philosophy goes well beyond the idle words from conservative talk shows that we hear today.

For a brief moment in the after-math of 9/11, most American people were united. That's where the comparison with World War II ends. What was the difference? Charismatic strong leadership with a conscience! Without that kind of leadership the country drifted apart, seeing so many more things going wrong than right. Those in favor of the Iraq war could be considered hypocrites, though many don't even realize it. They seem to be unaware how cheap it is to be in favor of a war while unwilling to partake in sacrifice. Wars are by nature not budgeted, and consequently, unless a war is of short duration, only by increasing taxes can war costs be paid. Tax increases are not liked but wars shouldn't be liked any better.

Yet, Mr. Bush and the Republican Congress decided that the war spending should be borrowed, apparently to be paid back by our children sometime in the future. Was their reason born out of fear that Americans would otherwise not approve of the war? To make matters worse, the President urged Congress to reduce taxes instead. It would sound incredulous when this story is re-told to our grandkids. Even if some tax cuts across the board could have been desirable in a weak economy, the Bush tax cuts went far beyond modest. The tax cuts were huge and favored mostly the rich, which wouldn't do much to jumpstart a weak economy. Pulitzer Price-winning tax analyst David Cay Johnston calculated that the tax cuts for the rich reduced their effective federal income tax rate to just 17.5%. While this further contributed to the abandonment of national social responsibility, the psychology of tax cuts while waging war is almost psychopathic and as immoral as borrowing the cost of the war on the backs of our children. If our soldiers aren't killed, they and others in their generation may have to cough up the money in the future to pay for this war and deficits caused by tax cuts for the rich. This is the warped sense of "fairness" among our so-called highly "moral" political conservative leadership today.

For Americans who still have a conscience, cutting taxes on the rich in wartime is borderline obscene. It contributed to the loss of respect for the Presidency. It was just another step on the path of cynicism that Lynn Cheney described as a phenomenon of our times. How did this all get started? How did our nation's political leaders lose their conscience to provide for the well being of all Americans?

Did they feel encouraged and emboldened by the deception, lies, innuendos, and character assassinations that have been flying around daily since the nineteen nineties? It sure poisoned the political atmosphere. While Democrats aren't angels either, conservative talk show hosts and other conservative politicians have continually trashed Democrats. For example, they allege that democrats will raise your taxes, as if taxes are something terrible that Democrats invented, instead of what it really is, *the consequence of federal spending*. This is one of the greater deceptive marketing stunts of modern times. While fiscally unconscionable, it is moral hypocrisy to bad mouth democrats for trying to balance the budget. Cut spending first, then cut taxes.

Likewise Democrats are now blaming globalization and in particular NAFTA for the job losses in our nation. They know better. These aren't the problems; they are just conduits for the indifference at the top of the economic ladder while our politicians lack the willpower to work together. The nation has become too polarized. Compromise and sacrifice are long forgotten qualities. We are facing the permanent loss of that part of our culture that made America great.

Might the American people get wise enough in time to stop the demagogues that have polarized our nation? How will we vote in November 2008?

CHAPTER 3

▼

JUSTICE

When Southern states ignored the Supreme Court in Brown versus Board of Education, regarding equal education for minorities, Congress passed the Civil rights Act of 1964. The main reason was to ban segregation of blacks. Congress thus handed special rights to blacks, and that was a good thing. Had it left it at that, our legal system may have worked fine. But in its "wisdom" Congress began to dole out rights to most people in the United States.

Older workers over 40 got an age discrimination act. Then came discrimination acts against national origin, race, color, religion, and sex. Education for All Handicapped Children Act was passed in 1975 requiring educational facilities for these kids at no cost to parents. In 1990 Congress passed the Americans with Disabilities Act that required access for handicapped to every public and private establishment, along with special parking places, elevators and bathrooms whether it made sense or not.

The Supreme Court helped Congress in 1970 in Goldberg vs. Kelly when it decided that due process was required for every holder of rights. It also affirmed that children have rights. Thus, except for the able white male above 18 and below 45, every American now had special rights. All these rights were wonderful in intent. As long as no right holder abused them, we would have a wonderful world. But the potential for lawsuits was frightening because every right holder had ample opportunity to sue for every possible treatment they didn't like, especially if due process was denied in their imagination. In 1977, the Supreme Court decided to allow lawyers the right to advertise their legal services as a form of free speech. The world of justice has not been the same since when the effects of that decision were combined with the growing indifference for fairness in our country. Ethically challenged lawyers were free to seek out clients and encourage lawsuits. Some focused their advertisements on classes or groups such as those injured in an accident or on the job, or fired without due process, or those that weren't cured in full by their doctor. It was this turn of events in the world of justice that has since clogged courthouses and changed the way we live, furthering a culture of indifference towards others in our society.

At first, the seriously injured gratefully responded to these ads. No doubt many "little" men had no easy access before to find lawyers willing to take their case for loss in income or physical ability. These seriously hurt Americans were followed by opportunity seekers aided by savvy lawyers who in addition to compensatory damages stressed or rather exaggerated damages for emotional distress and punitive damages. This development in the judicial system opened up a perfect way to enrich one-selves at the expense of an otherwise good and conscious honest doctor or fair employer. Many in our nation seemed outraged by this development.

We used to believe that these plaintiffs were mostly low-life opportunists that exploited our judicial system at the expense of taxpayers and innocent but deep-pocketed Americans. But with others getting large payouts, and the increasing attitude problems of indifference in our society many Americans loosened their standard of the threshold of decency. That in turn opened up an explosion of lawsuits. The prevailing attitude became: If others take advantage of the system, we'd loose out by not taking advantage of it as well. It changed the nation's attitude, many of whom had already felt the immense injustice committed by our economic leaders. Once, we accepted life as it came. Now, we sue if anything happens out of line with our expectations. Once, lawsuits were filed for employers who blatantly ignored safety or for doctors who made fatal mistakes through blatant negligence. The indifference that replaced our conscience for fairness is perhaps the most worrisome change in attitude today.

As a result, cities and counties, deemed with deep pockets, became the target of lawsuits for things, the thought of which decades ago would not have occurred in our mind. Were you told to remove your headscarf when you were booked in prison? Sue the county. Did you drive too fast over a road bump? Sue the city. Did you fall from a damaged ladder when you were breaking into a home? Sue the "negligent" owner who dared to leave a malfunctioning ladder on his property (and win). Unused food from restaurants or grocery stores subject to spoilage is often thrown out rather than dispensed to homeless shelters. Why? Because of fears of lawsuits by some homeless person! Security guards prevent kids from cooling off in fountains because someone might slip. Teachers or superintendents don't discipline kids because of liability risks. Parents are fearful of inviting friends of their kids because someone could fall or otherwise get injured on their property. Swimming pool diving boards disappeared because of liability risks. The litany goes on and on. Life changed profoundly.

If justice changed tort law, how did it change criminal law over the last twenty-five years? According to the Census Bureau, the population of the United States was 226 million in 1980. This grew to 281 million by the year 2000, an increase of 24%. According to the Justice Policy Institute, in 1980 there were 474,000 men and women incarcerated. This number grew to 2,000,000 by the end of 2000, an increase of 320%. One major factor contributed: The growing indifference in our nation; our hearts hardened.

In paradox with the teachings of Jesus, these statistics seem to indicate that we Americans have on average become more revengeful as well as a more fearful people. Criminals seem to have lost their status of human beings. Many of us can care less if a murderer gets the death penalty or if criminals are locked up for life, off the streets. And if they do get released, we want to make sure they are marked for life for everyone to see, especially if the convict had a sex crime to his name. Many of us sit in church feeling justified and righteous, while ex-cons, who paid their dues, are not given a second chance on life. Where has our Christian, or for that matter human, compassion gone?

On March 7, 1994, California's Governor Pete Wilson signed the "Three Strikes" law that Californians wildly endorsed, saying: "It sends a clear message to repeat criminals. Find a new line of work because we're going to start turning career criminals into career inmates." The governor forgot that when released from prison, there is no new lease on life. There are a few companies that hire ex-cons for non-challenging positions but company executives I have known would not hire an ex-convict at all. Their lawyers would recommend against it. They would argue that if an ex-convict were to be hired, and something would occur, say a fight involving the ex-con, the injured would no doubt seek a sympathetic jury finding the employer guilty of willfully putting the workplace at risk by hiring ex-cons; executives should know better than putting the work place at risk. And all the saints say: Amen.

Unless a prisoner was wealthy or had connections to wealth, most prisoners are out of luck in finding a challenging line of work. Not everyone's name is Pat Nolan, ex-lawmaker in Sacramento, who as lawmaker proposed the toughest laws on crime, then was arrested on corruption and spent 26 months behind bars. Today Pat is a crusader for prison reform. He landed a job with the Governor of California. Most ex-cons aren't so lucky. Want to try your luck as an ex-con getting a bank loan to finance your new business start-up? Good luck!

Most released prisoners soon run out of the pittance of money they received from the state upon release. Because most of them are not given a second chance to find challenging work, they are not able to provide for themselves and end up on the street. Hungry as they may become, they may get tempted to grab a mouth-watering hamburger or a Mrs. Fields chocolate chip cookie, without paying for it. On June 19, 2001, the headline in the Los Angeles Times: Court Upholds 3-Strikes Term for Cookie Thief. Yes, Governor Wilson got what he wanted. Another prisoner for life! We don't care about the injustice, heck, we have become so full of fear and revenge that we even ignore the fact that it costs us $75,000 a year to incarcerate a prisoner. Talk show hosts cry: "He/she should have thought about the consequences before committing the crime, don't you come crying to me; you got what you had coming". And so-called Christians speak these words.

Mike Huckabee, Republican candidate for President, was once the governor of Arkansas. A parole board released a convicted rapist, allegedly at Mike's urging because the convicted rapist became born-again and was "saved". Then the parolee raped and murdered a woman. The electorate was furious. After all, Mike did a "Dukakis". In American politics today, a politician cannot be successful unless being tough on crime and by playing it safe, never show compassion with criminals. Mike showed a rare face of true Christianity; forgive and give a second chance. When you don't play safe, you will win most of the time, but sometimes things go wrong. That's the American way in business but apparently it didn't work for Dukakis or Huckabee when they took a risk by showing compassion.

Ever watched the mobs in front of a convicted sex-offender's home? They are submitted to fear and aren't even rational. According to Jamie Fellner, Director of the U.S. Program at Human Rights Watch, 87% of all sex crimes against children are first time offenders, only 13% are repeat offenders. But the nation is obsessed about the 13%. The media helps them in highly publicized cases, such as repeat sex offender John Evander Couey, who committed horrible sex crimes against Jessica in Florida and then killed her. It made us scared. The probability of another John Couey is as rare as the odds of winning the lottery. Yet, the media hypes up these rare Couey cases as if every past sex offender is going to strike today. The result is that any released sex-offender has to pay with his life.

We want to make sure that they will never lead a normal life even after they paid their dues to society. How inconsistent for a nation of mostly Christians.

The purpose of doing time in prison should be two-fold: punishment to enforce our human law, and preparation for a second chance in life. That second part got lost somehow when we began to become tough on crime. In all developed countries except the United States, released criminals get a true new chance on life. Why do we feel more fearful or revengeful than those living in other developed countries? How could we possibly feel more righteous? How could the slogan tough-on-crime be one of the most successful political slogans ever? The politician using this is practically assured of re-election. The politician using the opposite of tough-on-crime, the compassion of Jesus of merciful forgiveness and revalidation, is assured of defeat in America.

In summary, in the three main areas of life, economics, politics and justice, we have discovered a staggering number of seemingly "minute and unexpected" causes that changed attitudes and that together are keeping America on a path "to ruin". The general mood of the electorate feels it. People want change. But we don't want to settle for just any change. We need the right change.

We need to replace the indifference in our society by a return to the unwritten rule of fairness, decency and social responsibility. We need to stop the terrible trend in the economy that the free markets are unwilling or unable to self-correct; the unbridled greed in the corporate office and Wall Street. We need to let go of the feeling of entitlement to life, curb lawsuits and our attitude of fear, and put a true Christian face on our nation. We need to re-learn how to save for retirement (that takes sacrifice). We need to protect our economic and military leadership, and protect American jobs the right way. We need a call for national unity to tackle the biggest challenge in over sixty years on American world-leadership, akin to Kennedy's call for the race with the Soviet Union to fly to the moon. On an individual basis we need to re-learn how to take responsibility for our actions instead of seeking scapegoats. We need to stop listening to the meaningless polarizing ideology of talk shows. We should give the boot to politicians that refuse to compromise by voting party line rather than what is good for America. We need to become doers instead of standing on the sidelines and agreeing with talk show hosts. We've got work to do instead of letting China take over while we blame one another in our country. We are all Americans; let's work together despite our differences.

SECTION II:
THE ECONOMY

Our economy, one of the major draws of America in the past, is in a precarious situation, facing a serious challenge. Under President Reagan a depressed economy picked up then blossomed during the Clinton years. But under President George W. Bush our economy did merely O.K. and was largely held together because of artificial boosts such as the economic benefits of the Iraq war and large tax cuts without federal cost cutting. The attitude of consumerism in our nation along with low interest rates played a strong role as well. It set the stage for an economy out-of-control with growing federal budget deficits, growing trade deficits, negative savings, inflated real estate values and creative financial instruments that proved disastrous for financial institutions and investors. Foreigners financed a significant portion of our irresponsible behavior. Our once almighty dollar took a dive when it finally lost the world's confidence that America had enjoyed since the dollar replaced the gold standard.

Recessions come and go, and should not worry us too much on a macro economic level. But what should worry us as a nation is the growing income and wealth gap in America and the rapidly growing professional skills in China and India that together are making our long-term economic future less secure.

Beyond some words of encouragement, our government has shown little initiative to help America retain its status as economic world power. China could surpass the U.S. in a short time span of just twenty years. If China were to become the world's leading economic power it will eventually also become the world's leading military power, and the world's political power. It should be said that the two-term Bush Administration has done much harm to our economic future and as a consequence our national security.

CHAPTER 4

▼

MARKET CAPITALISM

Adam Smith (1723-1790) was a Scottish philosopher and economist, who became the father of market capitalism. Smith explained that rational self-interest and competition can lead to common well-being. In his days this philosophy was a radical departure from reality but it turned revolutionary, eventually known as market capitalism.

As we know from Econ 101, the system of market capitalism works best without government interference. Smiths' theory proved that market capitalism creates more wealth than any economic alternative, especially central planning, the system underlying the workings of communism. Market capitalism moves capital from old industries to new industries where it is more useful. What makes market capitalism really work so well? The most powerful ingredient behind market capitalism is the common human element of greed. Greed drives us to compete for private gain, to set us apart from others or, at a minimum, to achieve no less than "the Jones". "Greed" unleashes our creative souls with the promise of reaping rewards. Adam smith's theory helped greed to maximize our gains. While counterintuitive, the word greed is actually healthy as long as it is contained. The word greed becomes a real negative, however, when the drive for more power, fame or money is accomplished at the expense of the unsuspected. For example, defrauding old people from their homes while falsely promising them a more secure retirement is caused by greed that was not contained.

One other amazing element of human greed is that once individuals have obtained significant wealth, more than they would need in order to live a very comfortable life, their greed continues to drive for more wealth. Their greed won't let them slow down, perhaps a few wise men excepted. It defies common sense. Once having attained enough money, why bother for more? Is it akin to an athlete that keeps on trying to improve his own world record? What more is there to prove? It is prestige that allows them to brag. These "bragging rights" for attaining the most marbles makes them stand out among equals, receiving recognition and adoration from media and friends. Other than for bragging rights, there seems no logical explanation why greed keeps us from slowing down the pursuit of more wealth.

Greed, this perhaps despicable human characteristic, has turned out extremely beneficial for societies embracing market capitalism. There is no logical explanation why greed and market capitalism together have accelerated the well being of an entire country. But it has worked, and worked very well. In America where market capitalism has been least encumbered by government intervention, it worked so well that we became the undisputed economic world power. An added result of holding economic world power is that we could afford to pay for the world's best national security and defense. Along with the unwritten sense of fairness and social responsibility that prevailed in our society (before the nineteen eighties) market capitalism, without much government intervention worked extremely well for our entire society.

Not surprising, some people feel that greed feeds immorality. But greed is the proven ingredient for economic growth and rising individual standards of living. In the days of Rockefeller, Ford and Carnegie, these giants capitalized on significant opportunities offered by new technologies in their days. They became super rich but their wealth did more than that. The successes of the industries they built spilled over to the rest of the country. Their opportunities became the opportunities of ordinary families all over the country with jobs at new factories and service areas, raising individual incomes that spread wealth across the nation. This process began to reduce the income gap between rich and poor in America. In the nineteen seventies and eighties, new technologies began to transform our world. The new Rockefellers emerged through the likes of Gordon Moore, Bill Gates and Steve Jobs. They revolutionized the way we work with personal computers, and standardized operating and application software. Along with fiber optics and satellite communications the world exploded in efficiency and productivity, opening up new jobs globally.

One great aspect of America is that it is possible for any person to become rich, irrespective of bloodline. In feudal economies, only those with the right bloodline would make it rich. This holds true for American bloodlines too. Think of the generations of Trump, Walton, Kennedy, Bush, Rockefeller, Ford. But in America one's bloodline isn't a restriction to make it rich. John Rockefeller and Andrew Carnegie came from poor families. Steve Jobs and Bill Gates weren't rich. Everybody in America can make it rich? Everybody? Well, in reality the vast majority never has a chance. But aren't we all having equal chances with free education and all? Yes and no. The requisites of making it rich in America is not in the bloodline but are God-given talents such as skills, intelligence, foresight, courage, drive, common sense and instinct for the kill. We can sing the praises of Andrew Carnegie, John D Rockefeller, Bill Gates or Steve Jobs as ordinary people, but all possessed that combination of skills, traits and instincts that made them wildly successful. Everybody has the will power to avoid destructive life habits, instead to choose a life to the best of their ability. But not everybody has the God-given abilities, talents and skills with intelligence, foresight, courage, drive, common sense and instinct for the kill, which are all required to make it big. In fact, only a few rare individuals possess those. Thus the chances of making it rich in America are stacked against the vast majority of Americans. What do we do with them? Use them as tools that can be discarded? Or should those endowed with God's extraordinary gifts treat that vast majority as valuable participant, as Americans, that should earn a fair share of the wealth created in our country along with a decent retirement income?

The masses of Americans are lured by "the dream" but will not attain riches no matter how hard they work. It is not their fault that they weren't endowed with great talent. What about those who cannot work at all? Disabled? Sick? Too old? Unemployed? Until the eighties, society at large recognized a social responsibility. The tax system back then seemed unfair to the rich but just about all Americans enjoyed real income growth and many companies provided job security and good benefits including pension plans.

According to the statistics, this no longer holds true in America. Real wage increases of workers have not occurred since the nineteen eighties while CEO pay packages got out of hand. Retirement benefits are no longer affordable for most Americans while CEOs retirement benefits have become outrageous.

Pension plans for workers before the nineteen eighties changed to 401Ks. They were touted as an equivalent form of retirement security. They are not. It is a lie. A recent report by The Employee Benefit Research Institute showed that 58% of all Americans have built up a 401K worth less than $50,000; another

13% up to $100,000, and another 8% up to $150,000. Let's be optimistic and assume that all these people-nearly 80% of Americans-would retire with $150,000 (in current dollars) in their 401K. Assuming a 20-year retirement span and a decent return on investment, it could result in an annual annuity of $10,000 per year. Along with social securities, this would not provide a dignified retirement for most Americans. With minimal home rents today exceeding $10,000 a year, that is a shameful treatment for American who contributed to the national economy all their lives; a painful outlook for America's future retirees.

The statistics in chapter 1 regarding income ratios and tax rates demonstrate that the current system of market capitalism has let greed run wild. American capitalism still works for America but it doesn't work anymore for the vast majority of Americans.

To ordinary Americans, the lack of fairness was symbolized by President Bush's promise to veto a Democratic bill in Congress. Instead of paying a low federal income tax of 15%, that bill would have taxed private equity managers (making $657 million dollars each) the same normal income tax rate that ordinary middle class Americans pay. Apparently, the President felt that 15% tax was enough for the obscene fees of these private equity managers. A President's action is symbolic and his veto threat was a clear demonstration to most Americans that they should not count on this President or his Republican Party to restore the fairness and social responsibility that disappeared in America.

In a span of some thirty years, the American society has drastically changed. Society has become indifferent. On average, those who received the God-given talents to strike it rich are indifferent to those who didn't. Our system of market capitalism has ultimately broken down because greed was no longer contained. Our system of market capitalism will need some help to contain greed once again.

CHAPTER 5

▼

CEOs and Social Responsibility

In the 1980s, Reagan's slashing of marginal tax rates was the unintended beginning of the loss of social responsibility in America. On the positive side, Reagan's optimism and great oratory ability helped stimulate the economy and his tax cuts helped movement of capital to burgeoning opportunities in technology and finance. With many new start-ups capitalizing on disruptive ventures thanks to the (Intel's) microprocessor, venture capital funds increased tremendously, funding many cash-strapped entrepreneurs. A visit to Sand Hill Road in Menlo Park became a must for would-be entrepreneurs. The successful ones created a huge positive impact on our economy. In the process, entrepreneurs made millions of dollars and their investors realized huge returns on their investment. Those were the days of success stories of Oracle, Sun Micro and many more. They were inspirations for many would-be entrepreneurs to pursue their dreams and make a difference. The key question here is, if marginal tax rates on the rich had remained high at 70%, would Larry Ellison or Scott McNealy not have started their companies and stayed on the sideline, or joined IBM?

Of course not, they would have been just as motivated! In fact, Steve Jobs and Bill Gates pursued their dream in the seventies before marginal rates were cut. High marginal tax rates would have made no difference to their dreams.

Paul Volcker, the Chairman of the Federal Reserve, successfully reduced the high inflation and interest rates that dominated the seventies. A low inflation is great for the economy and for retirees. But the event of low interest rates, after a decade of high inflation, also opened up a whole new avenue for savvy and smart opportunists. In the eighties, a brilliant young man by the name of Michael Milliken altered for good the business in debt financing through the creation of high yielding junk-bonds. In the end, it also landed Milliken and others such as Ivan Boesky in jail. That took away much of Milliken's momentum to stardom but his pure genius will and should always be recognized. Opportunists who succeeded Milliken understood the potential of Milliken's groundbreaking development.

These financially savvy opportunists had already accumulated some wealth. Besides unusual talents, they were endowed with courage, lots of courage. With lots of chutzpah they changed the prevailing reason at the time for buying out a business. That used to be centered on a sound long-term business strategy. They invented a new reason. Without much personal investment and heavily leaning on Milliken's invention of junk-bonds, their new reason for buy-outs was nothing else but "flipping a business" for pure financial short term gain. They targeted established businesses that had undervalued assets. They were the pioneers of American economic leaders that caused the loss of social responsibility for important stakeholders of the targeted business.

Some of the great companies at the time had amassed fabulous real estate wealth. That wealth was hidden on their balance sheets (the official accounting method required to account for assets at acquisition cost as opposed to replacement cost or market value). As a result, the balance sheets didn't reflect their true value. Typically, these companies enjoyed a relatively good partnership with their employees; most everybody shared in the wealth increase of the business, workers seemed relatively happy and many enjoyed a life-time career with one company, secured of a pension that allowed them to retire with dignity.

Unfortunately, these good companies were ripe plums for this new breed of leveraged buy-out (LBO) investors. The latter would take these ripe plums off the public stock market, sold-off undervalued assets and reaped huge profits in the process. Part of these profits paid-off excessive debts and part was available for distribution among their general partners and passive investors. But these investors didn't stop here. Their next step was to increase profits by cutting waste. In those days it was easy to find waste, in almost any company. Once that waste was cut, the knife wasn't put back in the drawer. The cuts continued into employee pension plans and job positions that were traditionally deemed necessary. This was the defining moment that started the breakdown of our nation's social responsibility!

The justification for their cost cutting sounded almost altruistic: The purpose of the buy-outs was to make the companies more efficient in order that they could better compete on the long run; in addition, freed-up capital would be allocated to new business opportunities. Once stripped to the bone with much higher profits, these companies were then returned to the public markets, reaping huge profits for the investors on the sale of stock. Most LBO investors were already quite rich because minimum investment requirements were often well in excess of $1 Million. This process had a snowball effect. Once "LBO'd", these companies showed much higher profits than competing companies, which were spared from LBO's. However, they might as well have been LBO'd because suddenly they found themselves at a distinct disadvantage to compete. As an economic consequence that forced other market participants to follow their lead with a snowball effect rippling throughout their industry. When globalization opened up world markets, this effect continued, not just in America but also had an effect on Europe.

LBOs work best in times of low interest rates that make high-leveraged debt possible at low cost. When interest rates rose in the nineteen nineties, LBOs all but disappeared. In recent years low interest rates had returned and so did buy-outs, now essentially renamed Private Equity Funds. The jury is still out regarding the benefits on society of LBOs or Private Equity. Certainly, it made these companies leaner and meaner, which freed up capital for newer opportunities. But did that justify the pile up of huge riches and concentrated wealth by essentially a legal form of "stealing" from employees and stockholders?

Some point to the roaring nineties as proof that LBOs were a success for the country. However, the roaring nineties were more a result of productivity gains from new technologies-including the commercialization of the Internet-that swept our country and the world. The biggest advantage of LBOs was re-allocation of capital but the damage was that uncontained greed flourished and it started the process of a precious loss that had no financial valuation, yet was invaluable to our country: Fairness and social responsibility for all Americans.

CEOs of companies that had not yet been targeted by LBOs took quick notice of a couple of things. One was that bloated companies with undervalued assets were easy targets. The other one was that extreme profits could be made in a short time, simply by manipulating earnings for a few years. That sounded more enticing than working a lifetime for wages. As we saw, CEOs of large companies in those days had relatively low annual income compared to today, perhaps 40 to 50 times the income of the average worker.

To avoid becoming the target of an LBO, many CEOs began to sell-off undervalued assets and become more astute in cutting waste. CEOs also began to warm up to new compensation packages that tied their personal income to the performance of their stock.

Another major change occurred when Wall Street as a whole began to focus more on short-term results, the quarterly earnings reports. As a retired CEO, I know how difficult it was to meet quarterly earnings, quarter after quarter, even in a good, stable company. There was always something going on that would change the estimated earnings, say 5% up or down without having any effect on the potential of future business or the long-term earnings picture. Yet, failing to meet expected quarterly earnings by just a penny could cause an immediate drop in stock price well beyond 5%. This would result in irate investors. If that happens twice, it could erode stockholders' confidence in the CEO and Boards of Directors would fire CEOs for erratic stock price movements. Whether CEOs intend to manipulate earnings or not, their job security depends on meeting Wall Street's quarterly earnings estimates. This new focus had to go at the expense of building a strong company for the long term. The President of the U.S. Chamber of Commerce, Thomas J. Donohue, gave a keynote address at a Wall Street Analyst Forum in New York:

> "The rules have now changed in favor of a culture of immediate financial gratification without regard to long-term costs. We've created an environment where a company's long-term value and health are all too easily sacrificed at the altar of meaningless short-term performance. We focus on a company's numbers and ignore its business-and that philosophy poses a significant threat to our future competitiveness."

> "While many U.S. CEOs are worried about the next three months, our global competitors are making long term investments in their companies and in their economies."

This speech was in 2005. We are in 2008 and things didn't get any better.

CEOs whose compensation packages included stock options were quick learners. Wall Street's emphasis on short-term earnings allowed CEOs to make huge amounts of money if they, legally or illegally, manipulated those short-term earnings. By caring less about employees' welfare, keeping raises down, reducing benefits, and sacrificing the long term, CEOs could legally manipulate short term earnings, beat Wall Street's expectations and make large amounts of money on rising stock prices (for as long as they could find more cost to cut). Shareholders loved it. Board directors loved it. Employees didn't (except those lucky ones that received stock options and cashed in). Employees with 401Ks invested in their company's stock loved it too, until, of course, the stock came diving down, often after the CEO cashed out or was fired with huge exit packages.

When most of our politicians embraced globalization, it took little imagination for CEOs to see huge opportunities for more short-term profits on the horizon. With the social responsibility factor on the wane it took certain CEOs little convincing to replace more expensive labor in the United States with cheaper labor in other countries. Opening up the globe with its immense supply of cheap labor would increase the labor supply in America, and thus products worldwide would become cheaper. This is what the economic theory preaches, and there is nothing wrong with that. Is it? Don't we have a responsibility to provide job security with good wages for Americans?

CEO salaries became more and more excessive but why did corporate directors do little to prevent these run-away compensation packages? If market capitalism is self-correcting, why did the market not correct the trend of excessive packages? Did Boards of Directors loosen CEOs character requirements of integrity and care? Al "Chainsaw" Dunlop anyone? Dunlop considered himself Rambo-in-pinstripes and if he cared for employees, it wasn't obvious to the world. It was in his days that psychologists suggested that the profile for the successful, modern CEO might include the characteristics of a psychopath that is with a mental state unburdened by a conscience.

There was a time, I remember, when corporations and in particular corporate directors were ashamed of excessive pay. Are there still boardrooms that find CEO pays excessive? A recent study by Heidrich & Struggles and USCs Center For Effective Organization concluded that 32% of corporate directors find CEO pay too high in most cases. But what about the other 68% of corporate directors? What do they think? We saw how CEOs increased their pay package by, mostly legally, manipulated quarterly earnings. Because of publication requirements, these huge gains found their ways into executive pay package surveys that are used to determine the annual revisions of CEO pay packages.

During the annual CEO pay package process, boards of directors commonly use professional executive salary consultants-or their executive salary surveys-such as Towers Perrin, Mercer Human Resource Consulting and the guru of them all, Graef Crystal. The motivation for directors to use these consultants or surveys is clear. It provides them with a base of "competitive" CEO packages, and it helps avoid shareholder liability lawsuits. After all, when you consult the experts, how could you be held liable if a pay package turns out excessive? The problem with these surveys is that it keeps driving CEO packages up. CEOs with big egos (and who among them doesn't have one) require that their package measure up to comparable CEOs. When hiring a new CEO, directors often appear in awe for striking a coup with their new CEO. Then shouldn't his package be higher than that of other CEOs, otherwise they didn't hire the best? No doubt, most boards intend to act responsibly. But because executive compensation surveys are used by essentially all of them, CEO packages only point one way, up and up.

The recent sub-prime mortgage events revealed another fabulous, though psychopathic, CEO strategy:

> In good economic times, go with the market flow with gusto and without concern for an unavoidable meltdown. The odds are that such irresponsible leadership would reward the company's short-term earnings resulting in a fast rising stock-price. It would enrich the CEO in good times with huge stock gains and often, huge bonuses. When bad times arrive, well, who cares? The company might risk chapter 11 and it might cost employees their job and shareholders a fortune. It would cost the CEOs job too, but unlike employees and shareholders who are left with a pittance, the CEO would laugh all the way to the bank with early retirement. While keeping the huge gains and bonuses, a huge severance always seems to be in the wings. CEOs can't loose. Sure, they'll get some bad press but they'll get over it. And soon the bad press will be forgotten especially when they donate some millions to charities.

Here are some CEO exit packages that raised eyebrows: Dick Grasso, who left the New York Stock Exchange as its CEO pocketed an alleged $140 Million exit package. Bob Nardelli, famous CEO of Home Depot, was said to leave with a $210 Million package. After the sub-prime crisis, according to David Lazarus of the Los Angeles Times, Angelo Mozillo from Countrywide Financial allegedly got $115 Million in severance related pay as a result of him driving the company into the ground. In turn this resulted in pink slips to as many as 12,000 workers while shareholders lost their shirt. Mozillo also pocketed $169 million in 2005 and $120 million in 2006, for keeps. According to the Associated Press, Stanley O'Neil, the ousted CEO of Merrill Lynch walked away with $161.5 million while Times Online reported that Chuck Prince, the ousted CEO of Citicorp received just under $100 million (poor baby) on the way out the door.

It seems that CEOs always win, even when employees or stockholders loose. That's why it is so important that Board of Directors seek CEOs that score high on integrity and long term focus, and low on psychopathy. It is important to point out that many CEOs have exhibited admirable focus, whether it is Ken Chenault of American Express, or A.G. Lafley from Proctor & Gamble or Indra Nooyi from PepsiCo and many others. But too many CEOs see the short term with huge payouts as their main interest. Long ago, I remember, directors demanded from their CEO a strong sense of responsibility for the well-being of the company, its shareholders and employees, even the community and nation. But things fell apart when pundits began to argue that character doesn't matter as long as the CEOs interest is aligned with shareholders interest. It seems that many CEOs found a way around that.

For what purpose do CEO packages need to exceed one or five million a year? It is hard to spend one million a year when you work 60–80 hours per week. Does a CEO really work harder when he gets a hundred million rather than five million a year? How do exit packages for failed CEOs in the tens or hundreds of millions fit the principle of accountability? And why do boards of directors approve any compensation at all to someone who failed? These are just simple questions that boggle the mind.

Free market economists need to consider that there is more to a society than just optimal economic growth when all the wealth is piled on the top. Would we rather grow at 5% annually without a sense of social responsibility, or should a society have a conscience and choose a 4% growth instead but with a sense of social responsibility? Indeed, it is a fine line as to how far the market should be left alone.

Consider the income inequality gap as measured by the so-called "Gini-coefficient" (or index when multiplied by 100). The Gini-coefficient, also called Gini-gap, was first published in 1912 by an Italian economist, Corrado Gini, and has been commonly in use, worldwide; to establish how equitable or inequitable income or wealth were spread around the world. If everybody in a country earned equal income, the Gini coefficient would be zero. A Gini-index of 1 would mean that only one person had all the income or wealth while everybody else had none; of course, there is no country where one person owns all wealth or earns all income. Likewise, there is no country where all people earn or own the same amount of wealth. In other words, the Gini-coefficients in all countries measured are between 0 and 1. The lower the Gini-coefficient the less extreme wealth or income inequality exists. This is commonly the case in developed countries. Undeveloped countries have a higher Gini-coefficient, indicating huge gaps between the have's and have-nots, typically without a strong middle class, such as Mexico. A Gini-coefficient over 0.5 to 0.7demonstrates the great divide in income and wealth concentration. As published by The Economist (August 11,2007) Japan and Germany, as well as other West European countries, all considered developed countries, have the lowest income Gini-gap, in the 0.25 to 0.36 ranges. In the seventies, America's Gini-gaps used to be close to these developed countries. However, in the last thirty years, the U.S. Gini-gap has been growing significantly into the wrong direction; by 2001 we had by far the highest gap among developed countries with a coefficient of 0.46 and as incomes on the top continued escalating, we are closing in on Mexico's coefficient of 0.54 (Source: Sustainablemiddleclass.com/gini-coefficient).

According to Professor Edward Wolff, professor of economics at New York University, the Gini-coefficient for wealth inequality in the U.S. is much worse, at 0.82, close to the maximum level of inequality a country can have. Consequently, the proposal by the Bush Administration to abolish the so-called estate or death taxes is just another moral lapse for our society that will just exacerbate wealth inequality in America to a point that would have King George of England (of the 18th Century) blush. These Gini-gaps demonstrate that the situation in the U.S. is out of control, skewed to the rich and potentially causing an environment of unrest that could turn ominous. This development in the American Gini-coefficient over the last thirty years is a result of the various changes in attitudes that we have discussed.

The only hope for the future of America is that the trend towards a widening income gap is reversed, soon. It is possible with some of the solutions provided in this book. One effective way of achieving these solutions is to get the support from American voters. And before that could become a reality, we need common Americans to stop insisting that they are "conservative". You can't be a conservative unless you belong to the top 10% or maximum 20% of income and wealth earners, and even if you did make that kind of money, you must not care about the other 80%. Your values and religion do not make you a conservative, no matter what Rush Limbaugh or your minister tells you. The conservative label was broadened on purpose to make many Americans think that they are in the true circle of conservatives. They are not. The true circle of conservatives is foremost concerned about letting the rich get richer at the expense of the middle class. Here is a test. If you continue to think that you are a conservative just like Rush Limbaugh, you ought to remember that he has a $285 million eight-year contract with Premier Radio Networks. If you make that kind of money, you can call yourself a conservative too. If you don't make near that kind of money, you are not a conservative. If you still insist on being a conservative, you need to accept that those who dominate the party ideology will shaft you. Think how they will retire and compare that to your prospects.

CHAPTER 6

▼

MORE ECONOMIC CONSEQUENCES

The widening income gap between the rich and American workers, and the growing indifference among our nation's leaders had an awkward affect on most Americans. "If nobody cares about me, I better take care of myself", seemed to be the logical reaction. But instead of becoming frugal to save for dark days and retirement, most turned a deaf ear towards the whisper of sacrifice. Instead they took care of themselves in the emptiness of a new kind of consumerism, seemingly without concern for the future. Consumerism here is defined as uncontrolled urge to satisfy instant gratification even if it consumes all our earnings or even built-up equity.

The average worker didn't fail to notice the spending sprees of Americans who had turned fabulously rich in just a few years of work through dotcoms or hedge funds and so forth. The Ferraris and fancy vacation homes in the Caribbean were testimony to easy money and instant gratification. The demand for this grew sky-high. The Los Angeles Times reported that premium seats at the Super Bowl were going for $75,000, and that concert lovers are willing to lay out $3,000 to watch a concert. At least John Rockefeller and Andrew Carnegie lived responsibly. But the new rich of today live differently, spending money in the face of the average middle class American. Of course, the average worker couldn't afford that material life but instant gratification became hard to resist. A new consumerism across the nation was born.

Because most consumer goods are now made overseas, a dramatic increase occurred in the national trade deficits. Had these causal reactions happened in other countries, the financial markets would have swiftly punished that country by dropping the value of their currency. Fortunately, or rather unfortunately, we were spared that punishment for much too long, solely because the world had trusted the once almighty American dollar. This only made matters worse as it lulled economic policy makers to sleep, while politicians and talk show hosts snickered at pundits who had warned that this couldn't go on forever. Well, nasty consequences are now striking us with higher inflation around the corner and a huge loss of American purchasing power. This will strike even harder on common, middle class Americans, who unlike the wealthy don't have money stacked away abroad.

President Bush said that we are addicted to oil. We are, but we are addicted to a whole lot more than oil. With instant gratification dominating our lives, we are obsessed with getting the latest consumer products, faster cars, the latest wireless gadgets, plasma HDTV, IPods, IPhones, and if possible a condo at the beach or lake; even porno blossomed thanks to our need for instant gratification.

Our individual savings, seen as a nation, are now negative. In 2005 this happened for the first time since the Great Depression in the early 1930s. The U.S. Commerce Department said that Americans spent more in 2005 than they earned. A negative savings rate of 0.5% is not good. Just for comparison, in 1985 as a nation we still had a savings rate of 11.5% of disposable income. What a significant attitude change when compared to our fathers who made this country great.

Even though Alan Greenspan observed that open borders drive savings in other countries our way, it can't be good for our nation that we don't save to bolster our capital investments and to secure our own future. After all, with a negative savings rate, other countries won't help out when we retire. It is not good that we have lost the will to sacrifice; without sacrifice a nation cannot survive.

On a national scale the government doesn't save money either. Logically, the national budget should run a surplus in good times to compensate the bad times. Yet, the Bush administration consistently ran a large deficit even in good economic years. Even though the federal budget is huge, little money was available to modernize our aging infrastructure. Without improvements it will be hard to compete with China in the long run. Our infrastructure is getting antiquated and comparatively is far behind the level of say thirty, forty years ago. Road are not wide enough to handle rush hours. Bridges are barely maintained. They crumble under loads that are much heavier today than when they were built. According to a 2007 Report by the International Organization of Economic Cooperation and Development, OECD, the United States ranks #24 among 30 countries in the developed world regarding of Broadband Internet Penetration of homes connected. One reason is the lack of standards in the communications industry. This illustrates one of the weaknesses of free market capitalism. It ignores the need for adopting a national economic and technology vision. As a result we fell behind other countries. Think about it. The United States is not #1, not #2, not #3 in the world. No, we are #24. How embarrassing!

We have seen that individual consumerism increased; yet individual real incomes remained at best flat for most Americans. How could people without real increase in wages satisfy their craving for consumerism? Besides using the equity in their homes, their hope was to achieve richness beyond the confines of their own job. Gambling became more popular through lotteries, racetracks, poker or slot machines. Indian gambling business on reservations mushroomed. With the growing indifference spreading to the rest of the nation, others became more creative, displaying Bonnie and Clyde mentality.

The growing indifference on the top expressed by obscene incomes at the expense of workers expanded the growing indifference towards many circles of Americans. Without social responsibility, it was just a short step for more and more people to seek their fortune in the vast borderline of dubious ethics. Scam artists popped up everywhere; a whole new level of opportunists. The number of cases of defrauding the elderly rose sharply. Creative mortgage fraud was seen all over the country. Identity thefts became astronomical. Internet scams are all too common, aimed at defrauding the unsuspected user. Fake drugs are not just offered over the Internet but entered the logistics channels that mainstream pharmacies relied on, endangering people's lives. It used to be that we were warned for the occasional con artist who would talk sweet old ladies out of their savings. But now we don't know where it is coming; the scams are all over the place.

Other more legitimate efforts to quick money resulted in a deluge of porno websites or on-line mortgage offerings. EBay presented a great opportunity for many honest entrepreneurs but also scam artists. The pre-2007 booming real estate markets turned into a bonanza for real estate flippers. A number of mortgage brokers seemed to come out of nowhere to sell no-down mortgages beyond the ability of borrowers to pay. Gone was the common decency of warning new homebuyers that they might loose their home when interest rates would rise. Nor did they worry about investors, the suckers, who purchased the sliced up mortgage debts that banks unloaded on Wall Street. Who cares in today's society?

Worse when the "sucker" got bailed out by the government, it turned the tax-payer into the real sucker; an irony for those with "common sense" who didn't partake in the smorgasbord.

While focused on consumerism, Americans became easy prey to enticement. It was common for me to receive at least ten invitations a month to sign up for more credit cards. Further, my existing card companies sent me in aggregate at least ten mailings a month with blank checks encouraging me to take out more money. This is not done because they cared about me. It is all about quarterly earnings per share and more commissions for the salesmen who sell mortgages, credit cards, what have you, regardless the damage to the social fabric.

Many American succumbed to the temptation of credit cards. Debt was piled up. Second or third mortgages were taken out on built-up home equity, and the monies received were spent. Even venerable banks advertised for taking out a second mortgage to add a room or take a dream vacation or whatever filled our insatiable appetite. These banks lost their sense of social responsibility they used to have when they urged homeowners to protect their home equity. In the 2000s they wanted you to give up your equity so that their salesmen could earn lots of commissions and their CEO could achieve higher quarterly earnings.

With their safety net gone, Americans may hope that their IRAs or 401Ks would provide some form of secure retirement. But many are finding out that this is not going to be in their cards. When businesses offered 401Ks as a replacement for pensions, they took away more than just a designed benefit. They took away the professional pension fund managers. The vast majority of Americans are not professional investors. The average self-managed 401K holders stand little chance of achieving results that match those of the professional managers of pension plans.

Without professional pension fund management, enter the domain of the financial planner. Many reputable financial planners exist but if there is any easy field for crooks, this is it. The number of scams has risen dramatically to defraud 401K holders, especially the more gullible elderly (which some day we all will become). In Con Artists Old Tricks, the Los Angeles Times recounted many cases of such fraud. Even the honest financial planner is no match for professional pension fund managers. The difference of 5% or 10% annual return over a career's time could be a 400% difference in assets upon retirement, enough to recognize the difference between comfort and poverty.

To add insult to injury, with the national savings rate as low as it is, contributions to 401Ks are not keeping up with relative pension contributions that were made available to workers decades ago. With many home equities already spent on consumerism, the future looks bleak for many Americans. The government has a role to play in breaking the culture of consumerism and instant gratification and in restoring a culture of gratification delay. That may not be good for the world economy but once the one time shock has past, the economy should return to a normal level.

The attitude of indifference and subsequent deluge of scam artists had another consequence; a growing lack of trust that Americans can have in one another. When I became CEO of a high tech firm in the mid eighties, I forcefully established a culture of trust within the company. No lockers, no closed desks, no closed closets, no tools locked up, no supplies locked up. There was resistance, especially from line management. Workers doubted that management could walk the talk. We did! The trust caught on throughout and flourished for years. During the next five years, not a single item was stolen. And this was done in a fast growing company that nearly doubled employment year after year. Rather than building a company on trust, most companies today prefer the security of locking up. Other businesses, particularly hotels and stores are displaying a greater level of distrust than ever before, asking identification for check-in or credit cards. You can't talk to your credit card or phone company before going through PINs and passwords and mother's maiden names. It is not as nice a society as it used to be.

In 2007, we spent a vacation trip in Germany and Austria. We were surprised that we could fill our car's gas tank before having to show money or inserting a credit card (with ZIP number). It felt great to be trusted. We checked into hotels in Germany or Austria and no one asked for identification. A hotel in Garmish-Partenkirchen, a lovely town in Germany's Bavaria, blew us away. Upon check-in, I dutifully pulled out my credit card to which they said; "We don't need that now", to me, a foreigner, "just bring it upon check-out." When you are trusted in a trusting culture, you respond with trust. Trust your clients and your clients will respond with trust. On the other hand, distrust responds with distrust and you'll get defrauded when you look the other way.

It is not a coincidence that school shoot-outs started when the attitudes of indifference spread to the rest of the nation. When social responsibility broke down and materialism increased while trust disappeared, kids see no 'heart' anymore in this society. What is left for them is that they are driven harder to achieving more and more, rather than spending quality family time. Rather than showering them with love and quality time we shower them with materialism. We are wrapped up in instant gratification so much so that our lives are dominated by the ways to make more money; less time is available for the family. This is an empty life for most kids. But the American drive for unrestricted ownership of guns helps some kids to express their feelings in a dramatic way. It is not guns that kill.

Because of Wall Street's focus on short-term results, businesses reduced their development of new technologies. Consider that in the first half of 2007, American oil companies booked a combined profit of $57 billion dollars, of which they devoted $23 billion to repurchase their shares instead of pouring that money into developing new alternative energies that could save our nation. When industry critics pointed to these buybacks of stock as proof that oil companies aren't interested in investing into renewable energies, John Felmey, Chief Economist of the Petroleum Industry, shot back, saying that by buying back stock, oil companies increased the share values of the "Joes and Marthas" (the little people owning a few shares).When companies buy back their stock, they remove shares from the marketplace; as a result the company's earnings are spread over fewer shares that remain outstanding; thus earnings per share will rise and consequently the price of the stock will rise. Here you have it. Mr. Felmey seemed to suggest that oil companies care about the value of the few shares held by the Joes and Marthas. But when oil gets more and more scarce it will get very expensive. It will take a lot more money for the Joes' and Marthas at the pump than the gain on the stock. The Joes and Marthas and especially America as a nation would be far better served if oil companies had spent that $23 billion on developing renewable energies. The big winners of the $23 billion stock buy-back are the top 10% of wealthier Americans. According to Edward N. Wolff at New York University on Wealth Distribution, 85% of all stocks and bonds are held in the hands of just 10% of the richest Americans while the rest of America, the 90% that includes the Joes and Marthas hold just 15% of all stocks and bonds.

It has become plainly tiring to listen to talk show hosts trying to undermine conclusive statistics that America is on the decline. It is as if they don't care, as long as they can pocket their fat salaries. Decline here is not meant in terms of personal morality, but in our collective willingness to stay ahead of other countries economically and thus militarily and politically. Other countries are renovating themselves and running harder than we do. Our nation is too conceited to realize that America's leadership in the world is faltering. It is embarrassing. Consider our President's speech in February 2008 at the Annual meeting of the Conservative Political Action Committee.

> "Our policies are working. The American people support our points of view. They share our philosophy."

Duh? What philosophy? The one of doing nothing? Or the one leading us downhill?

CHAPTER 7

▼

GLOBALIZATION

Globalization is the best thing that could have happened to the world at large; it offers the best opportunity to wipe out world poverty. Anyone honest couldn't argue with that. Open borders guarantee that the world uses the capital and production in the most efficient way. Thus much capital from Western investors goes to developing countries.

Globalization also reduces tariffs on our borders, allowing these countries, especially China, to export to America more of their products of lower complexity, such as apparel, toys, computers, etc. In doing so, they undercut these industries in the U.S. with jobs being lost or at best wages held stagnant.

However, globalization is not necessarily bad. According to L. Josh Bivens from the Economic Policy Institute, economics teaches that liberalizing trade [globalization] is a win-win proposition between countries. Labor jobs will disappear but professional jobs will increase. It is generally assumed that as developing countries get richer, that would stimulate their demand for our more complex products that they can't make themselves. These products are more professional worker intensive and thus an increasing demand for those products would in turn increase the need for professional workers in the U.S. The scarcity of our professionals will even drive up their wages, argues Bivens.

Yet, Bivens also continued that, even though economic theory argues a win-win position, it is not a winning proposition for workers who lost their job or for the workers that still have a job. After all, the unemployed will add supply of labor to the market that will cause all wages to be reduced. Further, according to L. Josh Bivens, production workers [manufacturing and service] constitute roughly 75% of the entire U.S. workforce, and workers without a four-year college degree constitute roughly 70% of this workforce [or 50% of the entire U.S. workforce]. In any case, the theory suggests it is extremely important for all Americans to get a four-year college degree to qualify for the increasing demand of professional jobs.

How many more jobs would eventually go offshore? According to Thomas Friedman, in "The World is Flat", in the next twenty years, China, India etc. will take every American job that is fungible. Friedman defines a job as fungible when that work can easily be digitized (communicated over long distance) and thus transferred to lower wage countries. Truth is that, except for prototype production, every job description on the assembly line could fall under that definition. Every accounting and tax preparation job could fall under that. Every product and service provider could fall under that. A hardware and software engineer could fall under that. Even investment banking could be done overseas. Common surgery could be done over remote communications robotically. Unless your job is personalized like a barber, waiter, gardener, in other words, a job that requires your work to be personally anchored at a geographical spot in America, Friedman says that your job is fungible and could easily be transferred to another country, without you, of course. Except for the very specialized person who built a name for him/herself, the best brain surgeon or an undisputed master of software, would continue to demand high fees and get what he/she wants. Otherwise, thanks to the amazing progress in technology, especially in communications and container shipping, the transfer of fungible jobs will continue, slowly eroding our well paying jobs.

Professionals working on sophisticated American products would, of course, retain their job, but how long before China catches up with us in making sophisticated products themselves, at a lower cost? Many economists have tried to forecast how many future jobs in America might become lost due to globalization. They just can't agree on the numbers except that many more jobs will be lost, ranging from 10% to 40% of the workforce. L. Josh Bivens of the Economic Policy Institute quoted Alan Binder, a Princeton professor, who rated 22%-29% of the U.S. workforce as potentially "off-shorable" over roughly the next one or two decades. If these jobs are not replaced, the economic consequences to middle class Americans could be devastating.

Thanks to globalization, the world's middle class, according to a researcher at the Brookings Institute, Homi Kharas, will have reached 52% of the world population by 2020. Further, globalization kept American inflation low, temporarily. Once our trade deficit began to worry foreign investors, speculators began to unload their dollar reserves; the dollar began its long, inflationary slide. Even the dollar slide had a positive side; it made our products less expensive for overseas customers. However, in addition to job losses, inflation is the big worry. Due to rapidly increasing standards of living in developing countries such as China and India the demand for just about anything scarce will increase and thus drive up prices. Their appetite for commodities has driven up world prices. But the rising world middle class also demands more food and has placed a huge demand on meat, corn, wheat, oil, cars and other luxury goods. According to the (magazine) Economist, food prices alone increased 30% in 2007 with wheat increasing almost 80%. Rising prices of commodities affects every country. Rising food prices affects every country. Unless the increased demand is offset with a similar increase in supply (of commodities and food), inflation worldwide will increase. This will be hard on us but especially hard on the people in underdeveloped countries that remain in poverty. Rising standards of living in developing countries will also cause price increases in the products they make. Thus the clothes, computers and toys we buy from China will get more expensive too.

It is easy to see that globalization is a mixed bag. Is globalization good? As an economist by training, I am a proponent of globalization. Most economists, even amateurs, tend to focus on macro-economic effects and less about the effects on certain groups of people or even countries. What if we confine the question to just America? Is globalization still the best medicine for America today? Globalization exacerbated the loss of social responsibility, widened the American income and wealth gap, suppressed middle class wages, and the unavoidable inflation in the future will hurt us all. How could we be pleased? Sure, globalization eliminated poverty for lots of people in China and India. But for an American in heart and soul, it is hard to maintain a rigid conservative ideology to keep American market capitalism unfettered.

Dr. Alan Greenspan in his book <u>The Age of Turbulence</u> is adamant that the greater the freedom to compete, the greater the material wealth would be produced. But he also fears that the Achilles heel of market capitalism "is a growing perception that its rewards, increasingly skewed to the skilled, are not distributed justly." His fear is well placed. So are Friedman's observations that fungible or "off-shorable" jobs would leave America. If and when that happens, we have to conclude that the magic of market capitalism has stopped for most Americans. Do we want to wait that long before we demand action?

Pundits would argue that tinkering with free market capitalism is un-American. But anarchy is also un-American. And a slipping off the cliffs of world power is also un-American.

We believe that our government must step-in carefully by forcing a change in attitudes that are the root cause of the negative consequences that we have seen and are seeing. The markets are not giving any sign that it is planning to correct these negative attitudes. So why not let the government help? Government intervention is nothing new. In fact, Adam Smith, the father of market capitalism, did not require that governments leave the market alone. For market capitalism to work, he demanded that governments create stability and freedom. Stability and freedom are subjective concepts and governments have used it to give advantage to their agendas. Stability often requires measures that are counter to freedom. Ask George W. Bush!

The potential of national unrest or even anarchy, due to widening income and wealth gaps, would certainly justify government intervention, well before unrest could become a problem. If we believe that democracy is supposed to benefit all Americans and if we believe that social responsibility should not be confused with socialism, then all Americans should profit from the increase in our nation's wealth. We gain nothing by creating a new super class of wealthy Americans while the middle class disappears. Securing a strong middle class is even more American than the ideology of unfettered market capitalism.

Globalization in itself is good. Market capitalism in itself is good. But a widening income and health gap will turn into disaster.

In conclusion, we asked a hypothetical question: What would have happened without Globalization? We would have had:

- Less prosperity as a nation
- A lower GDP
- A better trade balance
- More world poverty
- No threats to our world leadership
- A stronger dollar
- More secure borders
- Lower oil prices and lower material prices

- More job security and retirement security
- Lower riches for CEOs and Wall Street
- Lower stock market values
- Lower real estate values
- Lower food prices
- Higher real income for American workers
- Lower income gaps
- Higher average inflation (beyond food) and higher average interest rates
- More economic volatility in terms of inflation and recessions
- Less chance of terrorism (because borders and ports could be controlled better)
- And likely, less stress and more happiness

CHAPTER 8

▼

CHINA

Economically, it was nothing but a wonder and surprise that China could grow and sustain a fast pace growth without major troubles such as retractions that normally occur after such episodes. China claims that its centralized, dictatorial government is more efficient than a democracy. To substantiate this, the Economist reported that the incredible new airport terminal in Beijing, bigger than all terminals of London's Heathrow's airport together, was planned and built in just four years by an army of 50,000 workers. In Britain, it took four years to just conduct public inquiry into the proposed construction of Heathrow's terminal Five. Especially in building infrastructure, China's centralized government may well be more efficient than a democracy. The Economist continued that China built a network of highways crisscrossing the country that is second only to America's famed (but ageing) interstate highway system in length. The difference? They built it in 17 years while it took us forty years. China's infrastructure will soon be the worlds most modern, and will include the world's longest (36 km) sea-crossing six-lane bridge, and bullet-train links.

The great beneficiaries of globalization and market capitalism today are China, India and some other up and coming economic powers. It worked great for them because market capitalism allocated Western capital to them. After all, they have the most effective cost structure to produce the lowest cost products.

Countries such as China, India and others with abundant labor were eager to take over America's production processes. Of course they needed to provide us supporting industries and a limited infrastructure, along with the promise to establish a decent rule of law that would protect American property rights, such as patents and proprietary designs.

In the end, there is no denying that America helped China and India gain a foothold in the world market place. The outsourcing by American businesses and our appetite for low cost consumer products allowed the developing economies such as China and India to grow rapidly.

Developing countries increasing wealth also began to increase their demand for America's more sophisticated products that they couldn't make, such as airplanes. This increased the demand for professional jobs in America. But over time, these countries, especially China, are learning to make more complex products, and are beginning to compete with their "teachers" in America. As a result, the drive of CEOs for keeping profits high will force them to further subcontract out more and more sophisticated products to countries with lower cost structures.

How does the American economy stack-up with the rest of the world and China in particular? With $13.2 trillion in 2006, our Gross Domestic Product (GDP) is leading the world with a convincing margin. In 2006 it was about the same size as the next five countries combined (Japan with $4.4 trillion; Germany with $2.9 trillion; China with $2.6 trillion, United Kingdom with $2.4 trillion; France with $2.2 trillion. [Source: Wikipedia/list by countries GDP]

It is known that China with $2.6 trillion and India with $0.9 trillion are rapidly closing in because their growth is staggering. How long before China surpasses America? In 2008, China's GDP is expected to jump from #4 to #3. Often overlooked in comparing GDPs is that GDPs do not necessarily reflect purchasing power. A dollar spent here provides less economic output than the same dollar spent in China. In other words, when comparing China's GDP to that of our GDP, we need to realize that China's GDP is actually much higher in real purchasing power.

Our nominal GDP growth rate has been seriously falling behind China and India. With the present annual growth rates of the US (around 3% or less) and China (around 10%), China will have caught up with us in about 20 years. That may sound a long time away but it isn't. Not for your kids that will have to face China. Not only will they have to watch the vanishing riches of America as China takes center stage, our kids are also were saddled with our huge national debt that include the cost of wars in Iraq and Afghanistan. Thomas Friedland in The World is flat is convinced that China and even India are poised to overtake the

United States in economic power. The Chinese are motivated to overtake us, just as our grandparents were motivated to overtake the old European countries.

China has forecasted 800 million automobiles by 2025, just for China. Today the entire world has only 400,000 automobiles. Think of their immense growth opportunity for automobile companies, in China. Oh, and think of the adverse affect on the demand on oil, and the prices on metal and the price of oil/gas.

China's overtaking of the United States in GDP purchasing power would have serious consequences for us. For example, only the richest country can afford to pay for the best defense system, the best military and the most sophisticated weaponry. What would our place in the world be when China is militarily stronger than America? America has felt righteous in its decisions to attack other countries by military force, often unilaterally without even being seriously provoked, as in Iraq, or Grenada or Haiti. Once China's GDP has exceeded ours, they could feel justified in overtaking or at least copying that role from the United States, whether we like it or not. China already has influence over us, because along with other countries they are holding a significant portion of our national debts.

In an article on October 23, 2007, the LA Times staff writer Richard Verrier reported that Los Angeles has the largest manufacturing base in the U.S. He reported that this base was healthy and competitive [despite the high volume of copy-cats from China] because we have better service than China could provide, specifically in customization. Lacking proficiency in English, the Chinese couldn't deal with the demand for unique designs. The Chinese were not good in small lots either. But all that is changing as English proficiency in China is improving, and they are willing to take smaller lots. Customers are beginning to demand that the L.A. manufacturers match the lower prices of the Chinese. The Chinese now target even specialty-designed items. Several manufacturers have expressed their fear that they may not be able to keep their manufacturing business open. In Fortune Magazine of October 15, 2007, Peter Georgescu believes that creativity is the only possible way to avoid the commoditization of almost every product with ferocious price competition in which only China and India can win. But how would America be able to continue to out-create China?

In a sign that even American research and engineering jobs are not safe anymore, General Motors announced in October 2007 that it is building a facility in China near Shanghai. It is not just any facility. It will house the Center for Advanced Science and Research. Said GM in an interview with the Los Angeles Times: Researchers would explore technologies for producing ethanol from plant products, study new light weight materials that could improve energy efficiency, and work on new manufacturing processes that consume less energy, produce less waste and emissions and recycle more. There you have it. Except for stem cell research, all important new technologies combined are researched in China. The reason GM will build this in China: China's growing pool of engineers and scientists and their relatively low salaries; likely winning some Chinese government favors as China is exploring ways to reduce its reliance on oil. For sure there is another major reason for GM: No threat of strikes from the United-Auto-Workers in China!

Could we have done something to counter China's rapid rise on the world scene? Could we have continued our world leadership unabated? Could we have done something to lessen the threat that China would catch up with us? Yes, of course, we could have done a lot. However, the Bush Administration has pretty much wasted its entire years in the White House by essentially ignoring the China threat. The Administration has been too occupied with the war in Iraq and the possibility of terrorism threats.

Once China's threat to our leadership became clear, it should have been a wake-up call, much louder than Russia's surprise launch of the Sputnik in the 60s. Kennedy used that surprise to rally the country towards a national determination unseen since. Similarly, the Bush Administration could have used China's wake-up call to rally a national determination towards a more rapid pursuit of new technologies. Major emphasis should have been placed on private research and development of critical new technologies with the promise of standardized products for exciting new world markets.

Not everybody believes that we are shooting a hole in our economic foot. The optimist, Walter Russell Mead, senior fellow at the Council of Foreign Relations, wrote an Op-Ed in the LA Times on October 14, 2007 with some relevant excerpts:

> Conventional wisdom is that China is rising and the U.S. is on its way down but conventional wisdom is almost always wrong. Reason 1: It is not only China but many Asian countries that are becoming powerful; too big for China to rule. China, India and Japan are in rough balance. Reason 2: Thanks to it's one-child-policy; China's population may have peaked, weakening its economic prospects. Reason 3: China has huge problems including the lack of a well functioning financial system and a government system that cannot keep up with the needs of market capitalism and its people.

No doubt, China will face formidable challenges but they are resilient, and have defied all conventional wisdom. Who would have thought that the most valuable company in the world would no longer be an American company but a Chinese one? On 11/5/07 it was announced that PetroChina became the world's first company to surpass the one trillion dollar mark in market capitalization. We should not let ourselves be lulled to sleep by those who like to diminish the threat from China. It is real. China has proven to break all conventional economic and political wisdom. It is far safer for us to assume that Mr. Mead's pessimistic view towards China's rising star is misplaced. America might still rise to the occasion but only if we take the threat of China seriously.

CHAPTER 9

▼

EDUCATION

As expressed by L. Josh Bivens from the Economic Policy Institute, the theory that the demand for more complex American products would increase in a freer trade of globalization, assumes that developing countries are not capable of making these more complex products over time themselves, such as aircraft.

It seems presumptuous to exclude China from that capability in the next decades. While still a long way off, their engineering schools are taking giant steps to producing large numbers of engineers at low wages. Given the huge gap in wages between nearly identically educated Americans and Chinese, the theory that globalization favors our professionals might be correct for a decade but beyond a decade might turn to wishful thinking, unless our engineering skills are elevated quickly in quality and quantity. Economists have expressed hope for America if we succeed in improving our dysfunctional education system. If we were to fix our inadequate school system, Mr. Alan Greenspan in <u>The Age of Turbulence</u> expects that the reversal of the income inequality could be accomplished. Friedman added that the only thing that can be done to change the current trend is to massively upgrade the individual skills of Americans beyond the skills of the Chinese.

Unfortunately, our country hasn't done well in this regard. In the past, we were lucky in our ability to lure the brightest foreign students to America's great universities that were and still are by far the best in the world. America's brightest and the brightest foreigners dove into physics and science, discovering newer technologies and processes that accelerated the American economic success story. As a result we became patent-rich.

While our top universities are still the best in the world many of the brightest Chinese and Indian students are staying home to do research at their own universities, at the expense of the American future. For them, the opportunity is no longer in America. China and India are no longer waiting for innovations to come their way from the US. They are furiously developing them at home. Today we still have the most advanced products in the world as a result of past innovations, still requiring many professional workers with college degrees. But what about tomorrow?

If we want to have a chance at keeping China at bay, we need to greatly enlarge our pool of top engineers. Yet, this effort is hampered by Wall Street's appetite for hiring the best students, luring them with obscene bonuses. Instead of seeking a career in the innovation of science, many of our best students opted for a financially quicker success as investment banker, hedge fund manager or in other Wall Street jobs. The result is that we are now facing a dramatic uphill battle to increase our pool of super talented engineers while having an abundance of financial wizards on Wall Street, concocting sub-prime derivatives that have wreaked havoc on the world markets. Our technology companies need more and more math and engineering wizards to stay ahead, but our pool of American talent in science is decreasing while the foreign talent pool at our universities is diminishing. What gives? As a result, technology companies are paying more and more for less and less capable engineers and scientists. Can you imagine the talent that will be left for teaching math and science to our youngsters, our future hope?

Our kids aren't dumber than the Europeans or the Chinese, our K-12 education system is. There is little hope for improvement unless the job of teaching becomes vastly more valued and the size of the pool of aspiring scientists increases, vastly. Many leading businessmen and, of course, politicians believe that education should be America's #1 priority. Yet, they have done little to correct the national problem. We have not heard business leaders ask for an increase in their taxes for education so that we can afford to pay teachers more and thus attract better teaching talent. With mediocre teachers, our kids will get a mediocre education. This is not to suggest that all teachers are mediocre; there are many very bright teachers who are altruistic and willing to teach, forsaking a much larger salary in the industry. But the core teachers of the public school system at large are mediocre based on a low salary structure and arcane method of compensation that rewards seniority. Smart mathematicians are in extreme demand in business, fetching jobs well over 100,000 dollars a year and beyond. Yet math teachers are paid the same low salary as other teachers. Teachers are underpaid; many have not seen a real increase in wages for a long time. Besides the altruistic math genius who dedicates life to teaching, is it a surprise that the average mathematician that was attracted to teaching is not equipped to raise our national level to the level of other developed countries? The trend is towards even more mediocre teaching capabilities, unless something is done to drastically reverse that trend. Besides the failure of putting their money where their mouth is, our businessmen and politicians aren't willing to take on the teachers' unions. By and large, the unions defended an obsolete tenured system, refusing to take into account the market demand for specific skills. The solution is easy but the courage to get there is lacking. The tenured system had its advantages but it isn't working. If the unions are not willing to alter the system, Congress must step in. This is of national interest, at the level of national security.

Educational fixings at the federal or state level have done little to help. We may want to look to Finland for guidance. Finland boasts the best education in the world. How do they do it? By leaving their teachers alone and paying them well. Let's get rid of the federal educational department and much of the local bureaucracy and leave the teachers alone. Then do five things: First, set teachers' pay system based on market demand and supply for skill levels required, specifically to attract good mathematicians. Second, eliminate the tenured system that rewards incompetence and pay teachers based on performance to eliminate those who perform unsatisfactory. Third, encourage retired business professionals to teach (and waive state licensing requirements). Fourth, foster university enrollment in math, science and engineering (and keep them out of the hands of Wall Street). Fourth, reduce barriers for kids to enroll in any public school of their choice providing free busing within cities or within a limited number of miles from their home.

The elimination of bureaucracy would pay for buses and for pay increases to teachers. The side benefit of increased busing would be reduced traffic jams of cars with one parent bringing one kid to and from school, further it will free-up parents' time to be more productive, reduce demand on gasoline, and improve the environment.

CHAPTER 10

▼

A STRONG ECONOMY

Our government has a role to play in fostering today's new technologies to dominate the demand of tomorrow. This is truer than ever in the wake of increasing threats from China and other countries desiring to take over our world leadership. However, in the last seven years, our government has done little. It lacked economic vision either by incompetence or by following an ideology that markets are always self-correcting. Even the Bush Administration recognized that markets often do not correct when they stepped in "to protect the economy" with frozen mortgage rates and other incentives (that skirt the cause of the failure).

The Bush Administration and Republican controlled Congress (until 2007) abandoned the circle of trust of true conservatives such as the late William Buckley Jr. The Bush tax cuts pleased the late economist Milton Friedman who mistakenly believed that tax cuts would always be followed by cuts in spending. That didn't happen with this Administration. The Republican Party that controlled Congress gave up their constitutional duty of oversight; it agreed with just about anything the Republican President wanted. In turn, the President accepted anything Congress wanted including out-of-control spending. The 2009 federal budget of $3.1 trillion-with a $407 billion deficit-was an astonishing increase of $1.2 trillion since Bush took office, a 67% increase, not counting the funding for the wars in Iraq and Afghanistan. Nothing was done to reign-in ever higher government spending. What's more the Republican Congress allowed record earmarks in "pork", to be added to spending bills without concern to fiscal restraint.

The national debt mushroomed to an astonishing 9 trillion dollars, raising it by 1.28 billion dollars per day under the Bush Administration [Source: U.S. National Debt Clock, by Brillig.com, which keeps track on line of Treasury Department statistics]. After retirement of baby boomers, our kids will make up a smaller workforce, perhaps 100 million available workers. To get rid of the current debt, they would have to pay $90,000 per person provided that we stop adding to it. Thanks, Mom and Dad. Reviewed from any angle, this was not a government that managed the nation's money prudently. For shame!

Incredulously, Republican Glen Hubbard, the then Chairman of Economic Advisors, said in a speech in December 2002 that it made little difference whether the federal budget was balanced or not. Duh? Do we Americans have to turn to liberals to defend our nation's fiscal health?

When the President and Republican Congress enacted huge tax cuts, the argument was twofold. One was that Americans know better what to do with tax money than the government. This sounds convincing only if government spending was cut at the same time. The second argument was to stimulate a weak economy and to foster investments that would eventually increase tax receipts, not decrease. Republicans like to refer to select statistics of the 1920s and the 1980s that demonstrated their point. What they do not tell you is that the Reagan tax cuts produced bitter deficits of over $150 billion annually that continued under George Bush, father of the current President, and under Bill Clinton's first years. The argument that lowering taxes in the end produces more tax receipts borders absurdity. That theory suggests that we should eliminate all taxes; let's see what happens then! Clinton didn't follow that advice. He raised taxes early on as President. The results were major increases in tax receipts up to and including his last year in office that wiped out the federal deficit.

The Bush administration managed to keep our economy going by massive tax cuts and borrowed war spending. Anyone can understand that if you borrow massive amounts of money, we could all spend like kings. That borrowing made us look healthy in GDP growth but in fact it made our long-term outlook less healthy.

A strong economy, now and future, requires a government with low government spending and enough taxes to pay for them. Further, a strong economy will require strong stimulus by the government to encourage advanced technologies to enhance our future competitiveness as part of a long term economic vision. Some of the objectives of that vision should include:

1.   All real income levels across the nation should rise

2. A stronger middle class

3. Taxes should demonstrate the fairness principle

4. New mass markets must be dominated by American technologies

5. Factories and supporting facilities emanating from these new technologies should be built on American soil for as long as American patents are effective.

6. Tax subsidies should be based on economics, not on votes or political contributions from interest groups.

The most promising markets for the next decades are most likely those that protect the environment, producing renewable energies and extending the quality of life of an aging population. While not a new industry, the automobile market worldwide will undergo major renovations not seen since the gas engine. It will also see an unbelievable expansion in technologies and in geographic markets. In these four markets, we could have led the world in development and new processes. Not only did the Bush Administration do little to pursue an effective economic vision, it was also counter-productive.

The Bush Administration relaxed emission and pollution standards on our older, yet still vital industries of automobile, energy and environment. The argument was to save jobs at home, to keep the economy strong. But this was a flawed, short view argument that may have helped the economy while Bush was in office but it was without vision for a strong America in the future. Perhaps in our polarized political environment, the future was no longer important but that must change. Actually what the relaxation of emission and pollution standards did was remove all incentives for our existing businesses to spend research and development money to find the most economical and environmentally friendly technologies. Why should businesses spend money on something that is not required?

Likewise, the Bush Administration has been most unhelpful in developing alternative renewable resources. The one it finally pushed, ethanol from corn, was either lacking intelligence or was selected for political reason to secure republican votes from mid-west states. In either case, it defied the interest of the country. Finally, for religious reasons, the Bush Administration has been a barrier in research on (otherwise unusable) stem cells, keeping our country behind in the development of a vital new industry that with an ageing world population could spur economic growth tremendously.

In the automobile industry, the Administration hindered the market from becoming more competitive. For example, if the Bush administration had simply raised fuel standards, or taxed oil, it would have forced Detroit to develop and produce more fuel-efficient cars. It would have forced our three automakers in Detroit to become more competitive with Toyota or other Japanese and Korean companies. It would have helped reduce our imports of oil and trade balance. As it stands, the Bush Administration kept Detroit behind the rest of the world competition. Every quarter as new data are published, Detroit lost more market share. Slowly, Detroit's flywheel is turning to a halt. And history will be repeated when high paying jobs in the automobile industry will be lost to foreign companies with lower wage structures just as it happened to DVDs and TVs. When Harley Davidson was in trouble, President Reagan protected it temporarily through import barriers and goals to bring their house in order. The company roared back better than ever, and the import barriers were lifted. Reagan helped Harley Davidson's long-term future. And that is what smart government intervention is all about.

Given that healthcare is already the largest industry in the U.S., products that are bio-engineered to cure or replace diseased body parts are going to be the largest market of all. It will be an astounding opportunity. Stem-cell research will be a key development but has been hindered because of religious beliefs. Whether or not alternatives to fertilized eggs are technically better, the point here is that the Bush opposition to the research stifled the enthusiasm and kept many investors away that otherwise would have stimulated our nation's lead in research and product development. There is nothing in the bible to defend the murky opposition of stem cells based on religious arguments. Unutilized fertilized eggs can be thrown out but not used for stem cell research? That religious babble is not much different from the days of Galileo and Copernicus in the Roman Catholic Church. Science has always chipped away mundane religious beliefs and traditions (without challenge to core beliefs). Yet, the notion that earth was supposed to be flat stopped science in its tracks for centuries. So it is today with the vague notion that discarded embryos are human life and thus sanctified. If and when God wrote the bible, He would have clearly known that embryos could someday be used for scientific purpose. If He cared about this, He could have simply said so in the bible that it is a sin to use embryos for scientific purpose. In the meantime, other countries that didn't put the brakes on developing stem cell related research and product development could cause America's loss in its leading economic position in the world of bioengineering.

As long as Wall Street keeps focused on short-term results, existing industries will not invest sufficiently for the future. We can't depend on the market to pull us ahead of other countries. The Bush Administration missed an opportunity to stimulate the most promising markets. China, however, isn't suffering from conceit. They are moving on, relentlessly. Look at their GDP growing year by year. It is amazing and scary. What American jobs are really safe if our government doesn't step in? In 2009 when Mr. Bush leaves the White house, our country would have lost eight years that are characterized by lack of progress in stimulating economic prosperity for the future. Our nation must attempt to make up for lost time. Can it be done? Time will tell but without aggressive action, our place in history as a world power will be marked by its brevity.

The electorate must send a visionary to the White House who will stimulate our economy, not through the tired tax cuts as cure-all that dominated the vision of George W. Bush.

CHAPTER 11

▼

ENERGY AND
ENVIRONMENT

Energy and Environment deserve a special chapter within the discipline of economy. Since the Enlightenment started in the 18th Century, individuals in countries that adopted the Enlightenment, such as the U.S., became endowed with the right to seek their own destiny. Since then, mankind has made continuous progress in rising standards of living. Before the Enlightenment, the standard of living of the populace had been essentially stagnant for a thousand years. After the Enlightenment, continuous progress has staggered the minds. But progress came with a price to the environment when technological innovation took a toll on the world's resources. Fossils that took billions of years to develop into latent energy in oil, gas and coal have been exploited in growing numbers and will leave mother earth depleted in just a hundred years or two; a blink of an eye compared to the time it took to develop.

Recently, global warming as a result of fossil burning has concerned most of the world's leading scientists. Energy and environment are therefore intertwined. If mother earth's energy treasures can become depleted so fast, by our insatiable appetite, shouldn't most of our human energy be focused on developing renewable energies? Especially, when the side benefits are that renewable energy resources would reduce our dependence on foreign nations, restore the balance of trade, reduce terrorism and avoid an ecological disaster of global warming? Yet,

President Bush has been in denial for the need of renewable energies for most of his term, and when he finally took action, he took the wrong action that seemed more politically motivated than scientific.

In the process of turning fossils into usable energy, emissions are allegedly contributing to the global warming that the world is facing today. An entire circus has engulfed around the effects of global warming. Thousands of scientists attribute global warming to humans while others either deny there is global warming or deny that humans caused it or contributed to it in a major way. Those that believe in the catastrophic consequences of fossil burning want emissions curbed. This could be accomplished, though at great expense. Most executives of corporations that cause emissions don't want the burden of expense to contain those emissions. Lobbyists and conservative media succeeded to seed doubts in the minds of Americans. Many conservative republicans, who are for the most part on the industries' side, call the global warming movement a hoax. Many conservatives refused to admit the existence of global warming. They even succeeded to sway the public by discrediting 90% of the worlds' scientists. Senator James Inhofe of Oklahoma has been particularly vocal on calling global warming the greatest hoax on earth. The likes of Rush Limbaugh and Senator Inhofe believe that nature is so resilient that it will shake off whatever little effect humans have on the planet. Tell that to the fossils.

Newsmax, a conservative on-line magazine that also puts out a printed monthly, went as far as to write that the movie Inconvenient Truth, starring former Vice President Al Gore "may be disguised as a documentary, but in fact is a craftily fabricated infomercial". They ask: "Is the main message of Gore's movie accurate? In a word, no." It goes on to suggest that "global warming has spawned an entire industry that makes its proponents rich", (since when is this bad?) attempting to discredit Gore for personal gain. Further, Newsmax suggested (early on in the race for nomination) that Gore's platform is merely "to position him for another presidential run in 2008". No constructive word from Newsmax, however, how emissions should be curbed and who should pay for it.

The Economist reported on June 2,2007, that shortly after the establishment of the UN Intergovernmental Panel on Climate Change, the big carbon dioxide emitters set up the Global Climate Coalition in 1989 to cast doubt on the science and campaigned against greenhouse-gas reductions; likewise the so-called Competitive Enterprise Institute followed up with inane advertisement. If global warming is caused for the greater part by processing fossils for energy, the debate should be centered on the question of how emissions can be best contained, and who pays for the cost.

But perhaps the resistance to acknowledging global warming is changing. President Bush, who was in denial for nearly seven years, finally conceded that global warming is real. In a speech on September 28, 2007, he said that nations emitting the most greenhouse gases must reduce their pollution levels. The President acknowledged the widely reported and respected conclusion of the U.N. Intergovernmental Panel on Climate Change that in his words, "global temperatures are rising and that this is caused largely by human activities." And, "We acknowledge there is a problem and we commit ourselves to do something about it". However, the plans he outlined would unlikely result in any constraint of emissions in America for as long as he will remain in office. The only effect of his acknowledgment is that it took the wind out of the sails of the deniers to which he once belonged. In the meantime, seven years have passed since he took office without any steps taken to curb the growing problem. He knows that global warming is causing negative consequences. Unfortunately, he does not believe that it is the government's role to set emission limits because he thinks that the markets will take care of all problems and that carbon dioxide emissions will eventually be reduced through technological advances. He ignores two limitations of the markets. First, markets are slow to react. Second, markets have no interest in developing technologies unless there is a compelling demand. President Bush failure is to recognize that no demand for emission reducing products would exist unless governments create the demand. The question begs: Is Mr. Bush not smart enough or did he promise emission producers that he would place no burden on them under his watch?

We have heard some of the possible consequences of global warming. Rising seas would flood coastal areas and islands. Changing weather patterns would upset the world agriculture and thus our food sources. We learned from an op-ed on 8/9/07 by Jeremy Ripkin, author of <u>The Hydrogen Economy</u>: That as the sub-Artic region is thawing it would release methane, a so-called greenhouse gas twenty-three times more potent than $CO2$, the greenhouse gases most cited as the cause of global warming. Mr. Ripkin further cited Kathy Walter of the Institute of Artic Biology at the University of Alaska who called the melting of the permafrost a ticking time bomb, dramatically warming the atmosphere to a tipping point where there is nothing that humans could do. Mr. Ripkin continues that a global tragedy of monumental proportions is unfolding at the top of the world, and the human race is all but oblivious to what's happening.

Newsmax was correct in that a huge economy is developing with new technologies for products that will curb greenhouse gases. The good news is that it is good for entrepreneurs and for the world. The bad news is for America that this new industry is largely developing outside of our country. European countries, though emitting much less gases than America, have recognized the dangers of global warming to humankind. While recognizing that the largest polluters do nothing to curb the problem, they are trying to set an example. Even China is working hard to find alternative technologies to fossils. And guess what, Europe and China is where the new innovations are running high. If they stay ahead of us, that is where the new factories-with great paying jobs-will be built to produce emission curbing products.

It is understandable that conservative self-interests aren't willing to acknowledge the problem. But our government's priority shouldn't be in serving established interests and ideologies but in serving the interests of America's future. Innovation of new emission curbing technologies will only happen if the government mandates emission control. This is the best way to save Detroit from its current focus to satisfy Wall Street. Detroit, where the large automobile makers reside, is losing out. China has already raised its gas mileage requirements far beyond America. California, the traditional trendsetter in raising standards, was trying to raise its gas mileage average by 2016 to the level of China today. However, as Times Staff writer, Janet Wilson, reported on December 21, 2007, the head of the U.S. Environmental Protection Agency, a Bush appointee, ignored his staff's recommendation and refused to let California implement its landmark law to slash greenhouse gases from vehicles. It is absolutely insane that when the world is trying to beat us in anything, our President is stopping us from even keeping up.

In his address to the nation in 2006, the President told us that Americans are addicted to oil. Normally in a situation of addiction, such as with cocaine, the remedy pursued by governments is to curb demand. However, the President didn't follow up on his speech by curbing demand of automobile gas mileage. Instead, he pursued an unexpected solution that seems politically motivated because it will not help America or the world. In response to the increasing world energy crisis, this Administration decided late in its terms to save America's energy crisis by betting on ethanol, converted from corn. The Bush Administration, with approval from the Republican Congress in 2006, handed out rich subsidies to promote ethanol from corn and make ethanol competitive with gasoline based on oil. Of course, there are plenty of people out there that will support ethanol, just as many still support our involvement in Iraq, but the consequences for America and the world are not good.

Why is it a blunder to support ethanol from corn? First, the focus on ethanol is not a focus on true renewable energies. You might say we can grow corn every year. Yes, that is true but the purpose of renewable resources is to be an alternative to fossil resources without causing serious negative consequences. Currently, it takes more fossil energy to make ethanol (grain alcohol) from corn than it would take to bypass the ethanol and use the fossil energy directly. Of course, more efficient ethanol conversion processes will be invented but much fossil energy will be required to convert corn to ethanol. This makes corn a doubtful contender in the global race for new energies, and thus a slim contender for America to export the results of the new technologies derived from ethanol.

Why is it not smart to provide precious tax dollars to corn farmers: Because they were already using nearly all of the available agricultural land for corn. They didn't need more incentives. The following are excerpts from the LAT editorial of 8/20/07 highlighting the problem in numbers:

> The Senate's 2022 renewable-fuels mandate of 36 billion gallons using corn would require corn grown on 96 million acres. Consider that last year the entire corn crop, mostly for food, was grown on 80 million acres. Consider further that the only source of unused farmland is 37 million acres in the federal Conservation Reserve Program and that farming this land would critically damage wetlands and contribute to soil erosion.

Besides that corn production is an environmentally damaging crop because it needs more nutrients than other crops, the second major problem is that corn has been the primary food for livestock. Because corn farmers try to convert existing corn production to the more lucrative subsidized corn for ethanol, there is less food remaining for livestock. Thus corn for ethanol not only costs us our tax dollars for wasted energy, we will now pay higher prices for beef and other products that use corn. This Bush program has increased world food prices already. The Economist reported that in the period 1974–2005, food prices on world markets fell by three quarters in real terms. In 2007, however, wheat prices doubled and almost every crop under the sun is at near peak prices. The Economist Food-price-index jumped 75% since 2005 in real terms (after taking into account inflation). Dearer food prices are likely to persist. That, continued the Economist, has two causes. One is the growing wealth of certain developing countries such as China. Second is the self-inflicted result of America's reckless ethanol subsidies, it said. In 2007, biofuels would take a third of a record maize harvest. Fill up an SUV's fuel tank with ethanol and you have enough maize to feed a person for a year.

What with severe draughts? They happen. Would farmers divert the reduced harvest all to ethanol, causing world hunger and prices going through the roof? Or would they convert the reduced harvest all to food, causing a severe gas shortage? In any case, corn farmers are pleased because they win either way. What brainy people thought this through?

We have nothing against subsidies if used as a bridge to increased competitiveness for America. This isn't one of them.

It is hoped that ethanol, in the long run, wouldn't use corn but other biological material including the waste of plants such as corn stalks, though there are two major problems with that. As a Los Angeles Times editorial pointed out the first problem is that using plant waste would reduce the fertility of soil for agriculture, as plant waste is useful in enriching the soil. The second one is that such process doesn't even exist commercially.

It appears that this Administration enacted against the vital interest of America as well as the poor in underdeveloped countries. Why did the President decide on ethanol? With all his smart advisors, he must have known about the consequences?

The real answer to our energy crisis is not ethanol from corn but truly renewable energies such as solar, wind, batteries, hydrogen and the like. Even betting on renovated diesel engines would have been better. European diesel engines today run smoothly with reduced emissions, and diesel fuel can potentially be made without oil. Other measures that the Bush Administration should have taken are conservation of oil. It would have improved our trade balance immediately and could have helped reduce the recent slide in the dollar. Besides mandating lower fuel consuming vehicles, such as hybrid cars, the Bush Administration could have raised taxes on imported fossil fuels to discourage the demand for imported oil. This would have spurred the development of non-fossil fuels while maintaining the level of oil exploration in America. In an interview with Fareed Zakaria, published in Newsweek's issue of August 6, 2007, Amory Lovins believes that there is a cure that is painless and profitable to get us completely off oil by 2040. Amory Lovins, the co-founder of the Rocky Mountain Institute, explains that redoubling efficiency can save half of the oil. The other half of oil consumption can be converted to both natural gas and advanced biofuels.

The Bush Administration could further have spurred the implementation of solar cells for new homes. This could have brought America ahead in the development and production of affordable and more efficient, reliable solar panels, as well as with well-paying jobs for Americans in the future. As it stands now, Germany is leading the world in solar energy for home use. According to Reuters in an article printed in the L.A. Times on 8/1/2007, more than 300,000 photovoltaic systems, that is 55% of the world's photovoltaic power, is generated on solar power by Germany, a country that is covered by clouds for two/thirds of daytime hours. It is a thriving industry for them, generating tens of thousands new jobs. The bottom line is that Germany is today the leading exporter in solar systems. It could and should have been America. The problem is that there are no major constituents or lobbyists for the (as yet tiny) solar industry who can promise large amounts for campaign money or provide large blocks of votes.

Thanks to a handful of American companies such as General Electric (GE), the opportunities for the environment and renewable energy resources is not entirely out of sight for America. GE is developing environmentally sound products for export to countries such as China. Why are these products solely developed for export? Because the Bush Administration didn't require American companies to crack down on pollution and global warming. As we write this, new dirty coal plants are being built in America, and are exempt by President Bush from implementing even existing pollution requirements. Why? Is it to keep jobs in America? The answer is likely to generate short-term profits for the rich.

In the meantime, The Economist reported: Energy has become the hot new area for venture capitalists and universities. A major reason is the economic pressure from foreign governments that increasingly accept the need to put a price on the damage carbon does. Market capitalism does eventually take corrective steps. But it took the pressure of Al Gore, the movie Inconvenient Truth, and foreign governments to drive the shift. Even so, the market forces acted slowly, with venture capitalists moving seven years late. It may prove an insurmountable task for America.

Jared Diamond in <u>Collapse</u>, page 434, wrote a gripping indictment of the attitude in Washington today. Our government leaders have a 90-day focus, talking only about those problems with the potential to cause a disaster within the next 90 days, without regard for the future.

> Economists rationally attempt to justify these irrational focuses on short-term profits by "discounting" future profits. That is, they argue that it may be better to harvest a resource today than to leave some of it intact for tomorrow, on the grounds that the profits from today's harvest could be invested, and that the investment interest thereby accumulated between now and some alternative future time would tend to make today's harvest more valuable than the future harvest. In that case, the bad consequences are born for the next generation but that generation cannot vote or complain today.

A strong and inspiring leader in a united America would have developed solutions to the Energy and Environmental crisis that would benefit the American entrepreneur and the American worker. Proponents of progress in both environment and energy would have worked hand-in-hand because the issues of Energy and Environment are closely intertwined. Renewable energies that are going to provide us with abundant energy could be the ultimate solution to minimize greenhouse gases.

This Administration has been obsessed with short-term profits, tax cuts, terrorism and Iraq. Those areas of focus may not be wrong for America, depending on your views, but its focus was too exclusive. If the appearance of selling out to the energy industry was not true, perhaps it lacked competence to take upon vital economic responsibilities. But why then did it interfere in other parts of the economic market, including bailing out sub-prime "victims" who brought it upon themselves? Perhaps Jared Diamond is right. The Bush Administration's attention span was just 90 days forward. It could not see how to keep America competitive well into the 2001st century.

The American voter has it now in its power to vote for politicians who are able to see ahead and place renewable energies and carbon dioxide reduction on their agenda for a vibrant new economy, to save American jobs, and in the process truly lead the world to save the planet from its destroyers.

CHAPTER 12

▼

SOLUTIONS FOR THE ECONOMY

Alan Greenspan wrote in <u>The Age of Turbulence</u> that it is unlikely that our problems would "topple the U.S. economy from its place of world leadership". Presumably his belief is based on fixing the growing income inequality among Americans as well as fixing the educational system. But neither one is likely to happen unless we fix some attitudes first. How can we bring the attitudes where they should be? Shouldn't we follow the conservative mantra of letting the market run its course? The answer is a strong NO. The markets haven't corrected the problems nor are signs of the right corrections on the horizon, timely enough to avoid a catastrophe. Markets are slow to correct (remember the housing bubble or the sub-prime mortgage market) and if or when it corrects, it does so without concern for the middle and lower classes that stand to loose the most, relative to their wealth. The widening income gap between the top and the rest of Americans must be corrected more forcefully and quicker than the markets could. Since the nineteen thirties, market capitalism had been restricted by many regulations. That didn't hinder America's great ascent to becoming the world's economic powerhouse. After the deregulations of the eighties and nineties, our economic power relative to other countries didn't increase; it actually declined in the 2000's. This proves that appropriate government intervention does more good than harm.

Our Congress should enact quickly a two-fold plan:

STIMULATION:

We propose government stimulation of new research and development for technological solutions addressing the most promising markets such as the environment, renewable energies, the quality of life of an aging population, and renovation of the automobile industry. The objective is to accelerate the speed with which new technologies are developed to the extent that they advance disruptive commercial technologies necessary to keep America in first place in economic world leadership for generations to come.

As long as Wall Street's focus is on short-term earnings, existing industries in the unfettered system of market capitalism have little incentive in spending large amounts of money on research and development for risky technologies. It is too much to ask when CEOs are focused on short-term earnings to spend large amounts of money on research and development that may or may not become the industry standard for newly identified markets. Remember that any such spending would go at the expense of their quarterly earnings. Further, disruptive technologies would compete with their current sources of income and would destroy their own markets, the prospect of which few of their current employees could get excited about. Even with special tax incentives, it is far more difficult for existing industries to become committed to new technologies than it is for new start-ups.

The best approach is to provide strong government support for research and development of the most promising new and critical technologies at small but innovative companies (or PhD students) that are totally dedicated to developing new disruptive technologies. Disruptive technologies are the best way to advance progress in a society. But disruptive technologies often make existing processes and products obsolete. Therefore, disruptive technologies are rarely developed at large, successful companies. They have the money to develop them but they can't bring themselves to kill their successful products and processes. That's why oil companies are reluctant to develop hydrogen technologies. In practice, disruptive technologies are usually the brainchild of PhD students or other hungry innovators, often cash-starved. Without government research money their development would be delayed and in this crazy world of rapid technological advancement, other countries could beat us before we had a chance. To a certain extent, the government has had a long history of stimulating research and development particularly at small companies. However, most of these stimulants were granted through the lens of a military defense point of view administered by the Defense

Advanced Research Projects Agency (DARPA). Even though commercial technologies were derived from them eventually, the emphasis was not on a commercial economic vision. We need a focused approach on commercialization of disruptive technologies. Besides, DARPA's budget is not large enough to be useful for our long-term vision. Kei Koizumi at AAAS.org, reported that DARPA's budget for FY 2007 was only $3.3 billion.

Our proposal is to provide a federal commercial R&D stimulation budget of at least ten times DARPA's budget, to the tune of $35 to $50 billion.

How should the government use this budget? Not for tax cuts! Tax cuts are only effective for companies with profits. Small, new companies seldom make money, so tax cuts would do nothing to stimulate their development work. This stimulation should be through direct reimbursement, and even advances thereof. How do we pay for it? This R&D fund should be financed through the sacrifice of those who will eventually profit the most from them: America's wealthiest.

At the end of 2003, total U.S. Household Wealth, as reported by the Wall Street Journal, was 44.41 trillion dollars. The top 5% of Americans holds 59% of American wealth, or about $26 trillion. According to Edward Wolff, Professor of Economics at New York University, the top 1% owns 38% of all wealth ($17 trillion). These numbers show the magnitude of concentrated wealth. Given the increasing wealth concentration build-up in the last years, the wealth of the top 1% has increased considerably (though precise statistics were not available). Investment bankers and money managers have traditionally put the threshold of high net worth individuals at $10 million or more. Apparently wealth above this threshold is not needed for living expenses; in essence it is play money. The proposal is then to set a tax of no more than 2% per year on this play money, household's wealth exceeding $10 million, held anywhere in the world by American citizens and legal residents. Through their investments in venture capital and direct investments, the wealthy would on average be well rewarded far and beyond this 2% tax.

PROTECTION:

This consists of three sub-sets of protection. The first protection is to assure broad patent rights of new inventions as a result of government supported disruptive technologies. In this global world, strong and broad patents must be filed in all important geographic economies of the world, including China, India, Brazil and Europe, and other countries that compete with us. Due to the enormous costs and talent associated with filing strong and broad patents worldwide, our first proposal of protection is that the best patent attorneys are used, paid for by the government, to assist small innovative companies in filing broad patents. While this would protect the original inventors, it would also assure that the future of the United States economy is protected.

The second protection is directly for the benefit of the most important stakeholders of America, the American middle class. We propose that the new technologies that were funded in all or part by the government must be entirely developed in America and all products derived from these new technologies must be produced on American soil. This protection for America should last for the lifetime of the patents (approximately twenty years) and would include all subsequent developed products and services that benefit from the original patents.

In the event foreign based companies make a superior competing product at lower cost without infringement of the American owned patents, the American company could request a waiver from restrictions.

The effect of this proposal would be a strong America that will lead the world economically, while the future of American workers is secured with a well-paying, job stability. This program could last in perpetuity, and thus American jobs would be protected in perpetuity. Further, the country's wealth would be spread among a larger number of Americans and would contribute to reducing the seriously out-of-balance income gap in our country.

The third protection will be even more contentious but vital to the plan. Its purpose is to roll back the run-away, unbridled greed to a healthy level and thus stimulate and eventually restore social responsibility in America for all Americans. Besides the moral or theological aspects of unbridled greed, the current attitude in the corporate office and Wall Street must be changed forcefully to avoid an impending national social unrest caused by the huge income and wealth gap. Our Gini coefficient must be slashed in half to approach the more healthy Gini coefficients of most developed nations, as we had it in the nineteen sixties or seventies. As a rule, conservatives believe that corporate boards are doing a fine job firing underperforming CEOs or that corporate America does not need Congress' wisdom on how to run a company. Therefore, Congress should not set limits on how much CEOs could earn. Instead, Congress needs to restore a fair system of taxation that stimulates social responsibility.

The way to do that is to discourage excessive incomes of CEOs or boards of directors through higher marginal tax rates. The proposal is to raise the marginal tax rate on income from professions that exceed 200 times the income of the average worker, let's call this income "Z". Z is the average income of the bottom 40% of U.S. wage earners, for which statistics are available (see the Plebian Policy Study Group) and Z should be revised annually by a reliable government source.

If we believe that 200 times Z is an outstanding income level for top CEOs, then the only way to discourage higher pay packages is to tax the excess at the same marginal rate that President Franklin Roosevelt imposed in the 1940s; at 94%. Assuming that the average worker's income is $50,000, than CEOs could earn up to $10 million that would be taxed at current low tax rates. But anything they earn in excess of $10 million in one year would be taxed at 94%. In other words, if a CEO made $11 million, he gets to keep $10 million (at low tax rates) but of the one excess million he gets to keep only $60,000. It wouldn't be worth it for the company to give pay packages that exceed $10 million. This proposal would eliminate excessive pay packages, and would foster social responsibility. Of course, this marginal rate wouldn't be exclusive for CEOs but for anyone earning income from any profession. This tax rate is not unprecedented, and should restore a national feeling of fairness.

The income under this proposal would include every piece of compensation of a profession, including income from stock options, stock grants, salary, bonus or fees but would exclude income obtained from passive investments that are outside the activities of a profession. Thus Rush Limbaugh would bring most of his income exceeding $10 million per year to the Treasury. Would he defend this plan? The income of private equity managers that include fees would be subject to this tax; some of them "earned" $657 million income in one year. Under this system, they'd get to keep $10 million and most of the rest goes to our Treasury. Cool! However, the income that the private equity fund paid to a passive investor would be excluded from this tax. Another example: The income of Michael Dell, as Chairman of Dell Inc, that would be subject to this marginal tax are all incomes reported for him in reports filed with the SEC and include his gains on stock-options or restricted stock grants, however, his gain on his stock ownership in Dell would not be subject to this marginal tax but continues as long term capital gain at the current federal 15% rate. The intent is not to discourage investments but to discourage excessive incomes from a profession. Otherwise, no other change in the tax code is proposed (Note that enough reasons exist to revamp our tax system, however, they are beyond the scope of this book).

The assumption is that 200 times Z would reward the best professional more than fairly. And would still be three to four times higher than the average CEO income in Europe. If American CEOs want more money, then they should act as true entrepreneurs do. That is by taking personal risk and buy stock outright. After all, with the CEO rests the factual powers to make or break the success of the company; he/she doesn't deserve risk-less stock options or risk-reduced restricted stock grants. Employees could still be attracted with stock options or restricted stock grants. Their gains are not likely to exceed 200X Z, but in the rare event their income exceeds $10 million, they would pay this new marginal tax on the excess as well. They would be so lucky!

The incomes of CEOs at Wall Street's investment banks will of course be subject to this proposal. Guess what market forces will do to the bonuses of the folks below them; they will be vastly reduced. By reducing these bonuses, instead of going to Wall Street, the best and brightest college students might opt once again for careers in science and engineering to develop new technologies and thus add enormous value to the American economy, much more than they ever could achieve on Wall Street.

Sportsmen today derive insane packages from their profession. Asking $200 million to throw a ball through a hoop is outrageous, no matter how great an athlete or how many fans he would draw. Currently, there will be no end to the escalation of their pay packages. This new marginal tax would restore some common sense. Would talented players take up citizenship of another and play abroad? More likely, other countries will follow our lead and implement similar marginal rates on excessive income. If not, Congress could always make an exception for the sake of flexibility, and place a higher multiple on Z for a handful of first team All Star sportsmen. The point is not inflexibility but restoring decency.

Some companies, such as American Express, have attempted to make CEO packages truly pay-for-performance. If Ken Chenault delivers, and there is no reason to assume that this brilliant CEO wouldn't, his pay would still be astronomical, and thus excessive. Remember, the intent of the proposals is bringing back social responsibility by curbing excessive incomes so that the workforce of any company feels that decency and common sense in pay is restored.

When CEOs are no longer focused on making excessive pay, they might focus instead on the challenge of making a statement of brilliance in long-term strategy that benefit their company and employees. We need to recognize that many CEOs have never wavered from their responsibility to put the company's interest first. Our proposal makes that true for all CEOs. Our proposal will not challenge the American system of market capitalism rather it will protect it from self-destruction. Our proposals should have no negative effect on investors, or on the success of groundbreaking new companies.

What could be the worst scenario with this plan? We have seen private equity managers move to the Caribbean but as long as they remain American they would still be subject to this marginal tax. American citizens pay taxes on all income no matter from where they were obtained. Could we expect an exodus of American talent to forsake American citizenship for a Caribbean citizenship and move to foreign soil? Let them! We wouldn't miss those who want to leave American citizenship and live somewhere else just for the sake of unbridled greed. There is enough talent left. In the end, when decency has returned to American soil, and America has re-found its equilibrium in income gap, social responsibility with more domestic young talent pursuing teaching and science instead of Wall Street, we would be glad to have saved America from a disaster.

Many interested parties will object to these proposals but we can't risk the erosion of American power and unrest that Alan Greenspan predicted if we don't reverse income inequality.

Americans, especially the middle class, have everything to gain with these proposals and nothing to loose. Please demand that Congress implement them through your votes and action groups.

SECTION III:
POLITICS

Why is most everything government does subject to criticism or cynicism? It is because governments are by nature incompetent and subject to corruption. Do we need government, and if so, how much? It depends on whom you ask: libertarians, conservatives or liberals.

Many libertarians don't think that we need government at all or if any as small as possible, keeping it out of people's lives to the maximum extent possible. The former chairman of the Federal Reserve, Dr. Alan Greenspan, is a self-described libertarian. As proponent of free market capitalism he writes: We have to assume that people acting freely will ultimately make the right decisions on how to govern themselves.

Conservatives are a bit more complicated. They believe in free market capitalism without government involvement, however, unlike libertarians, conservatives are not in favor of letting individuals live their lives as they see fit but encourage government to infringe on individuals' rights for the greater good. They are also anti-tax crusaders and have turned the word taxes into something almost worse than death. Yet when in control of government, conservatives proved inconsistent as they grew federal spending faster than under any liberal President in the last forty years.

American liberals feel that societies share an inherent responsibility for the general welfare of society. Government should help the poor and disabled, protect shareholders, constrain polluters, avoid excessive income inequality, build and maintain bridges and roads, in general, care for society. At the same time, democrats are more inclined, as do libertarians, to keep government out of people's lives in making personal choices.

Should people be free in making personal decisions on how to live their lives as liberals and libertarians advocate? Should market capitalism be without government intervention and allowed to correct its excesses as libertarians and conservatives believe?

The answers depend on the socio-economic and religious group to which you belong. Any group that feels weak, concerned or powerless wants the government to step in. For example, a group of injured veterans demands that government provides them better healthcare (Walter Reed Hospital anyone?). Homosexuals demand that government stops discrimination against them. Small investors want to see a stronger government oversight to curb misconduct by corporate managers. The poor and disabled want government to help them survive. Religious groups may want government to go beyond our borders and help eradicate disease and poverty, and want government to outlaw social practices of which they don't approve.

Any group that is unconcerned wants to keep the government out of what they are unconcerned about. As a result, true libertarians are perhaps endowed with the highest confidence and self-esteem, as they trust that individuals will ultimately make the right decision, for themselves.

CHAPTER 13

▼

POLARIZATION OR
COMPROMISE

Decades ago, platforms were useful tools during election campaigns to demonstrate the difference with political opponents. In between election campaigns, however, political parties in Congress and the White House worked together in a bi-partisan approach to solve the most pressing problems and move the country forward.

Today's political parties have turned their platforms into an ideological stand-off, 24/7. Bridging differences through compromise used to be smart politics. No longer! Today, political compromise is considered a weakness, a character flaw, as talk shows remind us daily. Stand-fast insistence on ideology is now considered a sign of strong conviction and character. This attitude caused the political polarization of today.

Stand-fast insistence on beliefs has no precedence for success. Stand-fast insistence not only turned good politics into polarized politics but also paralyzed the country. In the economic process, we have seen that America is on a path of destructing our leadership position in the world. Our political leaders are directly responsible for that by focusing on populist ideology rather than on the good for the country. As we have seen, it began in the nineteen eighties by slashing marginal tax rates in half.

In business we learned (often the hard way) that stand-fast insistence on one's beliefs only results in flaws and stagnation. Good business leaders learned that the best path to success is through hiring a diversity of smart people with different thoughts on almost everything. Smart business includes the intellectual flexibility of working together with diverse people, all willing to compromise in finding the most compelling views on the best strategy. Once such team of diverse people selected the best strategy, that as a team they could agree on, everybody became committed, irrespective of their personal views. At regular intervals, diverse people would review the successes, or failure, of their strategy in an evolving world. If modifications were necessary to cope with external changes in opportunities or threats, they would modify the strategy, not based on personal ideology but based on full support from all team members.

Likewise, the People of the United States elected diverse and smart people to Congress for the purpose of working together and to devise the best strategy for our country that would be good for all Americans. Working together? Today?

Rightfully, the People of the United States have lost confidence in today's polarized political environment. As we saw, two-thirds of Americans say that today's leaders pale in comparison with those twenty years ago. What about the other 1/3? Perhaps they are ideologically obsessed and approve anything that comes from the White House, no matter what.

Stand-fast ideology is only possible when masses of people are constantly fed with ideology. A perfect example was the old Soviet Union or China under Mao Tse Tung and his little red book. In America, the constant feeding of ideology began with the modern talk show hosts. Largely conservative, they feed their listeners with populist propaganda and a hodgepodge of conservative ideologies.

America's greatest president, George Washington, believed that the President should be beyond partisan politics. His job was to uphold the Constitution, the laws of the land and the interest of all Americans, not just the majority but minority interests as well. After all, this is the hallmark of American democracy, the assurance that the opinions of minorities count. Ideology should never take an overriding place in the President's office. This is hard to do because no President was or is without political orientation. Yet, President George W. Bush, who campaigned as a uniter, ruled as if America's democracy had ended. For him, only the Republican ideology counted. If he cared at all about the view of democrats it must have been in his prayers. Law after law emerged between the Republican Congress and White House without the voice of the Democratic minority in Congress. That party was essentially ignored in debates or conferences. No wonder "the People" revolted in the November 2006 elections and sent the Republican Party packing.

The sharp edges of polarization and thus partisan politics began with the convergence of conservative radio talk shows and Newt Gingrich's 1994 Contract with America. That swept the Republican Party into power, first in Congress, and then in 2001 the Party consolidated all powers when it captured the White House. Compromise disappeared. Politics turned more partisan than ever; loyalty to party politics became essential. If some Republican Party member voted conscience rather than party line there was hell to pay. Tom Delay, House Majority Leader at the time made sure of that.

To stand up for what was right used to be a desirable character trait for politicians. Exhibit that trait today, and talks shows will label you a traitor. That's how talk shows view John McCain today because he used to stand up for his beliefs.

By suppressing personal conscience in their votes, the remaining conscience that representatives may have had, came under assault also. That's why an amazing number of congressional members couldn't talk themselves out of the temptation of corruption. In the last ten years, the stories of Congressional corruption became legendary, mostly by Republicans although some Democrats couldn't resist the temptation either.

We all know that personal values and beliefs are inseparable from our individual personality. Therefore, values and religious beliefs cannot be separated from a politician's decisions. For example, Gerald Ford or Jimmy Carter had trouble condoning the assassination of foreign leaders that America didn't like. Having said that, Congressional and Presidential policy decisions should never be based on religious beliefs but solely on the Constitution, the rule of law, and the general interest of all Americans. This may have changed. Besides the bizarre attention Congress rendered the plight of Terri Chiavo, there is a suspicion that major governmental policy decisions were in part based on religious beliefs. Suppose the president believed that God wrote the bible, word for word, and that he believed in eschatology such as one could find in the last book of the bible, Revelations. Would such President wage war in the Middle East that would corroborate with the Prophesies of Revelations, perhaps in seeking the fulfillment promised by the End of Times? If he had done so, he would have recklessly jeopardized the lives of Americans and foreigners while ignoring the interests of American citizens who do not share the depth of his religious beliefs. In the Chapter of Iraq, we have tried to understand the motivation of our President in the Iraq war.

Polarization prevented our President from keeping America united. And keeping us united was essential in the national interest of eradicating terrorism against

America. During the Presidency of George W. Bush, our country was marked by fear. Good leadership should never resort to fear mongering or should not let fear runs its course.

During this Presidency, the word patriotism turned into a euphemism of nationalism. Patriotism came to mean flag waving and rendering full support to the policies of the White House and Republican ideology. True patriots became villains. True patriotism should be reserved for someone with the courage to overcome fear while fighting, even risking one's life, for the good of our country, irrespective of the policies of the White House. A soldier giving his life heroically and voluntarily for our country is an obvious patriot. But if someone truly believes that the Iraq war is bad for our country, the courage of going publicly against mainstream could be patriotic. Today, in the comfort of their luxury, polarizing talk shows hosts and politicians, however, dare to call anyone unpatriotic for having the unpopular courage of speaking up and acting for what they feel is best for our country (without committing crimes, of course).

Terrorism has always existed. Think Oklahoma bombing! Think Peru, or Colombia or Northern Ireland. When terrorism strikes, it needs to be dealt with decisively without theatre, without circus, without personal religious beliefs. After 9/11 the entire leadership of al Qaeda should have been destroyed, quickly and decisively. No country should have stopped us. We were powerful enough to accomplish that task in a relatively short time. But our government didn't focus on the task at hand. Instead, it gave priority to Iraq. As a result, al Qaeda is considered more powerful today than it was in 2001. Instead of being wiped out, they have regrouped in the vast border regions between Pakistan and Afghanistan where they are training more aspiring terrorists than ever, masterminding new terror attacks. We know that the main objective of al Qaeda is to replace existing governments in Islamic countries with hard-line Islamic fundamentalists along with the imposition of the Sharia that embodies Islamic law. We suspect that eventually al Qaeda and other extremist Muslim groups want to transform the West to the Islam, beginning with Western Europe.

We are puzzled as to why this President forsook his promise to invade any country that knowingly housed terrorists who threaten American interests. Pakistan does! Perhaps history will show why the Bush Administration changed our united focus to root out al Qaeda. With the invasion of Iraq we even helped al Qaeda's goal of transitioning a secular Iraq to a more Islamic country.

During times of war that last more than a few months, Presidents used to demand sacrifice from all its citizens, not just from the men and women fighting on the front lines. Yet, in the over-six-years of wars in Afghanistan and Iraq, we have not sacrificed at home.

Wars cost the nation blood and money. While those at home couldn't shed blood for our country, the least they should have done is to pay for the cost of these wars by raising taxes on all Americans for the duration of the war. Such willingness to sacrifice would have demonstrated solidarity with the troops.

However, the staunch ideology of the Republican Party was focused on tax-cuts. Apparently, that ideology seemed more important to President Bush than demanding solidarity with our troops through universal sacrifice. Instead he called for tax cuts and borrowing the cost of the wars on the shoulders of our children, including the military youngsters that will survive the wars. The staunch proponents of the Iraq war, mostly conservatives, never talk about paying for the war by raising taxes. Their support for the war from the comfort of luxury without sacrifice is very cheap, and hypocritical.

The sharpening of ideological positions has made it nearly impossible to achieve much progress for America. Both parties are good at observing the splinters in the eyes of the other party while ignoring the beam in their own. Since the attack on Pearl Harbor and World War II, our country has not faced the extraordinary challenges of today. Yet, politicians and talk shows promote ideological babble and polarization that will assuredly get us nowhere.

The only benefit of ideological babble is that it sharpens the understanding of the political boundaries on any given position on the extreme left and extreme right. That is useful to know. But once those boundaries are determined, Americans and politicians should pay no attention to ideology but search together for the right vision and decisions that benefit all Americans. Perhaps Jared Diamond in <u>Collapse</u> got it right that "the attitude in Washington today is no more than a 90-day focus". But America deserves more.

Enough challenges exist today for that diverse body of people in Congress to work together and agree with compromise on the best solutions for our most pressing challenges in this global world. They are:

- America's growing income and wealth gaps

- Unfair taxation system

- Waning American competitiveness in a global market

- Global warming

- Insufficient energy resources, and dependence on foreign nations

- Proliferation of nuclear weapons

- Fascist Islamic Terrorism

- Health insurance (that is dysfunctional in service and cost)

- $70 trillion tab on entitlements

- Indifference in judicial and prison system

- Incoherent and arrogant Foreign Policy

- Consumerism, instant gratification

- Low savings rate

- Lack of job security and retirement benefits

- Lack of sacrifice

- Budget and trade deficits

These should be the priorities of our new President and Congress. It is up to you, the voter, to choose your selection wisely!

CHAPTER 14

▼

CONSERVATIVES

Conservatives, who commonly vote for the Republican Party, and liberals, who commonly vote for the Democratic Party, act as if they are at war, against each other. It is a clear sign of our country's deterioration when one political group sees another group of Americans as the enemy more so than the real enemy of Islamic fascists. This became further clear when Ann Coulter's books became best sellers.

Both major political parties today have laid claims to Thomas Jefferson's ideals. These ideals included Jefferson's pursuit of liberty and equality. Who could argue with those ideals or wouldn't want to lay claim on them?

The current Republican Party, officially founded in 1854, saw its roots based on Jefferson's ideals but also on Jefferson's fight for limited federal power. However, the Republican Party of today became a convoluted mixture of ideals that often contradict itself. While the late William Buckley was a highly admirable person for friends and foes, he was partly responsible for this hodgepodge. This was possible in part because of that meaningless word "Conservative" as is used in today's politics. The word comes from "conserve" that is "disposed to preserve existing conditions, traditional customs, avoiding novelty, holding the course, conserve." These are all words that one can find in the New Universal Unabridged Dictionary of Webster. A splendid example of these definitions is the way the Amish people live. Many Conservatives of today consider the Amish backwards but the Amish are the ones who truly live up to the meaning of the word conservative.

Here are some examples that have made the word conservative into a meaningless claim and Grand Old Confusion. Following the official "conservative" definitions, it would make sense that environmentalists, who want to conserve the environment, would be called conservative. Yet, most of them call themselves liberals while Conservatives in general hate environmentalists. Conservatives want to help developers expand everywhere in the nation with little or no regard to the environment. That is most certainly not holding to conserving of nature.

Many die-hard Conservatives are my close friends. Some call themselves proudly "…. more conservative than Attila the Hun". That sounds macho, tough and that is probably why Attila's name came up, but as I remember from history books, Attila the Hun was a progressive anarchist, not fitting the word conservative at all. Are my friends not truly conservative but rather progressive? They might kill anyone who'd call them progressive because that word is reserved for the hated liberals. Yet, I have more proof that my friends are in fact progressives. Most of them are progressive early-adaptors. Some drive Ferraris equipped with advanced technologies. They all carry I-Phones or Blackberry's, and IPods. They buy every new gadget under the sun, a habit that is not what one would consider a conservative life style. The true conservatives Amish would have nothing to do with those modern ties.

Conservative ideology is easy on the ear but I don't think that most Conservatives have a clue what it means to be a conservative. Most of my Conservative friends like to go out hunting or do anything they want to enjoy life. They truly love their liberty, their personal freedom and don't want government to intrude on their own personal lives and business. That would make them liberals or libertarians (The term liberal comes from freedom). Why would they support a Republican Party that wants to curb personal freedom even if some of those freedoms are generally disliked, such as homosexuality? Personal freedom is personal freedom. You are either for personal freedom or you are not.

Most Conservative families have embraced their gas guzzling SUVs. Shouldn't Conservatives conserve the world's energy resources? Shouldn't Conservatives demand that SUVs gas mileage be raised to conserve energy? But no, apparently Conservatives resist any imposition on conservation.

Conservatives are generally thought to favor free market capitalism. The right for business to fire employees at will. Business works best, they say, when left alone without interference of government. But that espouses freedom, liberalism. Of note here is that the original thinkers of free market capitalism, among which

Adam Smith, the father of the movement, got the terminology right when followers of Smith called themselves "classical liberals" instead of classical conservatives.

At times Conservatives fight for issues that contradict their own ideology. Take illegal immigration. As we have seen, Conservatives champion unfettered market capitalism. This implies that labor should move unrestricted, regardless of borders. The Globalization that Conservatives pushed opened up our borders for all the components in the economic process of which labor is one component. Putting restrictions on immigration, legal or not, should for true Conservatives be a grave violation of the theory of free market capitalism that assumes that the vast majority of immigrants, with or without valid visa, come here to work. Additionally, because America is graying, our expected wave of retirees of baby-boomers will put a serious restraint on the economy (who will work when the baby boomers retire?). Immigrants, legal or illegal, are the immediate answer to this serious economic problem. Therefore, it should be sacrilegious for Conservatives to bar immigrants, legal or not, to enter our country for work. Yet, who would have thought that Conservatives end up being their own stumbling block towards unfettered immigration by rallying against illegal immigrants? The only true Conservative ideologists here are John McCain and George Bush, both favoring to provide "amnesty" to illegal immigrant workers.

The word Conservative can mean anything today. It is a mixed pot of all kinds of thoughts, some of which are diametrically opposed. That has made it convenient for the Republican Party because every individual has some conservative thoughts no matter how contradicting they would be to another one. Here is an overview of groups that are commonly regarded as Conservative, which will prove the hodgepodge that the Republican Party has become. The following material is an amalgamation of old historic textbooks and particularly paragraphs taken from Wikipedia, the free Encyclopedia, on conservatism, in particular conservatism in the United States.

Among Conservatives belong the *Classical Conservatives,* followers of Edmund Burke (1729–1797), a British statesman who favored time honored states and institutions. They would have rejected Martin Luther when he separated from the Roman Catholic Church because that church was time honored. Mr. Burke didn't like the Enlightenment ideas of John Locke either. John was the father of "individual freedom" and as such an inspiration to America's Founders. So what do Classical Conservatives believe? They really have no political ideology as long as we don't change time honored states and institutions. Somewhat identical to Classical Conservatives are the *Traditional Conservatives* who oppose social change, not necessarily of religious beliefs but rather of traditional custom; they may not like racial integration for example, or they wouldn't like legalization of drugs, because they don't like change.

Another type of conservative is the *"Classical liberal"* (yes, liberal, not a typo) who favors market capitalism. This is in the tradition of Adam Smith and John Locke who believed in the freedom of the individual to achieve success without interference by the government. These classical liberals don't really like classical conservatives and vice versa. Alan Greenspan, the former chairman of the Federal Reserve described in The Age of Turbulence that he was greatly influenced by both John Locke and Adam Smith.

Another type of conservative is the *Fiscal Conservative* who favors a limited form of government with low taxes and a balanced budget. They reason that (excessive) taxation discourages investment and causes capital to flee our country. The purpose of taxation is, of course, to pay for federal spending that Congress approved; therefore, lowering taxes is only a good thing if spending is cut accordingly. But according to many conservatives today, they call for tax-cuts while condoning increased federal spending. Wonder where they got their accounting classes!

Among voters of the Republican Party are many *Libertarians (see chapter)*. Absolute freedom for the individual is what they want; if you want to smoke pot, that's your right, perhaps stupid but, nonetheless, your right, and governments should not interfere. Libertarians who vote Republican accept some limited form of government. As English philosopher Herbert Spencer pointed out: "Every man has freedom to do all he wills, provided he infringes not the equal freedom of any other man." And to ensure that no one infringes on equal freedom, we need government.

Further included in the term conservative are the so-called *Religious Fundamentalists* who believe that their moral issues, including family values, must be protected by the government. In essence, they want government to impose their personal morals on others, and in doing so they favor federal power over state power. By favoring federal power over state power, the religious fundamentalists are in fact against the true origin of the American Republican Party that favored states rights over federal rights. Needless to say that libertarians and religious conservatives don't mix well.

Another group included are the so-called *Modern or Compassionate Conservatives.* They appear to disagree with fiscal conservatives because they favor expansion of federal government powers, and they have no problem with budget deficits. The current President, George W. Bush, exhibits a modern/compassionate conservative approach. Finally, we have the *Neo-Conservatives* who broke the old Conservative preference of isolation from the world. Neo-Conservatives want America to play an active military and political role on the world scene. This group was believed largely responsible for planning the "war" in Iraq.

Note that the list does not contain *Tough Conservatives*, as in "tougher than Attila the Hun". There is really nothing tough in the ideology of Conservatives. In today's wars, many Conservatives sound tough but are in fact rather cowards by supporting the war from the comfort of luxury without demanding personal sacrifice. As a note of interest, prior to the Neo-Conservatives, Republicans didn't want to get involved in wars. Democrats were more likely to call Americans to arms as they did in all major wars in the 20th Century. Without going into history too much, our founding fathers would have felt uncomfortable as a Conservative today. They certainly did not adhere to the classical conservatism of Burke or traditional conservatism or modern conservatism or religious conservatism. They favored the Enlightenment ideas by John Locke and Adam Smith. In fact, individual liberalism was espoused by all the famous founders be it John Adams, Samuel Adams, George Washington, James Madison or Thomas Jefferson. Perhaps American Libertarians (those who favor some limited form of government) are closer to our Founders than any other political party today.

Making a gigantic leap from the Founders to the sixties and seventies, the most known Conservative at the time was the Senator from Arizona, Barry Goldwater. He was called Mr. Conservative. In those days, Conservatives mainly consisted of those who believed in free markets, small government and balanced budgets, summed up as classical liberals united with fiscal conservatives. It was a cohesive ideology. The great and late William Buckley Jr. was perhaps the father of the more modern and convoluted conservative movement. But this intellectual stood out among today's conservatives by seeing politics in a relative way. He didn't hate liberals. His best friends were liberals. President Reagan followed Buckley's footsteps. Most well known Conservatives today don't have friends among liberals. If they did they would be called traitors. Well, not all. Good Conservatives still exist: Christopher Cox, Chairman of the SEC, and Arnold Schwarzenegger, Governor of California, come to mind.

Beloved Ronald Reagan continued the Buckley revolution by uniting the Goldwater conservatives with religious fundamentalists. Reagan recognized that the word Conservative was a misnomer. In an attempt to define Conservatism, he said:

> "If you analyze it, I believe the very heart and soul of conservatism is libertarianism; if we were back in the days of the Revolution, so-called conservatives

would be called liberals, and the liberals would be the Tories [though Tories in Britain are the equivalent of our Conservatives]. The basis of conservatism is a desire for less government interference or less centralized authority or more individual freedom and this is a pretty general description also of what libertarianism is." (Source: Wikipedia/Conservatism in the United States.)

However, Reagan must not have realized that by adding Religious Conservatives to the party, it caused a departure of libertarian philosophy. After all, Religious Conservatives in politics seek to impose their morals on others, and that is a big no-no for libertarians. During the Reagan Administration, however, Religious Conservatives made little progress.

A significant change for Conservatives arrived when George W. Bush was elected President. All possible Conservative categories described earlier, were now united in the Republican Party. George Bush gave out big slices to everyone, here and there, somewhat incoherently. His excellent AIDS program in Africa and expensive drug program for Medicare showed compassion for Modern conservatives though his programs would likely have been loathed by the Conservatives of the Reagan or Goldwater years.

Fiscal Conservatives, among which Nobel Laureate, Milton Friedman, were pleased with the Bush huge tax cuts, yet they were displeased that Bush showed no attempt to restrain government spending. The Federal Budget grew from $9.7 trillion dollars in 2000, to $14.3 trillion estimate in 2008, the last year of George Bushs' term, a growth of 48% in Mr. Bushs' two terms. (Source: The White House). According to William Niskanen, Chairman Cato Institute and former acting chairman of President Reagan's Council of Economic Advisors, the growth of government spending tripled under George W. Bush compared to that under Clinton or other Presidents under a divided government.

Neo-Conservatives increased war spending and got us into Iraq, yet are not satisfied either because of serious mismanagement by the Bush Administration. However, Religious Conservatives got special attention. Even though at times the religious influence brought mockery to Congress, such as the Terri Chiavo case, they made a huge impact through the appointment of very conservative and religious judges both on the Supreme Court and Federal Appellate Courts. They also got a moratorium on stem cell research.

Classical conservatives got their share in the protection of big business, especially oil, logging, and car companies. Classical Liberals got the freedom to expand globalization. Yet, Libertarians, that President Reagan favored, didn't get many favors from George W Bush. For Conservatives as a whole, the results of the George W. Bush Administration were mixed.

Take nuclear proliferation. According to a speech on February 9, 2008 by ElBaradei, International Atomic Agency Chief, the nuclear threat in the hands of terrorists is higher than ever. Further, we saw that George Bush was the highest big spender since President Johnson in the 1960s. Trade deficits reached an all-time high, causing erosion of faith in the once almighty dollar. We are in the midst of an unresolved war in Iraq without a clear purpose. We've got Guantanamo Bay and water boarding, and a general feeling that we tinkered with the Constitution. We are left with an unfriendly world while the problems in the world are more demanding than ever. The nation is not prepared to compete with China.

This mixed bag has rightfully confounded most Conservatives (even though my conservative friends are still singing party line). The Republican Party tried to be something for everybody. That may work for a short time but long term it is strategically untenable. It also leads to manipulation of the American people. If the American people would expect integrity from the Republican Party, it would have to split up into ideologically matched political parties. The Libertarian party could certainly incorporate many conservative views such as fiscal responsibility, small government and lower taxes. The United States could use another one or two strong political parties. One could be a Christian Democratic Party that espouses true Christian beliefs and values within a secular government. Think of a strong social conscience, upholding human rights and individual dignity and a basic level of societal care.

CHAPTER 15

▼

LIBERALS

According to the conservative wing of the Republican Party, Democrats are "country destroying liberals". Ann Coulter, self-described conservative intellectual, went as far as the release of a book with the title: If liberals had any brains they would be conservatives. Is it true that liberals are do-gooders who are brainless by wanting to do too much good while destroying the country in the process? Do they want to tax all the money you have earned and give it away, redistribute, to the so-called poor that don't want to work and blame others for their problems? Under President Bill Clinton we have seen that these accusations proved mere myths. But what about Obama or Hillary?

Disputing Ann Coulter's book, a recent study reported in the journal of Nature Neuroscience concluded that Liberals don't get fooled easily and are more adaptable than Conservatives. Liberals might be better judges of the facts. In other words, Americans that tend to view the facts tend or trend to become Liberal. This might explain why Conservative talk shows are more successful than Liberal talk shows. Their followers accept freely daily slanted facts of America's politics. Conservatives have a tendency to follow leaders, such as Rush Limbaugh, similar to a herd of sheep. Conservatives tend not to question party gospel and are easier indoctrinated because, according to the study, they are not interested in or capable of exploring facts. This study may be applicable to the average Conservative, however, I personally know many smart conservatives who defy that rule of averages.

Webster's unabridged dictionary considers liberals "favorable to progression or reform in politics and religion." The word liberal indicates a free-ness, freedom, liberalism, and liberty. In the political sense, Liberals then should favor progression while affording maximum individual and business freedom; they should be open-minded and tolerant. That does sound very fitting of Jefferson's Declaration of Independence. But are they?

In general, liberalism in politics has two main, diverging streams: Classical liberalism and Social liberalism. Classical liberalism supports market capitalism and a small government. This branch of liberalism is somewhat akin to the American libertarian party. These liberals are not found in mainstream America but are common in Europe in their right wing parties.

The American branch of liberalism supports market capitalism but not unfettered. It does support individual freedom without government interference on how people lead their lives, akin to libertarianism. Otherwise it differs greatly from Libertarians. In particular, it favors a strong government role in promoting general welfare to help the poor, the sick, the elderly and the unemployed. In Europe, followers of the Christian Democratic Parties and labor parties would support the latter role. In reviewing the principles of Christianity, if religion should play a role in elections, true Christians should feel more comfortable with American Social Liberalism than with American Conservatism.

The Democratic Party is not a hodge-podge when compared to the Republican Party. If we try to capture the Republican Party in one word, we are at a loss. If we had only one word to capture the Democratic Party, the word "Care" comes to mind. Liberal is not the right term for those who support politics of care. For example, protecting labor, as unions do, seems very conservative, holding to tradition. Thus, logically, unions should be called conservative, yet nobody thinks of them as Conservative. Bottom line is that most American liberals are more caring than Conservatives for the welfare of all Americans; they also care more about the environment and care more about making us independent of foreign energy while caring more than Conservatives about global warming. All of that care, however, goes against unfettered market capitalism.

Democrats do not support the view of Conservatives that markets correct themselves fairly. American liberals point, for example, to the non-regulated mortgage brokers that sold teaser mortgages to new homeowners who couldn't afford to own these homes. The sub-prime mortgage disaster that followed was self-correcting but caused significant damage to the world economy and undermined trust in financial institutions. Liberals believe that with a little oversight of government, teaser mortgages could have been avoided.

Liberals also believe that if business were left alone, without OSHA for example or labor regulations; employers would not spend the money to keep workers safe. Or they would simply replace older workers with younger, less expensive ones. Liberals believe that without support from Liberals, America's black and other minorities would have had no chance to integrate, or women would still be sexually harassed at work. Liberals believe that your children might still be working in the mines if they hadn't pushed for laws that restrict child labor. They also believe that women trafficking would be more common. After all, women trafficking is only a market response of free market forces of demand and supply.

The problem with Liberals is, do they know when to stop? Because too much caring may sound good in church, but in practice, too much caring could harm the economy and reduce incentives to work creatively. Some American liberal environmentalists would stop expanding land development just to save a spotted owl or rat from distinction. So what if the rat dies, most Americans would ask. If one cares too much, one could loose common sense and become unrealistic about what can and should be done about societal needs.

It is sometimes hard to say stop. After all, when you pursue an ideal, that you will never reach, you often don't know when you might be going too far. This happened when Democrats were completely in control of the government under Lyndon Johnson in the sixties with too many welfare laws, or when communism had to be stopped at any expense in South East Asia, and Vietnam in particular.

It is perhaps the experience of forty years ago that justified Ann Coulter's observation that liberals can be brainless by wanting to do too much good. Since President Johnson, however, the Democratic Party has tempered its goals. For example, the Clinton Administration, albeit with a Republican Congress, dismantled much of the "welfare state" that had grown too much since Lyndon Johnson. Further, under the Clinton Administration, the nation's number of millionaires soared while the numbers of Americans below the poverty line were reduced. Additionally, the federal budget deficit disappeared. These were remarkable achievement under a Democratic President. It defied the general belief, especially among Republicans, that Democrats are big spenders.

Let's look at some more facts. Under the last Democratic President, Bill Clinton, the Federal Spending Budget stood at 18.4% of GDP or $1.8 trillion in Clinton's last year of 2000. Not counting the war spending for Iraq and Afghanistan, the Federal Budget under George W. Bush grew to $3.1 trillion, estimate, for fiscal year 2009, the last year for which George Bush is responsible, an increase exceeding 70% since Clinton, or when corrected for inflation a 48% growth.(Source: The White House).

While in Europe the term liberal in political parties is used correctly the term Liberal in America doesn't really fit the supporters of the Democratic Party. Comments such as flaming liberals are an insult to the true meaning of the word liberal. How would we find the right term for our Liberal Democratic Party? Some suggested the name of "progressives" but that doesn't fit the environmentalists. Ann Coulter might have some suggestions but they might fall on a deaf ear; perhaps Freedom with Care would work.

We believe that political parties would appeal more to Americans if their name would be in sync with their entire platform. As it stands today, the word liberals and especially the word conservatives are largely meaningless, leading to confusion and facilitating manipulation of the American voter.

CHAPTER 16

▼

LIBERTARIANS

Lately the term libertarian has become popular, thanks to Ron Paul, the Texas libertarian doctor who made a run for the Republican Party's candidacy for President. When viewing the number of delegates he got behind his name, his run was unremarkable. But in terms of buzz and excitement among young voters and the successes of raising money over the Internet, his run was sensational.

According to Wikipedia, the free Encyclopedia, libertarians' most distinct ideology views life and property as the ultimate rights of an individual. They oppose any law that restricts personal or consensual behavior including so-called victim-less crimes (such as drugs). The ideology of libertarians speaks readily to freedom-minded Americans. Yet most Americans realize also that government is a necessary "evil" while many libertarians would prefer to live without a government. Libertarianism as ideology isn't liked by a number of conservatives, especially religious conservatives or classical and traditional conservatives. Because Libertarians don't care about a government role in the plight of Americans, Libertarian ideology does not speak at all to American Liberals.

Critics have pointed out the pitfalls of Libertarianism. They view it as simple-mindedness removed from reality. Saying that we want freedom sounds good but is it always? Should we allow dumping of toxic waste in our ground water? Most Americans would want government to step in and set rules against pollution. Or should the government stay out of people's lives by letting the courts take care of problems such as industrial pollution. But courts are very expensive. Someone has got to foot the cost of plaintiff's lawyers, often up front, and often the low-income pollution plaintiffs are no match to deep pocketed polluting industries. As Michael Kinsley pointed out in the Los Angeles Times, the judicial system is also the most expensive, elaborate and inconsistent system of decision making in our country.

Kinsley further questioned the libertarians' preference for moving the responsibility of the nation's infrastructure to the private sector. Private industry would be attracted to high-usage highways but would have little incentive to get involved in roads less traveled. Let industry grab the efficient routes and leave the inefficient routes to the government? What about intersections of highways owned by different companies? Private companies are only more efficient than government if competition drives them to higher efficiencies, lower cost and lower prices. But competition would vanish once a private company built a highway, leaving the private company a monopoly, free to charge exorbitant fees to users who are without an alternative route. Further, without government oversight, who would set the rules of the road? Each company would set their own rules? Driving left or right?

On the surface simplicity often sounds good. But when peeling the onion a little bit, one wonders what our interstate highways would look like if libertarians had their way all along. President Eisenhower's decision to have government control the construction of interstate highways from East to West, South to North turned into the envy of the world, and was partly instrumental in the immense economic growth of America. These highways would not have been built without the government controlling the nation's infrastructure. Likewise, if the government had not required telephone companies to bring telephone infrastructure to rural areas, these companies could not have justified the high cost of bringing phone lines and central offices outside dense urban areas.

Libertarians would not support government subsidies for advancing critical new technologies that are the root of major economic growth in the future. In other words, our nation's competitiveness would suffer under Libertarian rule.

The list goes on and on. Libertarianism in its pure ideology is more a utopia than a practical solution for a thriving society. Even our founders realized that a limited government is a necessity. Yet, libertarianism is a very useful ideology to remind us that freedom should be central to our lives. Our lawmakers are too casual when they restrict our freedom with laws that may sound good but the cumulative effect is laws piling upon laws, eroding the precious freedom of Americans. Libertarianism does not lead to confusion and manipulation. Libertarianism is all about freedom. Unlike with Conservatives and Liberals, what you see with Libertarianism is what you get.

CHAPTER 17

▼

DECEPTION

Deception in politics has been around longer than America's existence. The masters of deceit found their roots in <u>The Prince</u> by Niccolo Machiavelli, the Florentine genius of the 16th Century. Machiavelli convinced the Prince that moral issues regarding good and evil be used not as an end but as a means to controlling power. Because men do not act in good faith, a wise prince is not bound to keep faith with them; however, it is best for the prince to "appear" to possess good qualities such as faith, integrity and religion. In other words, Niccolo advocated manipulating morals to achieve the support of the populace, or in modern America: your votes. In his view, deception is justified and morally acceptable because in the end it achieves a far greater good. This philosophy has had popular following by most of the not so popular figures in history such as Adolf Hitler, Josef Stalin and Mao Tse Tung. Unfortunately, Machiavelli's views are too popular in modern American politics today.

That <u>The Prince</u> is alive and well becomes obvious to the careful listener of politicians and "news media" as well as the popular conservative media of talk shows. Talk show hosts are often charismatic and gifted with a shrewd talent for rhetoric that sways the opinion of most listeners. If hypocrisy and manipulation were virtues, these people would deserve admiration for the cunning in which they manipulate high morals for the sole purpose of securing votes. It is not easy to pull off for people with scruples. It is not easy to adhere to a "no-spin" zone while supporting biased news and biased views.

How could one explain that middle and lower economic classes in so-called Blue States voted for the Republican Party that at the same time heavily promotes globalization, wiping out their jobs? Their votes were likely swayed through manipulation of "morals" such as the promise of a constitutional amendment to ban gay marriage. Their votes for the Republican Party helped wipe out their jobs while the constitutional amendment is never going to happen, simply because constitutional amendments provide rights of freedom, not restrictions of freedom. Yet, this is the way people are manipulated today for the "far greater good" as seen by the rich, at the expense of the poor.

I grew up as a Conservative by supporting the Conservative party in Holland. It stood for individual freedom and unfettered market capitalism. Thirty-five years ago the politicians and we could appreciate the talents and accomplishments of other political parties and their candidates. When I immigrated to the US, I found a similar appreciation in America. For example, Nixon, who was President at the time, was openly admired for his foreign expertise by many friends I had among Democrats. One such prominent accomplishment was the opening of China, a country that until then had been closed to the world since the 1940s. At the same time, Nixon was reviled by my Republican friends for imposing price controls, and needless to say, his disregard for the breaking of criminal law. Despite ideologies, people tended to be morally honest. They were not brainwashed, as most people are today, to automatically reject opposition just because they are opposition.

Today, only the rare independent Republican would fairly judge the President. Polls show that over 80% of Republican voters still support the President and the war in Iraq. This is an enormous partisan vote of confidence for a man who has spent our money like a "traditional flaming liberal", turned the world against us and is leaving us with a war without clear purpose or strategy. The President violated many conservative ideologies. Yet, it is as if accountability is of no consequence anymore for modern Republicans. Those in the Republican Party that do respect others or who would reach out to opposition have become an outcast today. On her show on February 6, 2008, popular conservative talk show host Laura Ingraham played a clip of John McCain in which he said that he respects his Democratic rivals for the presidency, Senators Barack and Clinton. Laura despised McCain for saying that and dripping of sarcasm asked, Great, you are not going after Clinton for being a big fat phony? Likewise, most popular conservative talk shows revel in their condemnation of John McCain, largely because in the Senate he had reached out across the aisle to work with the opposition.

What kind of America do we live in where it is considered a serious offense to admire other Americans from another political party? Why aren't we appalled? Why do we participate in the smear towards opposition? Why do we listen to brainwashing talk-shows that have polarized the country and make us hate our own fellow Americans, who mean just as well for America as we do?

The other day, I asked a smart, successful businesswoman in her forties if she saw Al Gore's movie <u>An Inconvenient Truth</u>. She snickered, and replied: Of course, not, why would I want to watch a movie by Al Gore? The way she pronounced his name was laden with contempt. I suggested, perhaps she should see it because it contained very important views about possible catastrophic damage to the earth, that could impact you and your children's live negatively; I added that the viewpoints in this movie were supported by most of the scientists in the world. Even if not everything is true, the movie is just interesting and allows you to shape your opinion about perhaps one of the most important changes affecting you and your children. She snickered again that she would never watch anything from Al Gore no matter how good it was, or for that matter from any liberal. Did I say that she calls herself a conservative? Oh, she did mention that liberal Al invented the Internet, ha-ha, but otherwise offered no substantive information. This is a classic brainwashed conservative woman, just one among tens of millions of brainwashed Americans today.

A great friend of mine said the other day that he couldn't vote for Hillary Clinton because she was too divisive. I asked him to give me some specifics. He couldn't come up with one example. He admitted that his opinion about her divisiveness was totally from, well, hearsay, particularly the media. He heard from radio talk shows, read polls, and thus assumed that she was divisive. He was brainwashed!

Not all conservative media or politicians use deceptive techniques. There are still honest and objective conservative media reporters though in the minority. William Buckley Jr. was one of them. He was a true believer of conservative principles and he was deeply disturbed by what is promoted today under the label of conservatism. He had common sense and personal integrity that is sorely missed particularly among many Republicans today.

Other old timers in the conservative media, who I used to admire and with whom I met, caught the disease of writing distortions. The other day, George Will wrote a scathing article about Jim Webb, Democratic Senator of Virginia, who, according to Will, seemed disrespectful for the office of the presidency. But what a short memory Will has that he didn't remember his own scathing articles towards Bill Clinton as President? Likewise, Dennis Prager, who I remembered as a wonderful and pragmatic conservative, is now writing disrespectful, conde-scending and blatantly generalizing articles about liberals such as his article that "Liberals must get over their desire to be loved". Cartoon jokes galore with accu-sations that Democrats are myopic, gutless, weak, and incompetent. Anti-Bush messages are doing the round too but at least many were backed up with relevant statistics. Conservatives who sent despicable messages about Clinton or Obama seem to follow Lenin's advice that a lie told often enough becomes the truth in people's mind. I often listen to conservative talk shows in hopes of hearing one nice comment about opponents; I am still waiting.

When did the smear and divisiveness in American politics get started? Joseph Ellis in <u>American Creation</u> describes the two friends, Federalist John Adams and Republican Party chief Thomas Jefferson, who found themselves on different sides in the party wars in the 1790s. In 1797 when Adams succeeded George Washington as America's second President, he pursued a bi-partisan approach with the Republicans. Adams heavily courted Jefferson to join him with a full cabinet status, an equal say in foreign policy, and enhanced political status just short of co-President. Ellis continued that Jefferson was willing to leave the door open for an Adams-Jefferson coalition and prepared a letter to that extent. But, according to Ellis, he decided to run it past Republican James Madison, who advised Jefferson that his long-standing friendship with Adams must not take precedence over the long-term interest of the Republican Party. Ellis continued, Madison was telling Jefferson that he had to choose between his affection for Adams and his loyalty to the Republican Agenda. Jefferson didn't accept Adams' offer.

That's about the time American partisan politics were born, and negative cam-paigning started. According to Ellis, Jefferson saw the Federalists (though not John Adams) as the evil empire that his party hoped to sink; instead of Federalists he called them Monarchists. Ouch! While that could be hardly called a smear in today's politics, in 1800, the smear became real during the election campaign between the campaign of John Adams for a second term and challenger Thomas Jefferson. As Adam Volland wrote in U.S. News, Federalists wrote about Repub-lican candidate Thomas Jefferson that "if elected: Murder, robbery, rape, adultery and incest will all be openly taught and practiced". That was bad, though at least that viciousness was not entirely pulled from the air as it alluded to the rumor, later confirmed, that Jefferson had fathered a child with Sally Hemings, one of his slaves.

Even though smear seems as old as politics, in the last twenty years we have seen a significant change in modern smear. Not only has it become more sophisticated but also often it seems campaigners no longer need at least a shred of truth in the allegation they make. Further, smear is no longer confined to the period of campaigning but seems now '24/7'. Rush Limbaugh, for example, never let go of his smear against Bill and Hillary Clinton even after Bill had left the White House and long before Hillary announced her candidacy.

It started in 1988 when Lee Atwater became campaign manager for George H.W. Bush, father of the current President. Lee Atwater was smart and shrewd and could be called the father of modern negative politics. From "Lee Atwater" in Wikipedia, the free Encyclopedia, Atwater used fake surveys by so-called independent pollsters that were often behind the negative rumors that were subtly spread. During the 1998 election, a number of false rumors were reported in the media about Dukakis, the Democratic candidate, that his wife Kitty had burned an American flag to protest the Vietnam War, as well as the claim that Dukakis himself had been treated for a mental illness, none of which appeared to be true.

Atwater's most memorable deception came with Willi Horton, a felon convicted of a 1974 murder. This deception had a slight shred of truth pulled entirely out-of-context. According to Wikipedia, Massachusetts had instituted a week-end furlough program for good behavior as part of a prisoner revalidation program. While working well, the revalidation didn't turn out so good in the case of Willi Horton who raped a woman while on furlough. Governor Dukakis didn't design the furlough plan, though he hadn't rejected it either, apparently believing that revalidation was the right thing to do (as a Christian). Wikipedia continued that George H.W. Bush, trying to overcome a 17 percent lead by Dukakis in early public opinion polls, used the name of Willi Horton frequently in his campaign. In the fall of 1998, advertisements came out such as Weekend Passes, showing a menacing shot of Horton and the words "every suburban mother's greatest fear", and another called "Revolving Door" with intimidating looking men leaving prison through a revolving door. George Bush went on to win the election.

According to Wikipedia, during that election, the current President George W. Bush, the son of George H.W. Bush, took an office across the hall from Atwater's office, where his job was to serve as "the eyes and ears for my dad," monitoring the activities of Atwater and other campaign staff. In her memoir, Barbara Bush said that George W. and Atwater became "great friends". Lee Atwater was also a political mentor and close friend of Karl Rove. After the elections, when Lee Atwater was dying of a tumor, he repented and converted to

Catholicism. Shortly before his death, he wrote a number of apologies to those he had attacked during his career, including Dukakis, adding:

> "..my illness has taught me something about the nature of humanity, love, brotherhood and relationships that I never understood, and probably never would have"

In a February 1991 article for *Life Magazine*, Atwater wrote:

> My illness helped me to see that what was missing in society is what was missing in me: a little heart, a lot of brotherhood. The '80s were about acquiring—acquiring wealth, power, prestige. I know. I acquired more wealth, power, and prestige than most. But you can acquire all you want and still feel empty. What power wouldn't I trade for a little more time with my family? What price wouldn't I pay for an evening with friends? It took a deadly illness to put me eye to eye with that truth, but it is a truth that the country, caught up in its ruthless ambitions and moral decay, can learn on my dime. I don't know who will lead us through the '90s, but they must be made to speak to this spiritual vacuum at the heart of American society, this tumor of the soul.

If the 80's were about acquiring wealth and power, the 2000s must have exceeded all Atwater's expectations had he been alive.

Atwater's timing to start this whole new level in political deception in 1988 was stunning. While the "end" should never justify "immoral means", if there was a time to do it, it was in 1980 when the economy was really bad with inflation roaring, family values under attack, an economy sputtering; and low national confidence after the loss in Vietnam while American hostages held in Iran. Yet, Reagan didn't start this new level of deception in his campaign against Jimmy Carter. That campaign was perhaps one of the more civil campaigns in memory. Probably the most memorable moment in that civilized campaign came when Reagan asked America in the only televised debate with Carter: "If you are better off today than four years ago, vote for Carter".

At the end of the Reagan era, inflation was held in check by the remarkable discipline of the Fed Chairman Paul Volcker; taxes had been slashed; market capitalism was freed of some restraints; family values were getting attention and our national confidence had made a remarkable come-back. In other words, in 1988, there was absolutely no compelling justification to resort to deception let alone to bring deception in politics to a whole new level. Yet, that's when it happened. It just coincided with the breakdown in our nation's social responsibility and with the growing indifference to fairness, care, truth, and respect. In short, all the things that bind a society were in the process of getting lost. And the process continued.

Fast forward to the Clinton years, when America enjoyed it's most remarkable economic growth. Poverty declined, crime declined, millionaires were born on the fly. Times were great and certainly no compelling motivation existed to use deception for the greater good. There was no real special "end" purpose. But there was Karl Rove who had learned from Atwater, and there was George W. Bush who had learned from Atwater. And there were the Rush Limbaughs. No one paid much attention to the repentance by Lee Atwater, or they thought that there would be time enough for repentance later.

Who doesn't remember the primary in South Carolina in 2000 when super war-hero and long time U.S. Republican Senator from Arizona, John McCain was running successfully against George W. Bush? As reported in Newsweek by Evan Thomas, Republican smear artists [for George W. Bush] began to spread false rumors that the former POW was "nuts" because he had been "in the cage too long". Other rumors circulated falsely that he had fathered a black child [he adopted a black child]. Even though they were lies without a shred of evidence, they fulfilled the end goal (though not for the greater good): George Bush got the votes. Once their end purpose was successfully reached, the lies about McCain were forgotten. Of course George Bush denied involvement. In 2004, who doesn't remember the Swift Boat Veterans for Truth that successfully, though cowardly, smeared war hero John Kerry? Bush, who didn't serve in the Vietnam War, distanced himself from that smear but not forcefully enough to stop the smear.

Another example is the manner by which tax cuts were sold to the American people. President Reagan did not hide from the American people that he was making important tax cuts for the rich. On the other hand, George Bush forgot to mention that his tax cuts were primarily benefiting the rich. He sold his rounds of tax cuts to the American people by suggesting that his tax cuts were intended "to benefit ordinary families". Perhaps Mr. Bush's advisors didn't tell him that as a percentage of income, the Bush tax reductions cut the taxes for the top 1% by 4.3% and for the bottom just 0.7%. (Source: Robert McIntyre, Director of Citizens for Tax Justice.) In other words, the top 1% gained the most. Another way of looking at the tax cuts was provided early 2007 by the non-partisan Congressional Budget Office about 2004 income taxes, the latest year for which data was available. It showed that the top 1% households with average income of $1.25 million received a tax cut of $58,000 while families in the middle income of $56,200 received a tax cut of $1,180. Did Bush lie? No, the tax cuts did benefit ordinary families. Was it disingenuous to omit that the bulk would go the very rich? Yes, it sure was.

This strategy of deception paid-off; the Republican Party got control of Congress from 1994 to 2006, and the Presidency from 2001 to 2008. What about the current campaign for the new president? Early on, the conservatives feared Hillary Clinton. It was rare to find a Rush Limbaugh show without hearing him rant against the Clintons. Yet, an intelligent listener would have remembered that Bill Clinton was a moderate and one of the most popular Presidents who made positive changes that even conservatives loved. He signed NAFTA, made serious welfare reform from a near welfare state to a more common sense welfare, he balanced the federal budgets, oversaw one of the lowest periods of growth in federal spending, while more Americans became a millionaire than ever before, he set conditions for an exuberant economy. In <u>The Age of Turbulence,</u> Republican Alan Greenspan, Federal Reserve Chairman, had more positives to say about Clinton in respect of the economy than any other President. Yet, the smear campaign against him attempted to rewrite history and erase all his successes.

In his loins Bill Clinton had an obvious weakness. But that shortcoming should not have defined his presidency. After all many brilliant and successful people for our country were caught (or deserved to be caught) for similar problems. It happened to hundreds and hundreds of well-known executives and politicians that were allowed to maintain their prestige. Think of top Congressional Representatives, Newt Gingrich, Bob Livingston and Henry Hyde. These fine upstanding and highly "moral" Republicans lead the impeachment charges against Clinton while they were having sexual affairs. Technocrats pointed to the difference of Clinton's lying under oath about it but forget to add that Clinton was set-up to fall in that trap, as any man would have done if he believed that his "secret" affair was safe. This is not in defense of his action but this has been the American way. In Europe, the public doesn't pay much attention to the sexual affairs of their politicians.

This writer is not a Hillary supporter, yet found it interesting to observe that the U.S. Senator of New York is despised by 40 to 50% of the nation (depending on the poll). No other candidate, liberal or conservative, is hated this much. What in the world did she do to become hated by so many people, including by many so-called Christians? Did she commit fraud? Did she kill someone? Did she antagonize people like Ann Coulter seems to do for a living? Why is she called divisive? Her resume appears positive or at a minimum neutral and contains nothing negative that justifies hatred. Ironically, she has all the proper qualifications and morals that are desirable by the Christian Right. She stood by her husband in turbulent and personal times; admirably she forgave him and did not divorce him. She did not commit adultery or other crime and has upheld the standard of high morals. She works very hard, is well respected as Senator by New Yorkers. She is fiscally conservative. Bright and experienced! Most Senators including Republican Senators like her. Above all, she is a devout Christian and she is against abortion. These are facts but you would never hear them from talk show hosts. For the Christian right and general conservatives, there should be no candidate for president better qualified than she is. Yet, the Christian right hates her. As the late Jerry Falwell suggested, if Hillary Clinton were to get the nomination for President, the Christian right will be galvanized to defeat her. Could it just be the one failure of the early nineties to propose universal healthcare? Why would it? Failure is good for the soul and sharpens wisdom. Besides, businesses all over America would love to see a national healthcare system that would take that monkey off their backs.

The late, genuine conservative William Buckley, Jr, founder of National Review, wrote a fairly positive article about Hillary and implied that he was against the mania against her. But most Americans are brainwashed. Some of my best friends regularly send me Hillary hate mail without knowing why. Apparently, it is just popular to participate in smear.

Lenin said: When a lie is told often enough, it becomes the "truth".

The conservative media, especially talk-show hosts, succeeded with their relentless smear, lies and half-truths. One of their interesting little tricks was so simple that it is hard to believe that the average American believes it. They began a campaign portraying all media as liberal biased. As proof they routinely cited articles that could have had a negative reflection on conservatives. As every common sense person knows, daily news could go against liberals, or against conservatives. Objective media would publish both conservative and liberal news in an unbiased way. But here is how conservative talk-show hosts interpreted the objective media: they took the negative articles towards conservatives as proof that the media is biased, and then spun the facts to make the negatives look better. Next, they would pound on the negatives regarding liberals but conveniently wouldn't tell their listeners that the same so-called liberal media also reported these articles. This left the listener with the conclusion: The media only reports negative articles about conservatives, and thus are biased. This amazing little trick was enormously successful. Newspapers became very conscious of that labeling and must have thought twice about reporting negative articles about conservatives. The result is that the average American is now convinced that all they read in the press is liberal biased. In a separate chapter, we observed the results of how liberal the mainstream media actually is. Another little trick was that talk-show hosts pretended not to be part of the media. Thus, Rush succeeded in gaining the confidence of listeners that he was a sort of judge of the media rather than being part of the media, and that he would tell them the truth, and nothing but the truth. Now, there is genius!

Another success from these talk shows is that most Americans believe that only conservatives can be trusted to fight wars while liberals are weak. How is that substantiated? Let's see. All four major wars in the last century were started and fought with Democratic Presidents. They won three out of four. They didn't even "cut and run" from the fourth. The fourth major war was lost, the Vietnam War, when a Republican President pulled out. The only major war that Republicans started was the Iraq war, mismanaged it while leaving Osama bin Laden a free man. Rush Limbaugh's brother, David Limbaugh, wrote in Newsmax that the GOP must prevail in war time because "the party of Neville Chamberlain (he means the Democrats) has only one solution: Embrace defeat, withdraw our forces and negotiate with terrorists." Why does that make sense other than fabricating a deceptive fantasy during campaigns? Assuming that he alluded to Iraq, every American should know by now that prior to our invasion al Qaeda was not in Iraq but that our focus on Iraq afforded al Qaeda a bonanza in recruiting new terrorists. Every American who listened to Hillary or Obama would know that they are determined to hunt down Osama bin Laden and destroy al Qaeda. Rush and David Limbaugh know all that. So why can't they tell the truth? Are they paid to not tell the truth?

Everyone knows that the Republican Party is fiscally more responsible than the Democrats, right? Why then did the Federal Budget under Republican George W. Bush and the Republican controlled Congress grow faster than under any President since the 1960s? Mr. Bush presided over an unbelievable growth in federal spending of 48% in Mr. Bushs' two terms, not counting the war spending in Iraq. Where did the myth come from that Republicans are more responsible fiscally than Democrats? It simply isn't true. George W. Bush proved it.

The question begs; what is the secret that a seemingly intelligent American public could become influenced and brainwashed by deplorable tactics of Atwater, Limbaugh, Rove, Bush etcetera? We believe there are three answers.

The first is the increasing knowledge in neurology and psychology in emotions that allow for refined techniques of manipulation and deception that are harder for our brains to detect. Second, our culture prevents the average American from becoming politically astute enough to detect deception. The average American finds it rude to discuss politics in company, and therefore has little opportunity to sharpen the mind with other people in places such as at the dinner table or luncheons with peers or at cocktail parties or at the ballgame. Lack of debate with people of different opinions leaves little room for serious thought. The result is an undeveloped sense for political manipulation.

Americans, in general, have a well-developed sense of judgment for their line of work, their career, or education of their kids. Those are topics that get discussed over and over. But when it comes to politics, most of the public gets their political knowledge from talk show hosts who pretend they are above the fray but in fact are central to the partisan deception, and are most often well paid to be so. As long as a media presents information objectively, the American public is served, though still not intellectually stimulated because of the lack of personal debate. When the media distorts news, on purpose, the American public gets misinformed in a believable manner.

An accomplished friend of mine recently wrote a letter to friends. It began: As you know I do not discuss politics". It seems like a badge of honor that in America we do not discuss politics. This attitude is the Achilles heel of American politics, and the basis of the success of Atwater's pioneering. This attitude becomes even more dangerous when people no longer read objective newspapers because Rush Limbaugh told them the media is biased.

The third answer as to why the public allowed itself to become manipulated is because most Americans were seeking answers of what went wrong in our nation and talks show hosts were all to eager to provide the answers. Blame liberals and the media. The true answers that the American people didn't hear were:

- The uncontained greed on the top

- The growing indifference in our country

- The widening disparity in income and wealth between the top and the rest, making us look more like a banana republic

- The lack of job security and retirement plans for American workers

- The lack of fairness in the tax system

- The polarization in politics

American people are smart but they lack political knowledge. That explains why many Americans vote from the gut, for example for George W Bush because he is a guy who we can drink a beer with, or because he is religious. Politically savvy people would choose their votes with the same care as they would in making business decisions. They would not ask if the candidate for President was religious. They would ask if he/she is competent to steer our country in this enormously complex world, making America energy independent and keeping our competitive lead over China. They would ask if the candidate would abide by the rule of law and keep us safe but not so safe that we forget what American freedom is all about. Could they restore fairness in the tax system, balance the budget and reduce the income and wealth gap so that all Americans share in our nation's wealth creation. We want a President that reunites America in one large patriotic American family who doesn't play up our fear but who destroys al Qaeda.

The best that Americans can do: To turn-off the partisan bias; tune-out the deceit from talk shows such as Rush Limbaugh; switch from Fox News to unbiased broadcast channels. Contrary to conservative beliefs, they are not pro-liberal. They are just not pro-conservative. They are by far less biased then Rush Limbaugh or Fox News. Invite political debate into homes and schools and work; seek out debate with those who have opposing views. We must become as knowledgeable about politics as about work or cooking or education of kids. Our country depends on it. Our children's future depends on it.

CHAPTER 18

▼

FEAR AND TERROR

"The only thing we have to fear is fear itself", Franklin Roosevelt, 1932

Is the whole world against us? It feels like it. Dangers seem to lurk everywhere. Iraq, immigration, al Qaeda, Hamas, Hezbollah, North Korea, Iran, the dollar's slide, drugs, gangs, liberals, gay marriage, China, India, Pakistan. Despite our military strength, the world seems to have lost its respect for America. If the results in Iraq are any measure, even God seems to have abandoned us.

9/11 got us very angry but also overwhelmed us with fear. Our anger was totally justified, even the fear was. But fear paralyzes and dulls the mind. For a year after 9/11, Americans refused to travel by air and airlines filed for bankruptcy protection. The nation was badly in need of a leader to lead us away from fear. Unfortunately, we didn't have that kind of leadership. The Bush Administration boosted our fear with rhetoric and color-coded elevations of fear. It utilized 9/11 to raise more fear during elections that only they could be trusted to keep us safe. Even in last year's press conference of 5/24/07, to secure support for his Iraq policy Mr. Bush said:

> [Regarding Iraq] It is their government's choice. If they were to say, Leave, we would leave. We are there at their request. Failure in Iraq will cause generations to suffer. Al Qaeda will be emboldened. It will cause them to recruit more. It will give them a safe haven. That would create an enormous turmoil in the Middle East, which would have a direct effect on the security of the United States. We are under threat. It's a danger to the American people. It's

a danger to your children. Al Qaeda will fight us wherever we are. It's better to fight them there than here. My point is; if we leave (Iraq), they follow us.

If we leave Iraq, they will follow us. Fear, and more fear! Some candidates that vied for Mr. Bush succession continued the fear approach. Quoting from Fareed Zakaria, Newsweek June 11, 2007, Rudi Giuliani warned an audience at a college in Atlanta: "They (terrorists) hate you, they don't want you to be in this college, this is reality." Even Barack Obama masterfully combines hope and fear.

Newsweek's Sharon Begley pointed out that in two breaths he denounced fear mongering and invoked terrifying images of suicide bombers and nuclear bombs as he assured us that you can't negotiate with them but as President he'd capture them, kill them, imprison them. Begley continued that a new generation of political psychologists are refining the understanding of the power of fear with new insights of how voters respond to having their anxiety stoked, and that the power of fear can be squared with the political truism that the candidate who best projects fear and hope tends to win.

Speaking of fear in our lives, Paula Spencer wrote an amusing article earlier this year in Newsweek: We protect our kids from everything except fear. We can't let kids walk to school without school administration approval. We fear the water; who drinks tap water? We fear child molesters! We fear razors in Halloween candies! We fear MySpace and biking without helmets! We are consumed with fear. It affects our life and health. Lynn Cheney, The wife of our Vice President, wrote in Blue Skies, No Fences that in the 1950s kids grew up feeling safe. Adults issued warnings, don't get into cars with strangers, and gave us telephone numbers to memorize. But they didn't see a need to frighten us, she said in an interview with Ronald Kessler in Newsmax. And yet, there is no reason to believe that there are more pedophiles today than in the 1950s!

Let's overcome fear because statistically the chance that a terror attack would hurt you is as likely as your chances of winning the lottery. Or as Dr. Fareed Zakaria reported in Newsweek, the odds of being harmed by a terrorist is as likely as being swept out to sea by a tidal wave. Yet, lotteries result in winners, and tidal waves do happen. Terrorist attacks will happen too. Accidents happen. But should we be fearful?

President Franklin Roosevelt was the kind of leader that was needed. Who can forget his cry that the only thing we have to fear is fear itself. In the 1930s, according to Dr. Richard Stuart, the U.S. military only ranked #18 or #19 in the world. Yet, by uniting us and ramping up production of tanks and military planes, President Roosevelt led our country into World War II to punish the perpetrators of Pearl Harbor. Four years later, with many volunteers fighting and a so-called inferior military, America was victorious. Japan and Germany, the largest aggressors the world had ever known, were decisively defeated.

In contrast to #18 or #19, George W. Bush led the world's largest military into Iraq. Compare the results of 1945 and 2008. In 1945, a nation without fear turned victor against all odds and we became admired by a grateful free world. Today, as a fearful nation with the mightiest army in the world, we are not victorious and disliked in the world. Leadership matters!

Roosevelt was not the only leader that rejected fear. President Reagan's charisma oozed optimism and set the stage that rebuilt our confidence and power. Inflation was just about wiped out. When our troops were murdered in a heinous terrorist attack in Lebanon, Reagan remarkably didn't resort to military muscle to retaliate. In his view, immediate retaliation against terrorism was unworthy of fighting with military lives, and would have far greater negative consequences. Instead, by building on psychological diplomacy and talking with the enemy, he got the biggest price. Soon after he left the White House, the Cold War enemy, the Soviet Union, collapsed like a house of cards. America became the ultimate victor on the world scene.

In a debate, one Republican candidate for President 2008, Ron Paul, U.S. Representative from Texas, was asked what he considered the most pressing moral problem in the United States. His perhaps surprising answer was: That we pursue preemptive wars against any country; with it we wiped out the "just war" principle of Christianity. Our country made a big moral mistake; we aren't justified to declare preemptive wars on Islamic countries just because we think that they may or may not have terrorists or weapons of mass destruction. That's why the UN is so important. We must use a severe screen to ensure that wars are just. But we didn't do the smart thing. We were obsessed with fear. We had to invade Iraq.

When should we strike militarily? Most Western religions developed a theory of a Just War. In WWII we fought a just war against evil that would have harmed the entire world if we hadn't stopped it. After 9/11 we struck rightfully back to defeat the evil Taliban that supported the evil al Qaeda, and we should have pursued al Qaeda with all our might to destroy them in the mountain region between Afghanistan and Pakistan. The mission would have been over by summer of 2002, and our troops would be home. But then came the war in Iraq. A just war based on fear?

A grandson of the famous Mahatma Gandhi lectured on world tours. His main theme was: "The world lives in a culture of violence based on fear, controlled through fear and therefore we feel that when something bad happens to us, we must retaliate with violence: Revenge, an eye for an eye, tooth for a tooth. Revenge is embedded in our system of justice. Unless we let go of fear, says Gandhi, we will always seek to respond to violence with violence and it gains us nothing." Gandhi's grandfather, Mahatma Gandhi demonstrated peacefully. He proved that a non-violent response to violence is the greatest force at the disposal of mankind. Prior to Mahatma Gandhi, the British Empire had no problem beating local resistance with force. Even though Gandhi was eventually murdered, his peaceful actions were too much for Britain and India gained independence. Gandhi proved that peaceful demonstration is mightier than the mightiest weapon of destruction ever devised by the ingenuity of man. Yet, any attempt in our country to talk about solving conflicts with non-violence is met with sarcasm from conservative radio talk shows.

Another man lived up to Gandhi's philosophy of peaceful resistance. He actually lived before Gandhi, some two thousands year ago. His name was Jesus Christ. Unless the house of God was defamed, he taught us to turn the other cheek (Matthew 5:39). In the garden of Gethsemane he told his disciples not to fight back (Matthew 26:52) "Put your sword back in its place because all who draw the sword will die by the sword". The bible tells Christians that Jesus did not tolerate vengeance (Romans 12:17–21), bitterness (Ephesians 4:31) and retaliation (1Peter 2:23). Perhaps that's why it didn't go too well in Iraq.

It is said that this "Gandhi talk" or "Jesus Christ talk" is for wimps, and is just not compatible with the American culture. Conservative talk shows impress listeners that negotiations are for wimps; all liberals are wimps they say, unwilling to be tough enough to solve our problems. Conservatives are supposed to be tougher than Attila the Hun, macho-men who have had enough of all that wimpy-talk. What the world needs, they say, is to see our military "kick ass". This macho attitude by talk shows and many conservatives sounds way tougher than their actions actually are. Their toughness includes sending our professional military off-to-fight while they, the macho-men stay home enjoying their luxurious life, drinking beer, watching football and shooting pool.

In real life, terrorism cannot be fought with just muscle because terrorists hide in places where our military can't find them. Sure, we might kill a few but many are waiting in the wings to take the place of those killed. If all Muslims would think that their cause warrants it, Islamic terrorists could bank on over one billion Muslims in a wave of terror that never ends. Our military commanders observed that hundreds of aspiring terrorist recruits cross the border of Iraq almost every week because our presence there infuriates Muslims all over the world. Is it our plan to kill them all? A billion people? There has got to be a better way!

As reported by Newsweek, U.S. News and the L.A. Times, over 4,000 of our soldiers were killed in Iraq, ten thousands were maimed, and it costs us more than a half trillion dollars. Further, 4 ½ million Iraqis (out of a total of 27 million) fled the country; terrorist recruitment became a thriving business; a once thriving Christian population became the target of fanatic Muslims. Muslim militants routinely kill women for failing to wear appropriate Muslim clothing and headscarves.

What exactly have we achieved in six years since 9/11? The statistics of terrorism released by the State Department has shown a significant increase in international terrorism since 2001. After six years of war in Afghanistan, the current President Karzai is inviting the Taliban back to join him in government. Illegal drugs, heroin, cultivation in Afghanistan is higher than ever. Osama bin Laden runs free and manages unabated terrorist training camps. After five years of war in Iraq, both the U.S. and Iraq are divided, almost literally. Red states, blue states. Kurds, Sunnis and Shiites. The only good news of the war was that Saddam Hussein is gone, for good. But did that justify the war?

We know that there were terrorists in Iraq but that was or is not a reason to have our military there because there are terrorists everywhere. We know there are terrorists in Britain. We know they are in Germany. We know they are in Saudi Arabia and we know that Saudi Arabia is still financing Islamic extremists. We know terrorists are in Spain. Those are not reasons to attack these countries. We also know that there are more terrorists in Pakistan than all other countries combined. And we also believe that they are here in our country. Why wouldn't they be? British spy chief, Jonathan Evans, gave a rare speech on November 5, 2007 that terrorists are methodically and intentionally targeting young people in Britain, radicalizing, indoctrinating, and grooming these kids to carry out acts of terrorism. And from what we hear, Islamic fascists are angrier about America than about Britain, so why wouldn't this be happening in the U.S.? It is said that in America, the Muslims integrate better; yet kids are vulnerable anywhere to demagoguery and re-indoctrination, and we are kidding ourselves if we believe that this is not happening in our country. Terrorists are everywhere. In the worldwide war on terror, how could we possibly use our military everywhere?

The Economist reported that Pakistan, the world's second most populous Muslim nation is now under threat from extremists on its fringes. Newsweek reported: Today, no other country on earth is arguably more dangerous than Pakistan. It has everything Osama bin Laden could ask for: political instability, a trusted network of radical Islamists, an abundance of angry young anti-Western recruits, secluded training areas, access to state of the art technology, regular air-service to the West, and there are no American troops to hunt them down. Further, Pakistan is an unstable nuclear power. Newsweek continued that Washington is chronically fearful that Islamists might get hold of nuclear material, equipment or know-how in Pakistan. Al Qaeda is said to be mightier and more sophisticated than ever. Why are we in Iraq instead of in Pakistan?

Fear and terror are a powerful combination. We see it in Tijuana just across our Southern border of San Diego. Drug cartel terrorists are torturing innocent people and spraying them with bullets to send a message of fear to the public. If you cooperate with the police you will be dead. Gangs in Los Angeles have used fear for decades by killing potential witnesses against them, warning people not to help the police. Nobody seems to know the power of the fear factor better than Osama bin Laden. The purpose of his terrorism is to instill fear by selective surprise attacks to demonstrate that they have no shred of restraint in murdering the most innocent. Then they target individuals who dare to speak up as the Islam moves to establish a position of power. There are numerous examples of this. Because he dared to air a film that exposed the inhumane treatment of women by Muslim males, Dutch filmmaker Van Gogh was brutally slaughtered in daylight by a fanatic Muslim in Holland. It instilled fear among many Dutch people that they might be next when speaking up against the (at times) inhumane treatment of women-as we see it in the Western world. In her book Infidel, Ayaan Hirsi Ali exposes the mentality of most Muslims in Holland. The picture she describes should make any government determined to stop their Islamic march to alter the culture of Western civilization. Yet, it seems that individual members of government are afraid that they or their family members would be next if they speak up against the Islam. The effect of fear is appeasement. In April 2008, Geert Wilders in the Dutch parliament released a short film called Fitna that highlights violent Jihad fragments from the Quran, in essence warning the Western world that the Quran demands violence upon Westerners. Almost every leader in Holland has asked Wilders not to release the film out of fear that the Muslim world will retaliate. Appeasement and fear seem to dominate European politics today.

Bruce Bawer in While Europe Slept gives a similar and frightening account of how the Islam is methodically sweeping over Europe. He describes how Islamic fascists use the weapon of fear to gain more and more power over European citizens. Political cowards and appeasement, according to Bawer, aid them. Wake up America. We can't let this happen to us. We must overcome fear, otherwise fear will keep us paralyzed and let terrorists achieve their ultimate objectives.

The question that scholars raise is whether or not the Islam in itself is evil. My Islamic friends have convinced me with passages of the Quran that the Islam is not a violent religion. They point to similar gory passages in the Bible and defend the Quran that if the bible doesn't make Christianity evil, then why would the Quran make Islam evil? They certainly have a point about Christianity's checkered past that included stretches of evil such as the Witch-hunt, the Crusaders, the Inquisition, the selling of penance. They argue that if those days are over for Christians, at some time in the future extremist Muslims could give way and that would make the Quran as peaceful as the bible today, so say my Muslim friends.

But we can't wait for Muslim "Enlightenment" to firmly take hold over its followers. The problem is what do we do in the meantime? We can't allow Islamic Fascists or Muslim Jihadists, whatever we call it, to slaughter innocent "infidels" until they see a new light.

George Weigel wrote in Newsweek about "Jihadism, which teaches that it is every Muslim's duty to use any means necessary to compel the world's submission to Islam." George Weigel, who wrote <u>Faith, Reason, and the War Against Jihadism</u>, is a Distinguished Senior Fellow of Washington's Ethics and Public Policy Center. Most Muslims don't accept the teachings of Jihadism. However, Weigel argues, that is beside the point because the Jihadists believe it, and these Muslims are our enemies. The failure of our government, Weigel argues, is to not openly discuss the Muslim Jihadists and their goals. To avoid bringing in religion, our administration calls it the war on terror but it is really a war against Muslim Jihadists. He feels that our reluctance to discuss religion in public is to repeat the mistakes the advocates of appeasement made in the 1930s [that allowed Adolf Hitler to invade Poland and other European countries without punishment]. While admitting the necessary use of military, Weigel argues that we can't win the war on Jihad terror unless we fight it on moral grounds. In the meantime, we must support the moderate Muslims who believe that the Quran is peaceful as much as we point to a peaceful Bible. But the Muslim Jihadists must be rooted out.

Weigel makes sense. We must not appease religions as our government perhaps inadvertently did. We are not fighting a war on terror. That is too broad and therefore meaningless. We are fighting Islamic fascism but we are not fighting the Islam. Because we are not clear about what we are fighting, most of the one billion Muslims believe that we are fighting the Islam. Yet, they desire peace as much as we do and they do not condone acts of terrorism. The key to winning the war against Islamic fascism is to convince the one billion Muslims that America is on the right side. For now, the one billion Muslims look at us with suspicion. It should be clear that the fear mongering policy that has dominated this Administration and the over-use of our military was a terrible choice. It even hurt our business of tourism and general standing in the world. Our fear made us reject foreigners. Fareed Zakaria reported in Newsweek that our country has become the most unfriendly, the most hostile to foreigners of any developed democratic country. Zakaria continued that every American who has a friend abroad has heard some story about the absurd hassle and humiliation of entering or exiting the United States. We don't need tourists you say? Discover America, a travel industry funded tourist organization estimates that this behavior on our borders has cost us 17% decline in tourism, costing America $94 billion in tourist spending, 200,000 jobs and $16 billion in tax revenues. Even tourists from our closest ally, Great Britain, are less inclined to visit the U.S. Read the travelogues on a British website. It's filled with horror stories about the inconvenience and indignity of traveling to America. The falling dollar should have overwhelmed our country with tourists but besides the brave ones to capitalize on the low dollar, most foreigners leave us in the cold. Of course, tourism should not trump our national security, but it is just another point that we are alienating the world at a time when we need it the most.

How can we get rid of this dogmatic belief, that military power will solve our problems? In business we are much smarter. Any CEO of a successful business knows that using forceful power may instill fear but is not a very effective approach to success, often it is a losing battle against companies that achieve success through soft power, the power that conservative talk show hosts snicker at. The power of leading by example, the power of persuasion, has proven far more effective than the power of intimidation. Successful companies in the world are masters of well thought-out strategic plans and attaining world leadership through a great product, great marketing, cunning, persuasion and a superb worldwide public image. Why should that be different in the case of terrorism? After all, terror only flourishes because of their ability to recruit those who feel the cause of terrorists is more appealing than our cause. We have competition here for the minds of Muslims.

There is a long-term approach and a short-term approach to rid us of the war on terror. We must begin by defining our war better and focus on what we really want to achieve. We must acknowledge that this war is not about eliminating all terror worldwide. We had the Oklahoma bombing by a disgruntled, yet decorated Army veteran from the Gulf War. We also had the Unabomber, a brilliant student and professor who for eighteen years terrorized, killed and maimed Americans. Terrorism in Northern Island has existed for nearly a century; it was a domestic conflict. That kind of terrorism should not be broadly included in our war on terror. Terror, like criminals, will always exist. But wars cannot and shouldn't be forever. The war on terror after 9/11 should be a specific war with a realistic end-goal. As Weigel pointed out earlier this is a specific war against "Islamic fascists that target the United States".

Hitler was the mastermind behind the atrocity against the Jews. Using half-truths, he made the Jews the scapegoat of all the problems in Germany that existed in the nineteen thirties. If the Jews went away, so was believed, all German's problems, and there were plenty of them, would go away. The prejudice became so high that it exceeded the threshold of respect and decency for other human beings. Thus began the well-documented genocide against Jews. The half-truth here is that Jewish people throughout history seem to have been blessed with darn good genes that were then, as is today, clearly visible through a more than average success rate in almost all categories of life (except basketball). The average Jew was just a bit more successful than the average blue-eyed German in those days. Pulling that half-truth out of context was an unbelievable stretch to blame the Jews for Germans problems. Otherwise decent people as Germans are, it has amazed historians how an entire nation could condone genocide against the Jews. At what point did their otherwise upstanding morals cross that threshold that turned many of them into monsters?

What does this have to do with us? A lot! We are the "half-truth". Islamic fascists are making the Western world and specifically Americans the scapegoats of the misery in the Islamic world. There are enough half-truths to go around because of our behavior in the last seventy years, supporting the Islamic dictators, the oppressors, to satisfy our materialism. Hitler's account tells us that it is very difficult to get rid of prejudice once it is running high. It tells us that it takes a lot of work to bring the level of prejudice below the threshold, the divide between peace and disaster. The prejudice that exists strongly about the evil Western World is fed to ordinary Muslims day in day out in the Middle East and Islamic Africa. Infidel by Ayaan Hirsi Ali may give a jolt of understanding that would make you crawl if you lived there.

So what should be our approach against Islamic Terrorism? In the short term, our nation must remain vigilant, but without fear. We should begin with ending the relentless attacks on the FBI, CIA or NSA; instead we should support them 100%. They are not perfect, but they are the ones who can best protect us from terrorist attacks. President Bush may have pushed legal limits but why is it such a problem to intercept international phone calls and emails without a warrant? Sure, there is always a possibility of abuse but should our President ignore the real threats of terrorists that want to blow up more targets in America? While he should have stayed beyond partisan politics that abused 9/11, his attempts to strengthen the security of America are laudable. When opposition screams about laws not being followed they are just being silly to dot the I's and cross the T's. Flexibility in real life is better than the mechanical dotting of I's and crossing of T's. As parents we do it all the time. Let's simply require that a log be made of all intercepted calls, gazillions, and let a Congressional committee take samples from it to see if abuse could be detected. Some of my siblings still live in Europe, so I do still call and send them emails. I don't care if these agencies intercept my calls or emails; I have nothing to hide or be ashamed of. Instead of seeing it as infringement on privacy, I see it as a necessary evil in these times when we know that evil people try to inflict large-scale harm.

Domestically, we must ensure that the FBI, CIA and NSA are equipped with superior systems and astute people with integrity to crack down on aspiring terrorists. That should prevent most terror attacks on our soil. But not all! Some are unavoidable. Sometimes you can't prevent a heinous act such as by Mohammed Atta and his peers on 9/11. We heard enough to know that Mohammed Atta and his peers could have been detected prior to 9/11 had these security units and systems worked as they should and had they been coordinated by smart and vigilant people. But people make mistakes. We all do. We cannot let that possibility govern our lives. All we can do is work with confidence to ensure that our federal agencies involved are well equipped and feel supported by us to work within the principles of our Constitution. If an attack happens, our military should respond swiftly but only if there is strong evidence pointing to a geographical location. Our military should then rapidly strike for punishment, and come home. Otherwise, our military should be used as bluff to deter governments from harboring terrorists. Today our military are too stressed out in Iraq to use bluff effectively.

For long-term success, we need something different than muscle on the ground. In Iraq and Afghanistan we achieved little but the loss of countless lives, and money. Our military presence provided ammunition to the fascist demagogues to recruit more terrorists. The more they can recruit, the more the chance that a few slip through our borders even under or over or through a ten foot wall.

The best answer to a long-term solution of eliminating terror by Islamic fascists aimed at Americans is by using an effective combination of the powers of leadership that demonstrate consistency in our values, public relations, education, and dialogue without fear. To some extent, the Bush Administration tried an approach to better international public relations. Karen Hughes, a long-time

Bush aid, headed the office of Public Diplomacy and Public Affairs as Undersecretary of State. With a budget of nearing a billion dollars a year, her efforts to improve the world's view of the United States were unsuccessful, and she resigned. Cutting through the innuendos of whether or not she was qualified for the job, our image didn't improve, simply because our nation's international walks don't match the talks of Karen's efforts.

The long-term effort to wipe out terrorism should begin with an assessment of our international behaviors and attitudes, and bring that in line with our values, then consistently apply that in all our interactions with the world. Our values include, among other things, freedom and true democracy. This means that we also value the rule of law. Shouldn't we begin to change our bizarre attitude of rejecting many rules of international laws, while expecting other countries to adhere to them, as if we are above them? Based on our values, it should also mean that we would no longer support dictators. But this cannot even be realized until we have become energy sufficient. (See Chapter: Iraq). Further, how do we treat foreigners when they come here? We expect them to speak English when they visit us; but do we speak their language when we visit them? How do we treat poor nations? Do we insist that they give up on their trade barriers (directly or through the World Bank) so that our subsidized farmers can undercut their poor farmers? Does our self-interest override well-intended foreign policy? Do we care enough about genocide in poor nations if these nations have nothing to offer in return? Do we care about disease that wipes out the poor in Africa and Asia by the millions? Or do we only provide some relief if these countries commit to live by American religious beliefs, no abortion, no condoms? Do we genuinely help suffering or only with a lucrative ulterior motive? Perhaps many of these questions go to the root of Christianity, and it begs the question; are we true Christians or do we tout the name when it is convenient? How could we expect Karen Hughes to be successful?

We need to diffuse the anger and hate against us that is taught in Madrasses and mosques. We need to take the wind out of their sails by beginning to value other cultures as we value our own and to show the world the consistent face of America as a great country with great people. In the meantime, there are many things we can do to accelerate the process. If we can spend nearly a trillion dollars to stabilize Iraq, which has had no visible negative effect on the worldwide strength of al Qaeda, perhaps we should spend ten billion dollars sponsoring new Boys & Girls Clubs in Pakistan that would bring hope, confidence and opportunity to their kids; this could start the Islamic Enlightenment. That would keep young Muslims away from the angry messages that they are now fed daily in

Madrasses and mosques by fanatic clerics. The most effective way to reduce terrorism in the long run is to stop the recruitment lines. And that requires neutralizing the power of Islamic fascist clerics. Even regular dialogues by the Pope and other top religious Christian figures with leading clerics of the Islam could be important contributions to neutralize fascist clerics. In the end, good strategy, education, psychology, hard work and consistent values work better than bullets. That's what we do in business all the time. It works.

First, let's begin to restore and improve upon our role as a world leader. Without the world behind us, our efforts to eradicate Islamic terror cannot and will not be successful.

CHAPTER 19

▼

STATISTICS OF TERROR
AND DEATH

This chapter attempts to bring some perspective to the folly of our fears for terror attacks. The following looks at the significance of 9/11 or similar recurrences through the cool eye of statistics. Statistics allow us to maintain a cool head and mind. Emotions never do.

Untimely deaths occur often. Untimely deaths appear more tragic for the loved ones that stay behind than an expected death. The hcinous crime of 9/11 put lots of loved ones into deep mourning while the entire country was in shock. But as deaths go, statistically, the number of deaths from 9/11 was not outrageous.

The annual U.S. death rate per thousand is 8.4, which would calculate to about 2,500,000 deaths per year. (Source: The Economist, World in Figures, 2007 edition). Accordingly, over 16,000,000 Americans have died in 6 ½ years since 9/11. On 9/11, 3,000 Americans died as a result of the al Qaeda attack on our soil. While heinous, statistically this was an under-whelming number of just 0.002%. When rounded off, statistics wouldn't even bother to give a 0.002% occurrence another thought, let alone a headline. Yet, 9/11 has dominated American politics for over six years, trumping far more important issues such as our ability to remain competitive or to become energy independent.

Some of the top causes of American death during the first six years since 9/11 were: Heart attacks 4,200,000; Tumors 3,600,000; Stroke 975,000; Chronic Disease 800,000; Accidents 700,000. (Source: 2004 National Center for Health Statistics' numbers rounded, multiplied by 6 1/2years)

If we need to be fearful, let's be fearful for unexpected death because of a heart attack or stroke or accident. The chance that since 9/11 your loved one would have died from a heart attack, a stroke or accident is about 2,000 times higher than one from a terror attack (of a magnitude of 9/11 every six or seven years).

We humans have a weird sense of fear. We even feared anthrax that has cost us zero lives since 2001. We fear it more than the flu that cost us annually a quarter of a million lives. Why isn't that bizarre? If we must be obsessed by deaths and fear of more deaths, let's tell our President to do something about deaths where it really counts, statistically. Statistics don't lie but fear does.

We realize that a dirty nuclear bomb might well cause a larger number of casualties then 3,000, but we have lived with nuclear attack possibilities during the entire cold war with the Soviet Union. Back then people shrugged their shoulders. If it happens, it happens, they said, we've got to die some day and we can't live in fear about it everyday because it would make life a living hell.

Despite the overriding concerns by this Administration about the fear of terrorism, if we get right down to it, with all the hundreds of billions of dollars spent, we should ask if we are safer from terror attacks than in 2001.

First, we should recognize that President Bush and his Administration have done a laudable job in strengthening the security of Americans. Also, we should recognize that Homeland Security and the FBI, CIA and NSA have been under enormous pressure to improve and get better and better. We should be proud of them. We are safer but not so safe that all terror attacks could be avoided.

As widely reported in the media, with all the hassle that Los Angeles Airport passengers go through to check-in, they learned in October 2007 that security screeners missed 75% of all fake bombs and explosives that passed through by undercover agents. USA Today reported that at the Chicago airport the security screeners missed 60% of fake bombs. Luckily, they didn't miss the toothpaste of old ladies in excess of 3 fluid ounces. Errors are made and these incidents are essential to improvement, just like in business, we learn all the time to get better.

It is impossible to prevent undesirable elements to enter our country. That's why everybody in the country must be vigilant to report anything suspicious to the local police or FBI. According to the Pew Hispanic Center, 500,000 illegal immigrants enter the south border annually. If you were a terrorist and you didn't have a false passport to smoothly pass border control, how much of a brain would it take for you to fly to Mexico City or Toronto and then jump the border like 500,000 of them do every year? So, let's assume for a moment that only one per ten thousand illegal crossings at the border would be an aspiring terrorist. That comes to 50 aspiring terrorists per year or since 2001, about six times 50 is 300 aspiring terrorists. Remember that the brutal 9/11 attacks took just 18 terrorists. Another legitimate claim is that Islamic fascists could enter unseen by boat on our vast coastlines. We can build thousands of miles of 12-foot walls on the South Boarder that will keep many illegal immigrants out and perhaps deter an unsophisticated terrorist-if there is such a thing. A professional terrorist might enter through customs at major airports. As shown on NBC Dateline on December 28, 2007, for $2,000 anyone can obtain an authentic passport with false identity from Peru or from consulates in Peru such as the Consulate of Spain. This Dateline program focused on criminals in black-markets in Lima, Peru, who bribe government officials of legitimate passport agencies. As was shown on TV, these passports have an authentic picture and according to Dateline, no custom agent at any port of entry in the United States would have any reason to suspect anything because the face on the passport is completely authentic; there is nothing to detect the criminal behind it. And why would we think that only Peruvian or Spanish governments are corrupt? The best way to protect ourselves is for all of us to be vigilant when we see something out of the ordinary. Sometimes, we might inconvenience an innocent person by it. But, c'est la vie!

How about ocean containers? According to the US Commissioner Robert Bonner, the vast majority of foreign trade, about 90%, moves in containers carried on huge container ships. The 360+ seaports in the US receive annually over seven million marine containers (source Gerald Nadler, Chief Scientist, Machine Talker, Inc). The Long Beach/LA harbors, the largest in the US, accounted for 36% of all the US containerized US imports and exports in 2004. Only a small percentage of these huge incoming containers are inspected. These containers are so large that you could hide dirty bombs or parts thereof without a problem. While our government has supported groundbreaking technologies to scan the containers for dirty bombs, parts of these bombs could go unchecked and perhaps nuclear material could be harnessed without detection. Besides, these new technologies aren't broadly on-line yet. There has been six years of unchecked containers entering our nation since 9/11. That is a staggering number of containers exceeding 40,000,000, largely unchecked.

If there is going to be another large-scale terror attack, it seems less likely to come from commercial airplanes than from the lack of security at our container seaports. As reported by Newsmax, Homeland Security Chief Michael Chertoff calls 100% inspection of containers impossible: "If I shut down [the ports], there won't be any risk but there won't be any ports." We just can't effectively secure seaports because 100% security would effectively stop the economy that brings in $2 trillion of goods into the US; in other words, we have to accept holes in seaport security. The interesting fact is that his statement drew little interest among the press and the public. While the public is fearful it is also irrational because it doesn't seem to care that dirty nuclear weapons or anthrax might have been or are being smuggled into our country. In this regards, Dr. Marvin J. Cetron in <u>The Future Face of Terrorism</u>, gives a sobering read.

The statements by our Home Security Chief are an admission that our own government already conceded that a terror attack will happen and that we are lucky that it hasn't happened yet.

We need to shrug off fear. Instead we should demand the capture of Osama bin Laden. More than six years after 9/11, the perpetrators, embodied by Osama bin Laden, our #1 terrorist enemy, and his protector Mullah Omar are still free, plotting more attacks on us. Now, Osama is not what you call a needle in a haystack. The allegedly 6'5" Osama bin Laden towers over the on-average shorter Arabs. His height seems to compare to short Arabs almost like a Shaquille O'Neil over the average taller American. How could a towering figure hide from our satellites, our CIA and our military intelligence for over six years? Obviously we haven't done enough.

Let's choose a President who leads us without fear instead of with partisan politics. Let's recapture the American spirit of fearless freedom, do the best we can to stay secure but above all live life to the fullest the American way, as long as we can.

CHAPTER 20

▼

GOVERNMENT

It has become popular among Americans to dismiss government as bureaucratic incompetence. Some even suggest that it is more efficient to outsource government tasks to private business. Libertarians often suggest that we would just do fine without a government in our lives. However, that appears naïve. In a society, we need rules, and rules need to be enforced. We can't even live in condominiums or track homes or even luxurious developments without an association that established rules of how we live. And we get upset if the association doesn't enforce the rules that our neighbor violated. It is the same as in sports. Without rules, sports become chaos. We need rules. And whether we call it government or association or sports league, someone needs to set the rules or laws, and that someone needs to be paid (call it taxes). Government is needed but not too much!

Our Founding Fathers were very wary of government. After all, their experience with the autocratic, non-democratic, British government was less than enlightening. As a result, our Founding Fathers built into the Constitution the requirements of checks and balances to avoid that any government branch would yield too much power. The Founding Fathers also believed in the autonomy of individual states. But they saw the need for a limited federal government that would bind the states into a single defense with consistency in foreign relations, and protection of the Constitution. Upon the founding we were a country of endless opportunities with few rules. Today, however, we are inundated, overwhelmed with federal and state services as well as laws and rules on how to live. In fact so many laws dominate our lives that our Founders no doubt would have rejected living in such a country. But most of us have gotten so used to these laws that limit our freedom that we demand more. Others have come to accept government services as entitlements that they wouldn't want to live without. Governments have a tendency to grow. Federal government, State government, County government, City government, they figure out a way to expand and raise taxes to pay for their expansion.

Through their services and laws, federal and local governments exercise power over American citizens. And the more services and laws they create, the more power they acquire. This is precisely what our Founders feared the most: A too powerful government. The Founders' defense of checks and balances that they built in the system were insufficient to stop government from developing more power. Congress' job was to check on the Executive branch and vice versa, but when the Republican Party controlled Congress and the White House, they turned a blind eye, wiping out the founders' intentions. The Judicial branch is also politically motivated and manipulated, which one could conclude combines to make one crazy, inept "ménage a trois".

A consequence of government is the inherent opportunity for corruption. When government exercises the power to say yes or no, citizens are inclined to influence that power through bribes. It has happened in the past and will happen in the future; and the more powerful government is the more leverage for corruption. Corruption can happen through bribes of money, or gifts such as Superbowl tickets, or promise of lucrative jobs in the future, or through promise of votes in re-elections.

Every new law provides opportunity for corruption. The more detailed a law, the more opportunity it provides for corruption. In Philip Howard's words; "because at the edges of words there are always interpretations." The more words written into law, the more edges exist.

We know that we need government but how much do we really need? How powerful do we want it to be? One of our political parties championed a small government. That was during the time that it was not in charge of government. This party was the Republican Party. But from 2001 to 2007 when they swept total power over Congress and the White House, they forgot their own promises as they grew government spending faster than at any time in the last forty years. This is the hypocrisy of the Republican Party. Or is it just the tendency of people when they have power to expand it no matter what their platform said? The Bush tax cuts didn't do the trick either. The late Nobel Prize winning economist, Milton Friedman, believed that "if you cut taxes, cuts in spending will follow". As we know, that turned into a myth under the Bush Administration and Republican Congress. It seems that the only way to keep the growth of government down is to agree on a maximum federal spending expressed in a percentage of Gross Domestic Product (GDP), and to find a similar limit for state budgets. At one time, liberal governments were accused of turning this country in a welfare state. But when a Democratic President worked with a Republican Congress in the nineties, government spending slowed and was close to 18% of GDP (18.4%-Source: White House). Today under President George W. Bush it is approaching 20% of GDP, a huge difference. We propose a law that limits the federal budget to no more than 18% of GDP.

Our governments are so large and have succeeded so much in interfering with our lives that it seems as if we can't spend an active hour of our days without dealing with some law or regulation or government service. The irony is that we, the taxpayer, fund the intrusion on our American freedom. Yet, we, the taxpayers, have become powerless to scale back this interference in our lives. Because most Americans have come to depend on certain government services, interest groups would lobby hard enough to make sure that the service they like will continue. That breeds corruption. That's why a maximum percentage of GDP might be the only solution, and if preliminary budgets exceeded that percentage, all services should be cut, prorated, including defense and entitlements such as social security and Medicare. A responsible President and Congress could pass that into law, if they were courageous enough to stop the lobbyists.

A serious problem for governments is attracting good people. As with any business, dedicated and competent management is needed to run an efficient and smooth organization. Yet, top jobs in the government are often given to political cronies who helped the political campaign of the President or governor. How do we find good people that would be willing to take upon themselves huge departments, running billions of dollars, larger than most public companies? The pay is comparatively low and CEOs don't like to dance to the tune of partisan politics. It seems that it is theoretically impossible to get superior leaders for government jobs. If it wasn't for their sense of patriotism (or ego), we could not have capable people running government services such as we had at the Treasury Department with Robert Rubin under Bill Clinton and Henry Paulson under George Bush. But by and large, there are not enough of these superstars willing to serve in government. No wonder that government services are often slow and wasteful even though the underlying service they provide is considered a necessity. Besides the clear cut cases of the over-hyped $750 hammers that incompetent bureaucrats used to buy, it becomes less clear as to which particular government service is more waste than benefit. This ambiguity is the source of discontent and one of the reasons that political parties thrive.

Government power also leads to abuse. Governments are made up of people, and we saw that people are caring less and less about fairness. On March 20, 2008, three State Department employees were fired because they looked improperly into Barack Obama's passport files. It was called an outrageous abuse of security and privacy. In 1992 papers of Clinton's passport files had been removed. (U.S. Presidents were known to spy on political opponents.) With power comes abuse. We realize that wiretapping is necessary to avoid acts of terror but the authority to wiretap will also lead to abuse.

Just for easy reference, here is a list of government services that just about everyone, except for "anarchic libertarians" agrees is essential for a proper functioning society:

> National defense and security; Foreign diplomatic corps; Customs and Immigration; Treasury (tax-collection, banking regulations); Management of government owned lands; Energy (mining, drilling, oil reserves, alternative energies); Education; Environment (pollution, clean air, wetlands); Infrastructure (roads, bridges, airports); Safety (clean water, safe food and drugs, safe vehicles, workplace safety, building safety, road-rules and licenses, aviation); Technology (Defense, NASA); Permits and codes; Veteran administration; Fair elections; Anti-corruption oversight; Justice (tort laws, criminal laws, workers rights, minority rights, rights to unionize, law enforcement, prisons); Social benefits (social security, Medicare, Medicaid, food-stamps); Business oversight (SEC; Anti-trust; Licenses for legal businesses; Stock-markets.)

While everyone agrees in principle with these government services, that doesn't mean that everyone agrees on the extent to which these services are provided. We want a strong Defense, yet how strong? Are we just swayed by a politician's cry that "we must strengthen our defense' without asking how much is enough? Does everyone who agrees with more spending for defense know that America spends more on Defense than all other countries in the world combined? Wouldn't an American defense still be by far the most powerful in the world if it were to spend say 50% of all the spending of all other countries in the world combined, some 190 countries? We would still be able to knock out any country, and our defense would still be a powerful deterrent. I agree that our defense should be the most powerful but we need to be reminded that under President Roosevelt our defense was only #18 in the world, yet we defeated the most powerful military countries during World War II. Cunningness of brave generals such as General Eisenhower could count for more than all the power in the world. Why are we so easily persuaded to increase defense without asking, when is it enough?

Back to government services: we'd all agree that providing food stamps to veterans or truly disabled people is the right thing to do. But what about giving it to everybody that is too lazy to work? The principle of Medicare is good but the Bush Medicare drug plan, passed in 2003, seemed excessive and wasteful to many Americans. Every necessary government service is essential to one group and a waste in other people's eyes.

The bottom line is that for the vast majority of Americans, the need for government is clear but not the size of it. One thing should be clear. We, The People have the power to elect representatives who have the power to determine the spending budget for government services. And once they decide on that budget, it is also clear that We, The People, must pay taxes to pay for all that government spending. Even the most uneducated American knows that you can't (or shouldn't) spend more than the money you take in. Yet, conservative political leaders find it normal to promise tax cuts without specifically telling us what services they would cut hand-in-hand with the tax cut. In fact, the Bush tax cuts were passed in the Republican Congress while increasing spending. And borrowing the deficit is expensive. Not only do we have to pay the loan back in the future, but also there is interest to pay.

Because government is inherently inefficient, some conservatives argue that most public spending should be farmed out to the private business sector. They argue that business is always more efficient than government. Additionally, die-hard conservatives teach that we must leave the economy alone, undisturbed from government regulations. Markets correct themselves, they say. These arguments are a distortion of the facts. As a (aspiring) market economist myself, I should be inclined to support these statements. But black and white ideology is always just too simple to be true. Let's look at some examples that disprove simple black and white statements.

- Market economists admit, right from the start, that government is needed to provide political stability and guarantee the rights to property. In other words, the keep-the-government-out folks beg the government to step in on behalf of the market. So, everybody wants the government involved.

- Markets do not correct themselves in time to avoid disasters. We know that the income gap widened to dangerous levels. CEOs and corporate boards can't seem to stop the trend of excessive pay packages. Eventually this could result in an uprising, warned Alan Greenspan in the <u>Age of Turbulence</u>. In general markets do self-correct and when they finally do, should be left alone (such as with the sub-prime mortgages), but corrections are not made in time. If disasters could occur, better to have the government step in before disaster strikes. The problem, of course, is that disasters are subjective, and only disciplined, non-partisan people should head the Federal Reserve.

- The housing market and the sub-prime mortgage market were fine until euphoria set in. Aided by excessive money supply, low interest rates and negative attitudes of indifference combined with unconstrained greed, the financial markets became extremely creative without any care for the consequences to our country. Bankers and mortgage brokers didn't bother to check the solvency of mortgage loans because they would sell these loans off, who cares! Then, Wall Street's young wizards bundled, sliced and repackaged these loans, which made it impossible for investors worldwide to assess the quality of what they bought. The bubble could have been avoided. While Alan Greenspan was brilliant for most of his tenure as Chairman of the Federal Reserve, the Fed could have reduced the money supply, raised interest rates and above all used its psychological influence to halt the euphoria in the housing market in 2003/2004 when everybody with a brain could see that a bursting bubble was inevitable. Enough government regulations existed but conservative managers didn't use their responsibility to interfere.

- Corporations have only one responsibility: To make money for its stockholders. Without government regulations, many a CEO whose income was coupled to the price of its stock could and would manipulate earnings to deceive stockholders by creating a fictitious demand for the stock. With high stock prices, CEOs could sell off their own stock before it plunged. Luckily, with government regulations (SEC) that CEO would find himself in jail today, if caught.

- Without EPA and OSHA, CEOs would skimp on investments for employee safety. They would freely dump toxic waste in our ground water instead of buying expensive equipment to neutralize toxic waste

- Before the FDA came around, butcher shops, bakeries and restaurants didn't invest in cleanliness; that would cost them profits. Butchers processed meat along with rats and other animals that were trapped in abattoirs. Bakeries used to process flour into bread with traces of poison that they liberally used to combat rats. Bread used to include feces of cats and rats.

- Enron, WorldCom, Tyco, anyone? Their CEOs cooked the books that eventually destroyed shareholder values, jobs and retirements of ten thousands of employees. The market corrected but not before the damage was done. In the eighties and nineties, government regulations were watered down. The results showed. But even with government regulations it was still far too easy for CEOs to cook the books. At least the government regulations didn't let the crooks go unpunished.

- For a good reason Local governments regulated utilities: To make those services available to all the people. If utilities and telephone companies had a say in it, they would never invest in utilities and phone services outside cities where the investments would be spread over too few families to make a profit. Governments required them to bring services outside the cities at affordable cost to the users. That helped development of suburbs in rural areas. A case in point, the government did not regulate telephone companies or cable companies to bring broadband services to rural areas. That's why those living in rural areas have typically no access to DSL or broadband cable services.

- Many conservatives argue that government jobs can be better handled by the private industry. As a black and white statement, this is pure nonsense. The private industry works best when there is free market competition with all competing companies pursuing maximum profits. This is market capitalism at its best. But government work is never a competing business. In a non-competing business, the inefficient government still works more efficiently than private business. Take the security guards in Iraq. Our Defense and State department awarded (without bidding) a security contract to Blackwater, an American company. This outsourcing was supposed to be more efficient than using our military personnel. Even ignoring that the Blackwater security guards committed crimes in Iraq (because they were not subject to tight military rules) these guards make three to five times as much money as their military counter parts, well into the six figures. So what is a military officer to do? They quit their military commission and promptly joined Blackwater for much more salary with lower legal risks and free from rigorous rules. It was also a great deal for Blackwater to get well-trained personnel at taxpayer expense. But wait a moment, why is that more efficient? We, the taxpayer, get to pay three to five times more than if the same people had continued the same work as a military officer at a fraction of the cost, and without the embarrassment of out-of-control private guards spraying bullets into civilian crowds.

- Let's pretend that our military would be entirely outsourced to satisfy the myth that private industry is always more efficient than government. How would we feel about the U.S. Navy under Northrop-Grumman, the Air Force under Boeing, and the Army under Lockheed Martin? An efficient military requires years of strategies, discipline, tactics and training throughout the ranks, for only one purpose: To be ready for warfare. In private environment it would be impossible to move such forces or other contractors through annual bids. Once completely under the wings of a business, they would become a monopoly for profit. We know that a private business has only one overriding job, to make money. What would CEOs do to increase profits in a monopoly? They would cut waste. But what is waste? Probably low-cost young MBAs just out of school would get to determine that. They would suggest that there is too much training and drilling going on. They wouldn't listen to the generals; after all business MBA's know best; their message from the top was clear; cut costs to increase profits, not to reduce the tax bill. Who would find out unless there is a war? Patriotism couldn't trump profits because private business has no other motive than maximizing profits. One could predict that within a few years, the military would be dysfunctional, at perhaps twice the cost to the taxpayer, but not ready when needed.

- Imagine our police departments under private companies. Or how about the judicial system in the hands of Halliburton? How about putting our National Forest Management under Boise Cascade? And our controls to prevent over-fishing in the hands of Star-Kist? How do we think that will work out?

- Here is what Homeland Security did. In 2003, the U.S. government handed out just 3,512 contracts to perform domestic security functions such as data mining. In the 22-month periods ending in August 2006, the Homeland Security Department had issued more than 115,000 security related contracts to private industry. The war on terror has become a sprawling new economy, where the government acts as a deep-pocketed venture capitalist at taxpayer expense without securing the profits for taxpayers that venture capitalists would secure for investors. Homeland Security handed out loads of monies to start-ups that are overwhelmingly headed by former employees of the Pentagon and Homeland Security. (Source: Naomi Klein, author of "The Shock Doctrine", excerpt published in the Los Angeles Times). You think that these people left government to save the taxpayer money? Think again! No wonder that the cost of government increased under the Bush Administration more than any other government in the last forty years.

- Many contracts for services were doled out without a bidding process, jeopardizing all the rules against corruption. The Associated Press reported that one U.S. army officer, stationed in the Middle East, awarded about 6000 U.S. military contracts, worth $2.8 billion, that are all linked to bribery and fraud.

- A news article in January 2008 points to government in an entirely different area, in simpler things that hardly makes us stand still, until … they fail. A recent L.A. Times article described the piles of uncollected refuse reaching six feet high in and around the city of Naples, Italy and surrounding cities. It swallowed sidewalks, parks, bus stops, parking areas, schools, and poisoned the air with breeding grounds for rats and disease. Not surprisingly, it is killing local businesses and tourism. How could this happen? Garbage collectors couldn't pick up the refuge because all landfills were full. And nobody wanted new landfills or incinerators near their neighborhood. Only authorities could break this problem. However in Naples and surroundings, governments broke down. Could this have happened here in America? It could. This story demonstrates that often we do have effective government, but we just don't realize it … until it breaks down.

Regulating our banking system began in the era of the depression in the nineteen thirties. In subsequent decades many more regulations were added in banking, affecting Wall Street and corporations. These regulations didn't prevent America from becoming the world's richest and most powerful nation. Yet, conservatives fought hard to get rid of regulations. And some were indeed onerous. Who remembered the lack of progress when communications were overregulated protecting the monopoly of old AT&T with Westinghouse and Bell Labs? The deregulation of that industry spun into a whole new industry that has benefited us all. The drive to deregulate continued under Reagan in the nineteen eighties and under Clinton in the nineties that motivated more entrepreneurship. But the pendulum swung too far again. The repeal of the Glass-Steagall act that separated banking from investing, and the repeal of many security laws by the Republican Congress in 1994 may have been overdue but Congress wasn't bright enough to replace them with less onerous regulations that could have prevented the massive frauds at Enron, WorldCom, Tyco, the Savings and Loans disaster in the 80's, as well as the sub-prime mortgage disaster of the present.

We could fill a book with examples to disprove the popular myths of die-hard conservatives that demonstrate black and white myths. At the same time we could gasp in horror about galloping government spending that "do-gooders" in the extreme left wing of liberals could impose upon us if we'd let them. There are only a few good rules to a sound government:

1. A maximum federal government spending of 18% of GDP, and similar rules in the various states of America to be binding on legislatures for sixteen years with automatic rollover unless The People desire to change the percentage for another sixteen years.

2. Let markets be free but with government oversight to ensure that the fruits of the markets benefit all Americans, and to punish anyone in business for making personal money at the expense of employees and stockholders.

3. Keep private business out of government services unless there is solid evidence of competitive bidding from private industries along with independent government oversight to punish corruption

4. Vote for a President and Congress that will restore a strong sense of social responsibility to our society.

CHAPTER 21

▼

THE WORLD

Without the world behind us, terrorism cannot be defeated. The world is not behind us.

Once, the world thought it knew us and was overwhelmed with gratitude for our role in liberating the world from the Nazis and Japanese imperialists. And that we didn't take advantage as past conquerors did to enlarge the empire. Past world powers, such as Great Britain or Spain, were indeed less altruistic than America. Brutally occupying foreign countries, they grabbed indigenous treasures while subordinating, enslaving, murdering or pilfering the indigenous people. America wasn't imperialistic but the world recognized that we were not without vice. They frowned upon our culture of individualistic materialism that trumped family life, and they were well aware that our materialism trumped our stated democratic values. If we needed a stable supply of scarce materials for our economy, that we didn't have, we wouldn't hesitate to sign agreements with dictators that promised to supply us if we supported them regardless of their human rights abuse. Yet, despite our serious vice, the world trusted us because they thought they knew us and because the benefits of America to the world exceeded our vices. Not everybody was happy, of course. Fidel Castro wasn't. He was a dictator yet had nothing to offer us but cigars. Our support of dictators, who did have something to offer us, began to work against us when indigenous people began to organize against their dictators and supporter, America. Muslims began to sympathize more and more with Islamic fascism that taught them that they were superior over infidels and that infidels harmed them unjustly. It was time to rise, and the rest is history.

All American Presidents since Franklin Roosevelt, except apparently the current one, understood how important it was to keep good relationships in the world. Yet, even they couldn't avoid acting as hypocrites. Since Franklin Roosevelt, we have catered to the dictators in the Middle East. As Newsweek and the Economist reported:

> There are over one billion Muslims, many of which hear stories from their imams that the West committed enormous injustices for a thousand years. Over the last seventy years, America has supported their dictators for oil, which, if you think about it, made us indirectly responsible for the suppression of the Muslim people. And it violated our own moral sense of justice and Christianity. No doubt, imams used this truth to seed hatred and convince Muslims that America, and thus Americans, are evil and cannot repent. Aspiring terrorists then sign up because they feel the injustice must be revenged by force. If there would be a belief that America can change and remove the enormous injustice of the past, these Muslims couldn't be recruited anymore, at least not in droves.

But the Bush Administration went far beyond common American hypocrisy of supporting dictators for oil and other materials. It began to alienate friends, apparently not understanding the value of friends in the world.

Even before 9/11, the world had become suspicious of the George W. Bush Administration as it negated international agreements right out of the starting gate. While first negating the Kyoto Agreement that his predecessor had signed (though never ratified by Congress) the Bush Administration signaled plans early on to pull out of the 1996 Comprehensive Nuclear Test Ban Treaty to test a new range of nuclear weapons. For the world leader to signal a possible rescinding of international treaties is just mind baffling. What would stop any other country from testing nuclear weapons when the leader was going to pull out? Russia would for sure. We had just lost moral authority to world leadership. How could we prohibit Iran from testing if we plan to do it ourselves? If America chose to violate the rules that the world lived by, any other country should now feel free to break the rules too. Countries were aghast.

Immediately after 9/11, this lost leadership was restored when almost all civilized countries showed their full support for us and condemned terrorism genuinely. Instead of fully utilizing that unique opportunity of unanimous word-leadership, the George W. Bush Administration butchered it by its arrogance. This was a once in a generation opportunity to truly lead the world and would have been the first time in world history that the world and entire UN Security Council would have helped as one united body with a common goal, to eradicate terrorism. Instead of capitalizing on this monumental opportunity, we began to stray from the pursuit of terrorism when we unveiled plans to invade Iraq. Next our Administration began to belittle and antagonize the world for not agreeing with our plans to invade Iraq. George Bush turned America into the school-bully. Most countries including old friends didn't know what to think. In the end the world's support was all but gone. No one would follow us unless enticed with money contracts. They feel they are on their own and they have their own problems to worry about.

When we attacked Iraq, we had a suspicion that Iraq might have weapons of mass destruction but we weren't sure. On the other hand, we had a stronger suspicion that North Korea had these weapons but we had no plans to invade them. Iran, an enemy since Jimmy Carter was President, was suspected to develop these weapons, yet we didn't make an argument to invade them either. We insisted on Iraq, a country that the world knew had helped keeping Iran at bay but also had become belligerent about weapons inspectors that the UN imposed on them after we kicked them out of Kuwait. But they were no more dangerous than Iran or North Korea. Why invade Iraq? It didn't make sense to the Security Council. Iraq's current status demonstrates that we aren't always right and that it pays off to listen to other countries, especially our traditional allies. They didn't abandon us; they gave us advice that we choose to dislike. And the overextension on the war in Iraq caused us to fail in our objective to punish Osama bin Laden. It seems that the Security Council may have had a better grip of reality than our Administration.

Mr. Bush's decision to unilaterally invade Iraq without the blessing of the United Nations may have made us feel good but was a blunder from the view of world reputation. It was also a bad precedent. What would prevent another country from invading its neighbor they don't like? After all, we are the leader and the leader sets the tone, sets the example by action. We couldn't possibly send our military to all corners of the world to punish those who did the same as we did, could we?

Another example of negative world opinion came after the Bush doctrine of preemptive strikes. That sounded to other countries as if America would declare countries guilty before they had their day in court. "If you are not with us you are against us", added President George W. Bush. It was a raw emotional statement, actually quite understandable by the American public after that heinous crime of 9/11.Yet, this simple black and white statement was not so simple, and smart government leaders should have known that. Sure, it made us in America proud to have a President determined to punish the perpetrators and to root out evil. But it scared the hell out of every other country. We sounded like the big paranoid school bully that would attack anyone for the slightest suspicion unless they did exactly as we pleased. Actually, it sounded worse than the school bully. At least, the school bully could be avoided by walking a couple of hundred feet around him. The Bush statement could only be interpreted to mean that every country had to agree with us even if we were irrational because "If you are not with us you are against us." That left little room for respectful disagreement. We could attack any country if their leaders dared to disagree with us? It would not surprise us if countries without nuclear weapons decided to play it safe by paying lip service to us but to explore what it would take to develop the weapons. Still, some countries became coalition partners in Iraq by sending a few thousand or just a few handfuls of soldiers to Iraq, often in return of a rich reward in contracts. But the majority of people of these countries opposed their leaders for becoming coalition partners. We didn't capture the world's hearts and minds. Our invasion of Iraq proved to the world that we would invade, as we pleased.

The world lost respect for America when Congress re-labeled French Fries to Freedom Fries. That was more than symbolic. It was childish. To the world, our government exhibited immature behavior that was not worthy or capable of leading a serious and dangerous world. The Bush Administration's doctrine of not talking with enemies, because he saw that as rewarding them, was further seen by the world as proof that naïve and immature cowboys led us. It confirmed that powerful America had in fact turned from wisdom to a school bully that for sure you couldn't ignore but you certainly wouldn't trust it with leading the world. It scared everybody that this "child" had the finger on nuclear weapons that could destroy the world.

Administration officials exacerbated the damage to America's standing in the world by their callous trashing of countries that didn't rubberstamp our wishes. Today, the world doesn't know what to think, and has become withdrawn. Some perceive us as more dangerous to world peace than any other country including Iran. After seven years of the Presidency of George W. Bush, it is sad to observe that despite our military might, America has become weaker, not only in moral world power, but also in economic power, and in military power compared to pre-9/11. Naturally after six years of war, our defense has become exhausted. But there was no need to loose our moral authority and political world leadership.

The world further observed the shroud of secrecy of this Administration, its continued arrogance, its disregard for world or even domestic opinion, its contempt for anything foreign. But it also saw a good side of the Bush Administration. Among many questionable foreign policy decisions, the Bush Administration should have gotten more world media mileage from the Bush world aid program. As the Economist reported the Bush Administration made a huge effort to curb the epidemic of AIDS. The President's emergency plan will have spent nearly $19 billion, mainly in Africa, while he has asked Congress for another $30 billion for the next five years. America also supplies anti-malarial bed-nets and drugs while giving poor countries monies if they come up with a good plan for what to do with it. These laudable efforts were unfortunately overshadowed by bad policies but it did get lots of good will in parts of Africa where America still rocks!

With so much focus on Iraq and domestic security, our country did nothing economically to counter the enormous rise of China. Suddenly as if overnight China surprised us with its relentless growth that is now a threat to America's economic power, and thus political power and eventually military power. The inability of our government to recognize this great shift in the world could be a travesty for our country.

A study by Goldman Sachs assumes that by 2043, the economies of China and India would have surpassed America.

Of great consequence to America, China's political prestige in the world has grown formidably. Chinese representatives can be found today in many countries. China smartly engineered a positive influence in mineral, material and energy rich, underdeveloped countries. It did more than just taking resources it needed; it assisted those countries to win heart and soul. For sure, China has huge problems but they have had huge problems for a long time and managed them well. They beat conventional wisdom that a central government could work successfully in a system of market capitalism. Pundits are quick to point out all the problems China will be facing in the near future. But similar challenges were pointed out a decade ago, yet China overcame them all. Even though pollution and the graying of China (due to their one-child policy) seem formidable problems, let's see if they'll stop China from becoming the new world leader or if China is able to handle these with the same ease as they handled other astonishing accomplishments.

Our system of democracy has to be superior to China's politically centralized system of government even though China's centralized system was one reason for their fast paced success. There are no polarized, partisan parties that stifle progress as it is in America today. Yet, conventional wisdom assumes that over time, China's political system will slowly give way to a democratic system, and that might slow them down. But don't count on it.

Regarding world opinion, a good conservative friend of mine told me, "Ask me if I care." So, should we care or should we just say to the world, go to hell, we don't need you, we are going to isolate ourselves as we did in the first half of the 20th century? Here are some reasons why it is so important that the world thinks highly of us. We need the world, more than most Americans think.

- Without agreements among countries to catch and destroy terrorists, they could freely train and travel anywhere. Countries could harbor terrorists. We couldn't possibly invade all countries, when just one, Iraq, took all our might without much success.

- In this day and age of globalization, few products are made in our country. By isolating ourselves from the world, our economy would be dead, massive lay-offs would occur and a long-term depression would follow. Decades ago our economy could have survived without the world (except those countries that provided us with basic materials and minerals that we didn't have).

- Our Homeland Security Department, wishes it could close off all borders and ports to make our country safer but it knows that it would kill our economy so it knows that it can't be done. Economically the world is one.

- We are up to our ears in a global network of economic supply systems. Our economy could not survive without the world. Killing an economy is easier than you think. Look what happened in Nairobi, Kenya. It went from a flourishing economy to total anarchy just because of a rigged election. Thank God that didn't happen to us after the 2000 Florida election. Yet, killing an economy would certainly raise the possibility of anarchy.

- With nuclear weapons all over the globe, the world has become a dangerous place. The oceans that used to protect us from invasion are powerless to protect us from nuclear weapons. Sure, we could fire back but much of our cities could be destroyed while radioactivity would make life unsafe for decades. We could only secure ourselves if we would work together with the world to curb nuclear proliferation and avoid that these weapons get in the hands of suicidal terrorists. Yet, today the world isn't cooperative because we have lost moral authority. Only if the world would see us with respect and would trust us for the long term to take treaties seriously, might they want us to take the leadership role that would make our influence felt. As it is today, we violated world treaties and few countries really trust us.

- With true moral leadership that can only be gained by embracing the world, we might see less infighting in the Security Council so that effective steps could be taken to end the spread of nuclear weapons, and other good things such as an effective answer to ethnic cleansing.

- Without respecting the world, there would be no adherence to treaties. Crime would increase in the U.S. because all a criminal would do when an arrest seems inevitable is to flee the country and he'd be safe. Without international agreements, anyone could kill Americans at random without fear of extradition. What would we do? Attack that country? All of them?

- Without us connecting to the world, countries could refuse to give us information about financial transactions of American citizens or of terrorist organizations. This would massively increase tax fraud in our country and would raise the taxes on abiding citizens.

- Countries could close their borders for goods or services that we want to export.

- Countries could refuse to acknowledge our patents and copy our product designs without punishment.

- They could refuse to cooperate in our wars such as the one against drugs.

- Countries could spew increasingly the worst pollution into the air and oceans that could significantly reduce the health and life expectancy in the United States. They could poison the oceans and kill the fish the world needs.

- Without friends, we couldn't send inspectors to harbors in other countries to check on sea containers for smugglers or nuclear weapons.

- Without the world on our side, countries rich with materials and minerals see a friendlier China that is just as hungry as we are for scarce raw materials. If they favor China, the stable supplies of raw materials to America might become less stable. This could interrupt the supply chain, thus bringing our economy to its knees.

- Countries could lay claim on borders much like it occurred before the United Nations were born. Without friendship and treaties, countries could wage wars for little reason.

There are hundreds of real important reasons why we need the world. So why do we keep antagonizing the world? Why do we keep showing contempt for the world? Why do we turn up our nose to the UN? The world is a very dangerous place. And it is even more dangerous for us when we choose not to care for the world.

Diehard conservatives are still telling us that we need to show the world our military power instead of pursuing negotiations. Negotiations are for wimps they say while real Americans fight. Appeasement is the preferred word of the right wing to condemn negotiations with unfriendly foreign countries. Every President since WWII, including conservative Presidents Eisenhower, Reagan and Bush, were accused of appeasement for talking with the enemy-even when their negotiations were successful. In election year 2008, conservatives compare Democrats, who intent to talk with enemies, with ill-regarded British Prime Minister Arthur Neville Chamberlain who appeased Adolf Hitler. Conservative hawks argue that we must show the world our military power; that will get respect quickly. Really? Well, we have seen what our power achieved in Iraq. Our military weakened and we accomplished exactly what? The hawks seemed to believe their own macho language. Yet we know them. In their own career, they behave differently. They studied how to win through negotiations. Negotiations, they know, can win competitive wars in business. Muscles don't do much but antagonize. If muscles were used in business, someone would be knocked out but who would win the customer's heart and mind, and specifically his order? Not the violent one. So why is this suddenly different when we confront nations? Is it the movies that make us dream about power while we sit in the luxury of our offices and homes?

Most Presidents understood the power of diplomacy and negotiations, the need to make and keep friends in the world. These Presidents didn't have a reckless disregard for other countries. They negotiated with enemies. The current neo-conservative hawks believe that meeting with enemies would reward the enemy for sitting down with us. What naïve arrogance! It is hard to believe that this thought could penetrate the highest office of our land. Perhaps, the electorate got what it asked for. Polls showed that George Bush was liked because he seems to be a man that we could have a beer with. Duh? We prefer a man we can have a beer with over a proven, experienced intellectual who would obviously need to be much smarter than we are. Our leader should be able to outsmart our enemies and lead the world.

After we showed disregard for international treaties, we didn't stop there. Over 90% of the world wanted us to take a leadership role by setting reductions of carbon dioxide emissions. After seven years of denial Bush finally conceded that global warming is real and that humans were largely responsible for it. Did he use that enlightening to lead the world? As widely reported, the Bush Administration refused to take the lead at the December 2007, Bali world conference on climate control to set CO_2 reductions. Even though it admitted to the problem it practically refused to take global warming and pollution agreements serious, infuriating some 180 countries that were participating. Reductions in CO_2 may hurt short-term profits and cost jobs, argues our President, letting the world know that he is more concerned about today than about tomorrow. So why would China or India or Brazil get serious if the world leader in emissions doesn't get serious?

The Bush Administration openly defied international courts, even threatened a friendly country with military invasion if the International Court would serve justice on an American (who would have had to gravely violate international laws before getting indicted by this court). The world perceived that America is only concerned about itself and that it feels it is above the rest of the world. Not a very good basis for assuming world leadership.

The Geneva Convention doesn't apply to us, ruled conservative lawyers that were prodded by Dick Cheney. Moreover, Don Rumsfeld, then Secretary of Defense, belittled European countries. That went over well!

Another tactic of the Bush Administration angered the world. Ben Wizner, attorney of the ACLU, described in the LA Times, the saga of Khaled El-Masri, a German, who was forcibly abducted while on holiday in Macedonia, a country in Europe, handed over to the CIA, beaten, drugged, transported to a secret prison in Afghanistan for harsh interrogation. Five months later, the CIA realized they had a mistaken identity, and dropped him off at night on a hill in Albania. This case got front-page news media coverage around the world and has been the subject of criminal and intergovernmental investigations. Yet, the Bush Administration won a suit in a U.S. court on grounds that any litigation would reveal state secrets. Apparently the ACLU wasn't after state secrets. This El-Masri case was clear, a mistaken identity. Stuff happens so why not admit it and settle out of court? Wouldn't that be fair? Yet, the Bush administration refuses to acknowledge responsibility. Its mode of operation has been to duck responsibility for mistakes. Challenges against this administration are typically answered with a refusal because somehow it might reveal state secrets. It has added fuel to the world's opinion of America as an arrogant country that doesn't admit to its mistakes, and lacks values such as taking responsibility and accountability.

Our foreign policy priority appears to be materialism. Benjamin Barber reported in the Los Angeles Times that the developing country of Malawi was under pressure from the Worldbank and the United States to eliminate its subsidies for fertilizers thus undercutting the local farmers from being competitive against heavily subsidized American farmers who subsequently sold our products to Malawi at the expense of the local farmers. The result was the "Malawi revolution" by the poor farmers who couldn't make a living anymore. It is hypocrisy to subsidize our rich farmers, which keeps poor countries from developing a healthy agriculture of their own, and the world sees it. We can point to Europe but who is the leader here? We talk about morals of alleviating hunger by "teaching them to fish instead of giving fish", but staying with this analogy, our behavior is that, after we taught them how to fish, we come in with power boats and take all their fish away so that they remain hungry.

When 184 countries (out of 188) in the United Nations voted to lift trade embargoes against Cuba because they are hurting the ordinary people of Cuba, the United States refused to do so. Everyone understands that our embargo exists to get the votes from Cuban-Americans in Florida. Our embargo is not hurting Fidel Castro but the people of Cuba, and is not a sign of a humanitarian act. Are these Florida votes that much more valuable than the poor people of Cuba? What does that say about us? How do these 184 countries feel about us? Hypocrites? Votes are more important than American values? Our embargo surely couldn't exist because we are defenders of democracy; we disproved that a long time ago by supporting other brutal dictators.

Without friends and moral leadership, the world moved away from us. It goes its way, doing things against our interests while perhaps paying lip service to what we promote. Those who can defy us openly will do so such as Russia and China. We may call them obstructionists in the Security Council but we have our own attitude to thank for that. They see our political maneuvering and believe that in this atmosphere they do what is best for them. The world can be a dangerous place and we made it more dangerous by isolating ourselves through bully tactics. Conservative Americans hate to admit that with all the military power we have, our military might doesn't change the world opinion in our favor. We hate to admit that we cannot force a democracy with our military; just like the bully cannot overpower us in the end. Even forcing that on a small country, as Iraq with just 27 million people seems, well, insurmountable.

The invasion of Iraq could have been less infuriating to the world if we had been consistent with our past behavior of American materialism. That is if we had stated that our invasion was for two reasons: To search for weapons of mass destruction and for protecting Iraq's vast reserves of oil in the wake of a world full of energy uncertainty. This might have had practical support because we would have acted exactly as the world thought it knew us to be. But our President ruled oil out as a reason.

An interesting question is why have we focused on Iran and Iraq while Pakistan is by far the world's most dangerous country? Pakistan could become America's worst nightmare. With nuclear weapons in this unstable country, it is more likely a source of supply of nuclear weapons to al Qaeda. Memories of Pakistan's hero Dr. AQ Khan still linger. He supplied nuclear technology to Iraq, Iran, Libya, North Korea, and who knows to what other country. And he is still a hero inside Pakistan, living a splendid life? Who is to say that he didn't supply to his own landsmen, the fanatic Islamic terrorists? As we know, al Qaeda and affiliates have regrouped in Pakistan, and are training more terrorists than ever. Supporting Pakistan's dictator Musharaf may or may not have been a good idea but why we didn't force our military to penetrate the border region of Pakistan to eradicate al Qaeda with or without Musharaf's blessing is still unclear. We believe we would have received full support from the world because that's where al Qaeda is hiding.

Newsmax, a conservative Internet media that also prints magazines, concluded that we haven't achieved much in foreign policy. It summed it up when it issued a report card of a C- to Condaleeza Rice as Secretary of State:

- Foreign officials such as Russian President Putin keep her waiting outside his Moscow office.

- She has yet to offer a plan for political reconciliation in Iraq.

- Rice's department is struggling in its stated effort to improve the way the US is perceived around the world.

- Karen Hughes, long time Bush-aid, stepped down as US public diplomacy chief with her $900 Million budget as polls show little improvement.

- Morale at the State Department is at historic lows; only 12% of Foreign Service officers feel that Rice is fighting for them.

But this may be unfair to Dr. Rice. After all, she serves at the demands of the President, and the world's reflection on her is what the world thinks about us.

The world needs a leader that uses different tactics than bullying. We were losing the war in Iraq against insurgents until General David Petraeus decided on a whole new tactic. Defying the Bush Administration's doctrine of not talking with enemies, the general did just that, talking to enemies. While knowing that in the recent past, some tribal aggressors killed American troops, he didn't use the extra 30,000 troops to kick open their doors and shoot but he used them to make friends with these local tribes, helping them with their problems, winning their hearts and minds, bringing them on our side. Ann Simmons, a staff writer of the Times observed that engaging villagers is now a key part of the U.S. strategy to win the hearts and minds of Iraqis. By helping broad services such as medical aid and humanitarian supplies, the military hopes Iraqis will become more tolerant of coalition forces based in their homeland. The hope is that they provide intelligence and cooperate with efforts to create a stable environment. "We are just trying to give them a taste of what could happen if they quit turning their heads and stop cooperating with al Qaeda," said Captain Terry Hilderbrand Jr. The Economist reported that a new manual on counter-insurgency co-authored by General Petraeus overturns the notion that America doesn't do nation building. It says that counter-insurgency is armed "social work". It requires more brains than brawl, more patience than aggression. The modern soldier should be less Terminator and more intellectual, preferably a linguist with a sense of history and anthropology. Since the departure of Secretary Don Rumsfeld, the entire Pentagon's attitude has changed. The U.S. military is now working with U.S. civilian anthropologists. Anna Mulrine reported in U.S. News that these anthropologists work with local tribes and act as advisors to brigades in Iraq, mapping the relationships of the power players and the local people. This is the correct face of the new America if we want to win. Even if we do, it is still unclear why we are in Iraq to begin with.

After seven years of policies that antagonized the world, the President seems to warm up towards the more sound foreign policies of his father and of President Clinton. Professors Steve Weber and Bruce Jentleson observed that not so long ago President Bush called the North Korean leader Kim Jong II a tyrant and Pygmy. Recently, he sent a letter to Kim Jong II, reiterating the U.S. commitment to security guarantees for Kim Jong. Duh? Mr. Bush, who had refused to be involved in brokering peace between Palestine and Israel, suddenly changed his tune and is now involved. Furthermore in his final year, the President has made an exhaustive trip through the Middle East building friendship with leaders, as well as in Africa. How we wish he had attained this wisdom seven years ago.

With baby-steps towards moral authority, other countries would slowly follow us if they believe that this America can be trusted. We must take the lead first in abiding by international treaties and champion them in Congress instead of fighting them. Our American values must become consistently applied. We must also begin to have genuine respect for other countries instead of condemning them just because they do something we don't agree with or vice versa. Attacking Afghanistan was a no-brainer for any country, but otherwise we must follow the Just War theory. Violence never gets us what we want but deaths, maimed, loss of a fortune, and a breeding ground for terrorists. Forceful punishment should be swift, and withdrawal prompt. Soft politics are sweeping the world. The Economist reported that even Indonesia has set up programs to "de-radicalize" Islamic militants, not by violence but by winning their hearts. A soft approach to win hearts and souls wins in the end.

Might Mr. Bush change his negative opinion about the UN too? We know that the UN is far from perfect; neither is our own government. But we need our government, and because we need the world, we need the UN too. If we want a better future for America including better security, it is time to embrace the UN. Of course, it needs to be improved as much as we need to improve Washington.

CHAPTER 22

▼

THE UNITED NATIONS

Many Americans have shown contempt for the UN and conservatives have called to pull out of the UN. It is easy to have contempt for a large bureaucracy, and many have contempt for our own government but that doesn't mean we should pull out.

Instead of throwing fuel on the fire as talk shows and conservative senators do, let's focus on the positives, and build enthusiasm rather than negativism. Anyone who lost the confidence of a partner or peer knows that it is becomes harder and harder to achieve successes. Enthusiasm builds results.

Ian William wrote <u>UN for Beginners</u>. He observed that the United Nations often acts slow and inefficient (we observed the same about our government). When it does things, it often does them too late, or it is too deferential to certain perpetrating states. But on the contrary, simply by existing, Williams argues that it is supremely effective. The very existence of the UN acts as a catalyst for a truly global society and is like the speck of sand in the oyster, the seed of a growing pearl of international order.

When a country obtains a UN seat, it surrenders freely some of its own sovereignty. Yet, conservatives try to appeal on impulsive emotions of people that America should never give up control to the UN. That argument is naïve at best but more likely misleading demagoguery. When you voluntarily become part of something bigger, you always accept a trade-off for the benefits you gain.

That trade-off is just a tiny bit less than having absolute independency. That holds true for ourselves when we accept the laws of our own country. Comparatively, the freedom we gave up to the UN is nothing in comparison to the benefits we gained. The same holds true for businesses when they participate in an industrial standards association. By accepting industry standards, a business gives up a little bit of its own independence but what they give up is nothing compared to the enormous benefits of developing a faster growing market potential based on agreed upon crucial standards. The other extreme is if a company decides to merge it looses its independence. Well, we don't have to worry that we, America, would ever merge into one giant world country. But some misleading conservative voices try to make us believe that it is exactly what would happen, merging into one giant world country. This is nonsense. America is America and will always be independent America. We would never have to worry about loosing our independence by accepting UN rules governing international relations even as we streamline our laws to agree with international laws, even as we eliminate borders to facilitate market capitalism in the increasing sophistication of international trade.

Diehard conservatives are seeking a scapegoat for what really happened. We lost a great deal of independence, not because of the UN but because of Globalization that has made us dependent on many countries in the world. The short-sightedness of many conservatives could cost our country dearly. For example, conservatives in Congress have refused to ratify the 1994 UN treaty on the International Law of the Seas. By refusing to accept the treaty on grounds of their opposition to UN sovereignty, as Fortune Magazine reported on August 20, 2007, this is now seen as a lapse of judgment that could cost us billions of dollars. The reason is that the North Pole may contain vast amounts of oil and gas. The Treaty would have allowed the U.S. to grab Arctic territory half the size of Alaska. Russia is already claiming half the Arctic, and other countries are busy doing the same. U.S. oil companies worried that because of our refusal to ratify the treaty, the U.S. will have nothing to say as the Arctic is being sliced up. Fortune Magazine continued with optimism that President Bush might come out in support of ratification, apparently responding to the oil lobby.

Another example of how the conservatives' negative attitudes towards the UN, and the Administration's foreign policies, are hurting us is that the world doesn't trust us anymore and goes its own way. As the Economist reported in September 2007, many American squabbles are already being decided in Brussels and Luxembourg where the European judges are. The European Commission has become the de-facto new standard setter for the world, and America has no choice but to accept it. This has nothing to do with the UN but stems from the attitude of the nation's leading conservatives that turned the world against us. It is already going to cost the American companies, and thus the American people. Company after American company is giving in as they are now adhering to European standards simply because the global world of trade is exceedingly following Europe, not America. In the last six years, our influence has been waning while the European influence and that of China are winning.

We are no longer the true superpower, and can thank our leading conservatives' arrogance and childish naivety for it. It is incomprehensible that conservatives such as Senator James Inhofe can't accept that globalization (that conservatives championed) caused us to loose independence and that globalization requires international laws. Inhofe is fearful about everything foreign and has a strong following of similarly minded people. Championing global trade while otherwise ignoring the world and the UN on false pretenses? Not very smart. It is the sign of a falling superpower unwilling to be flexible and adapt. Let's get with it America, and win the hearts of the world. We need them, and they are longing for us to become mature and lead them. Instead of fighting international laws, we should lead the world, and set the example of living by it, as true leaders do.

The UN is the place to exert our influence in the world, not by bullying but through smart negotiations. Often when looking at the U.N. in operation, the principle of consensus is frustrating, especially when we are on the sidelines. So is our U.S. Congress. Yet, trying to achieve a consensus is not a bad thing. The good thing about trying to achieve a consensus is that we are talking.

Improvements could be made. Some argue that decisions in the UN Assembly shouldn't be made by a simple majority of one vote per country. Each member of the Security Council can veto any decision of the Assembly—how is that fair? Perhaps a better solution is to give voting rights commensurate to our Congress (The House based on population per country and the Senate based on equal representatives per country). Should the Security Council be abolished? How should we finance the UN? John Bolton, the previous UN Ambassador from the United States proposed voluntary contributions to the UN. That may sound reasonable to some, but not more reasonable than suggesting that American taxpayers should be voluntarily paying taxes to our government.

Ian Williams observed that when the members of the Security Council voted against the invasion of Iraq, it was in itself an important victory for the United Nations and for its existence. We may not have liked it but operating in a global environment, the rule of international law should be important to everybody including us. Except for the United States, many countries in the world have applied international rules in their courts. The irony was that within months after our invasion of Iraq, the Bush administration had to return to the U.N. Few countries would otherwise buy Iraqi oil for fear of litigation because the invasion was rejected by international law. This was another reason that many countries would not help us because of the absence of a U.N. resolution. They considered our invasion a sign of international lawlessness. It is perhaps hard to appreciate that members of the international community refused to be bullied into what America told them to do.

It made us, Americans, furious. Who are they to resist our President? But were they wrong? Should Bush have taken a step back? In hindsight was it worth going it alone (with a handful of other countries)? Let's see! Over four thousand dead Americans; 28,000 American soldiers badly injured; cost of war exceeding six hundred billion dollars on the way to a trillion. And all we got for it is a divided Iraq with a paralyzed government that is turning from secular to religious while millions of people were displaced. And, the winner, Iran, is just waiting for us to leave, so they can pick up the spoils. Perhaps we should have worked a bit harder to let France and Russia convince us instead of changing French Fries into Freedom Fries.

Despite all its inefficiencies, the UN may be a more effective organization to world peace than America has given it credit. The UN has earned its place in the world. Williams observed that in any government organization especially as large and multi-ethnical, multi-cultural as the United Nations, one could count on forces of abuse and corruption. It happens in our Congress and government too. We can focus on that and lambaste the organization or we can strengthen controls and oversight with a policy of zero tolerance for abuse or corruption.

Do we want to go back to the history prior to the UN? Genghis Khan, Attila the Hun, Nero, Henry VIII, Hitler, Stalin, Mao, Franco, the list goes on. The world has known terrible times of wars, pilferage and genocide. Under Hitler, The Nazis may have killed some 20,000,000. The Soviet Union under Stalin appears to have set the record of the greatest mega-murderer of all times, 60,000,000 people died. In nationalizing farms and lethal forced labor in gulags alone, he was responsible for some 43,000,000 deaths. (Source: R.J. Rummel).

Yet, of all those monstrosities, only the worst German criminals were brought to Justice, and that was because America saw to it. Stalin went unpunished. Many Japanese generals and the Emperor went unpunished. Franco went unpunished.

The good news is that because of the United Nations, globalization and improved communications, immense atrocities of the past no longer go unnoticed or unpunished. And if abuse still persists, eventually the monsters will be brought into court, if not in the courts of the country, in the courts of the international community of the United Nations. Its role is to prosecute those who commit serious crimes against humanity but only when they were not seriously prosecuted in their own country. In 2002 the UN member countries established the International Court of Justice under the auspices of the UN, established in The Hague, The Netherlands, a country that has been a long trusted friend of the U.S. We should be very pleased.

The beauty of this International Court is not only to punish those that escape just punishment but also that it acts as a deterrent for future dictators that may think twice before going into a frenzy of human atrocities. They now know that they will get punished one way or another. The court had a precursor during the landmark trial in 1945 in Nuremberg, Germany. It was here that men like Herman Goebbels, Martin Bormann, Rudolf Hess and Julius Streicher faced an international panel of judges from the United States, Great Britain and France, in essence an international court. Twelve criminals were sent to the gallows and others received long prison terms.

So far, so good but what happened next was an international embarrassment. In 2002, 139 Countries signed the agreement for this new International Court. This included all civilized countries of the world. Well, except one: The United States of America. Of course, you would think that rogue countries would not sign, those with rogue dictators who would be afraid they might be sitting there facing international judges some day. Indeed rogue countries headed by monsters such as Iraq under Saddam Hussein, North Korea, and Iran did not sign. Interestingly, Cuba did sign. Hmmm! But the only civilized country that refused to sign was The United States of America.

In all its arrogance and hypocrisy, the conservatives in the Republican Party and the Bush White House decided that the International Court is only good for the rest of the world with 95% of the world population, but that court is not good for the 5% living in the US. This is one example of why the rest of the world distrusts us. We don't walk the talk when we talk justice.

The U.S. President made the following statement: "We are determined to protect our citizens from the International Court of Justice". Protect our citizens? Duh? From what? The only thing that this court does is prosecuting crimes against humanity that our country would not prosecute. It is unthinkable that we would not prosecute atrocities committed by Americans abroad or inside our country. We prosecuted those involved in the Abu Ghraib prison in Iraq. A case that wasn't even up to the scale of human rights abuse that this court would undertake. As long as our own country prosecutes crimes committed by Americans anywhere, we have nothing to fear of this International Court. So why is the Bush Administration and the Republican Congress against this terrific court? Argued the previous US ambassador to the UN, Negroponte, echoing Bush: "We are especially concerned that Americans are sent overseas as soldiers, risking their lives to keep the peace or to protect us from terrorism and other threats, be themselves protected from unjust or politically motivated charges." What nonsense. Was he suggesting that we'd let our troops mass rape, pilferage and commit genocide and that our judicial system would let them get away with those crimes? Who are we trying to kid?

In August 2002 the last governor of Indonesia's East Timor was prosecuted in Indonesian Court and sentenced to three years for atrocities against its people. Therefore, the International Court of the United Nations didn't indict this man because he was already indicted in his own country. Why would anyone in the U.S. fear this court if a) no Americans would commit atrocities against mankind, and b) if any American did, we would try him in our US court system? Our refusal to recognize this is because of a leader who doesn't walk the talk.

That court does more than prosecuting criminals. For example, the court decided recently on a case between Honduras and Nicaragua in regards to disputed waters. Instead of these countries going to war about a dispute that their domestic courts can't solve, the International Court functioned as a supreme court for international disputes. Instead of war, the rule of international law prevails.

The Republican U.S. Congress passed a law, signed by Mr. Bush that allows the United States to attack The Netherlands by force militarily, if ever an American citizen is brought to the International Court of Justice for crimes against humanity that the US would refuse to prosecute. Do you really wonder why the rest of the world community shakes its head? Do we understand how world animosity keeps building up against us? As superpower, we have the responsibility to lead or to isolate. We can't isolate. Conservatives have worked so hard on global trade that it made us dependent on the world. Therefore, there is only one good option left. Lead by example.

What does the US have in common with Brunei, Somalia, Sudan and Oman? We are among a handful nations on earth that refused to ratify the United Nations Convention on the elimination of all forms of discrimination against women. Jesse Helms, U.S. Senator at the time, said: "I do not intend to be pushed around by discourteous demanding women." We in the U.S. may not need those rights but women out there are facing rape or genital mutilations. Holding up ratification sent a message to the rest of the world that America, who believes in equality, doesn't care about the rights of women. It is so embarrassing, and it is hurting us.

In the twisted minds of conservatives, a non-American organization should never have any jurisdiction over any person from the United States. They play to the emotions of naivety and so-called "patriotic" card while playing a double role in advocating global trade that naturally comes with disputes. International disputes need international laws that are accepted by both parties. These diehard conservatives have made our position as the leader of the world untenable. They are aiding anti-American sentiment in the world and thus are playing in the hand of foreign terrorists.

It is time to stop our hypocritical embarrassing attitude in foreign policy, stop the brawl and become a true leader. We must support the UN for its legitimate place in the world. It is time to recognize the International Court. It is time to accept the rights of women. It is time to work with the UN, to make it more efficient through leadership, persuasion and enthusiasm.

It is time to stop pounding on our chests that we are better than others. Even if we were better, good leaders stay humble. Let's become a true leader because only through example and leadership can we eradicate the breeding grounds of terror.

CHAPTER 23

▼

FOREIGN POLICY

past and present.

According to Robert W. Tucker and David C. Hendrickson in <u>Thomas Jefferson and American Foreign Policy</u>, Jefferson's desire to change the world was at war with the desire not to be corrupted by the world. Jefferson pursued a policy of neutrality, just like George Washington. Yet, Jefferson's early sympathy for the French Revolution and his desire for American territorial expansion effectively supported Napoleon Bonaparte in his war with Britain. Tucker and Hendrickson continued: "No man had a greater impact on the day-to-day conduct of American foreign policy than Jefferson … where Jefferson's name has been invoked on all sides of the ever-recurring debates on the nation's diplomatic stance".

Joseph Ellis in <u>American Creation</u> wrote that the Louisiana Purchase by Thomas Jefferson in 1803 "was in the end a triumph on par with the winning of independence and the adoption of the Constitution. The Purchase opened up a new chapter in American national security by removing in one fell swoop all British and French imperial ambitions in North America. A colossal and fully continental American empire was now almost inevitable." Spain was the only European power left but was not much of a military threat anymore.

America had secured its place as independent nation without threats protected by vast seas. Jefferson established the policy of neutrality on the one hand while at times putting that aside for our nation's gain. That policy has worked well for over two centuries, until … we embraced globalization. Because of globalization we no longer have the luxury of the option to move between neutral isolation and active participation on the world scene. Isolationism includes neutrality in conflict as well as the power to establish legal barriers to influence trade and cultural exchange with other countries. If we want isolation today, our world power will be taken over by China and others. If we want to have a chance at remaining the world leader economically and in military power, we must scrap the thoughts of isolation and neutrality for good. That is the consequence of Globalization.

The following briefly summarizes the history of our foreign policy over nearly two hundred years, a zigzagging maneuvering between isolationism and active involvement in world affairs with one single thread running through, national security. The first full century of our independence, the 19th Century was really a policy of isolationism.

In 1823, President Monroe declared the Monroe doctrine consistent with isolationism: The U.S. would not interfere in European colonies as long as European countries (who controlled pretty much the rest of the world through their establishment of colonies) would not interfere in the Americas.

In 1846 President James Polk started the war against Mexico. The reason? He accused Mexico of crossing the Nueces River. When that war ended, we had taken a big chunk of Mexico including California and Texas. Polk adhered to the policy of isolationism, yet he used territorial defense to expand our borders.

In 1898, when our battleship Maine was blown up in the port of Havana, Cuba, President William McKinley declared war against Spain. We still considered ourselves neutral isolationists, yet this war rendered us Cuba, Puerto Rico, Guam and the Philippines, reminiscent of a colonial power.

In 1904 Theodore Roosevelt expanded the scope of foreign policy. He declared the U.S. the policeman of the Western Hemisphere and promised to intervene in any nation that threatened our interests in this hemisphere. This added some aggressiveness to our neutral isolationism.

In 1917 the question about our true position in the pursuit of neutrality was solved, when President Woodrow Wilson joined the massive Great War against Germany, now known as WW I: "Our motive will not be revenge or the victorious assertion of the physical might of the nation, but only the vindication of right, of human right, of which we are only a single champion".

In 1920, President Woodrow Wilson tried to expand his aggressive international policy by working with other nations with the creation of the League of Nations, a precursor to the United Nations. However, the U.S. Congress defeated it. Many Americans felt that our participation in World War I was a waste of lives and money.

As a result, America retracted itself from the world. It spent its time and energy on domestic issues only. Isolation was still technically possible back then because we were essentially self-reliant in energy and we made all products at home. Many other countries also closed their borders or put up trade barriers. Ultimately this isolation was seen as the cause for the depressions that followed, particularly in Germany as well as the one in the United States in the early 1930s. It also led indirectly to World War II.

The 1941 Japanese attack on Pearl Harbor changed our policy of isolationism overnight, and for good. President Franklin Roosevelt declared war on Japan but also on Germany, taking sides in this huge war. After WW II, the U.S. continued its influence in the world. This began with the Marshall Plan and increasingly invoked a massive U.S. interest in Europe and Asia, both economically and militarily. We had troops maintaining military bases around the globe, not to fulfill the role as conqueror but to keep an eye on the conquered nations as well as on unfinished conflict. Even today, more than sixty years after World War II, our troops are still stationed in many countries including Germany, Japan and South Korea. Franklin Roosevelt also laid the groundwork for a close friendship with the royal family of Saudi Arabia that has continued until today. The purpose, of course, was to secure a stable supply of oil.

In 1947, to stem the expansion of communism, President Truman put our country on a new course, the Truman doctrine: To support free people in the world who are resisting attempted subjugation by armed minorities or outside pressures. Obviously this was directed at the Soviet Union and at communist insurgents financed by the Soviet Union to overthrow governments in "free" countries. This policy was pretty much followed by succeeding Presidents. To enforce the Truman doctrine, military forces were stationed around the world.

In the early sixties Soviet leader Nikita Khrushchev decided to bring their nuclear war heads a bit closer to the United States, in Cuba, just South of Florida. They now could strike us in a matter of seconds. When our spy satellites discovered their activity in 1962, President Kennedy faced this missile crisis with a strong and clear warning to the Soviet Union: War now or retreat. At first Khrushchev thought that Kennedy was bluffing. However, it didn't take long for the Soviet Union to discover that Kennedy was no sissy and that he was prepared to stage war. The Soviet Union retreated. Gone were their nuclear missiles from Cuba. Never before and never again did the world come this close to a nuclear war. Since its independence, this was the only serious threat of war America faced on its soil caused by another country. Later, President Kennedy followed the Truman doctrine to stop the march of communism in South-East Asia when he sent military advisors into Vietnam. Under President Lyndon Johnson the Truman doctrine escalated into massive deployment of American troops in Vietnam.

Not surprisingly, after the "Vietnam" debacle, America became reluctant to continue the Truman doctrine. President Ronald Reagan pursued a more cautious policy. He withdrew from conflict rather than confronting it. For example, he withdrew our military forces from Lebanon after a Beirut terrorist attack killed 146 American service men on October 23, 1983, blown up by a truck bomb. On the other hand, he did pursue the policy of Theodore Roosevelt as policeman of the Americas, as he invaded Grenada. On that tiny island, a bloody coup occurred by a Marxist regime, allied to Fidel Castro's Cuba. Mr. Reagan didn't want to see an expansion of communism in the Caribbean. More important than Grenada, President Reagan played war on a different level, far more successful than a military war could have, as he banked on psychological warfare with the Soviet Union. We all remember the stunning outcome of Reagan's warfare, aided by Pope John Paul and Gorbachev's perestroika. The Berlin Wall fell and a few years later, the Soviet Union crumbled like a deck of cards. Yet, President Reagan did not revive the policy of isolationism as he championed free trade.

The first President Bush, the father of the current President, was as reluctant as Reagan to engage in interventionist wars. The only engagement of war by President George H.W. Bush was to drive Saddam Hussein from Kuwait. Hussein had invaded Kuwait to control more of the world's oil supply. Fearing that Hussein would continue his aggression and take over oil fields in Saudi Arabia, the senior President Bush drove Hussein back into Iraq but not before he had gained UN approval. He didn't pursue Hussein's troops back inside Iraq because he was reluctant to commit our troops for a long and drawn out presence in that country. He intervened but not more than was necessary for our interests in a stable oil supply. What foresight!

President Clinton followed Reagan's suit with great reluctance to commit our military forces. He did intervene in Haiti following Theodore Roosevelt's doctrine. Further, reluctantly, he intervened with humanitarian air strikes to stop the Serbian killings in Bosnia and Kosovo, yet he refused to let our military play policeman and nation building in those countries. Thanks to our aid, our nation's standing in that region is still very good to this day. Clinton also championed free trade, especially with his signing of NAFTA.

His successor, the current President, George W. Bush, campaigned on even more restrictive use of our military forces. But 9/11 changed George W. Bush forever. In an about face, 180 degree change, he allowed Neo-conservatives to dictate America's foreign policy. Declaring that pre-emptive strikes were now necessary to defend America, the Bush Administration argued successfully before Congress and the American people that Saddam Hussein had a relationship with al Qaeda, had weapons of mass destruction including nuclear weapons, and that this combination imposed an imminent threat to the United States. With the American public still in frightening panic, Congress authorized the attack on Iraq. The polls indicated strong endorsement by the American public.After his allegations were proven false, President Bush changed the objective for being in Iraq and subsequently changed foreign policy to the most aggressive interventionist policy in American history. His 2004 State of the Union further emboldened this aggressive policy, when he said that it is the policy of the United States to seek and support the growth of democratic movements with the ultimate goal of ending tyranny in our world. He added that spreading democracy abroad is vital to America's liberty and the war on terrorism.

In America's history, the pendulum of our foreign policy had never swung so extreme far of center to such a strong interventionist approach to alter the world to our views.

How did this Bush doctrine of democratizing the Middle East come about?

Natan Sharansky, well known Jewish Soviet Union dissident and author, argued in his book The Case for Democracy that foreign policy should embrace the promoting of freedom and democracy around the world because they are fundamentally connected to peace. He also accused the West, in particular the United States, of lacking moral clarity. As he sees it, a world without moral clarity is when people in a free country come to see their fellow citizens as their enemy, and foreign dictators as their friend. Sharansky continued that a world without moral clarity is also a world in which the only democracy in the Middle East, Israel, is perceived as one of the greatest violators of human rights. A world without moral clarity is a world where dictators speak from one end of their mouth about human rights while from the other they instruct the killing of thousands or millions. Ron Demmer wrote a preface to Sharansky's book, suggesting that Sharansky's thinking had an enormous impact on President, George W Bush. In 2003, Sharansky was invited to the White House. After that meeting the President declared in his 2004 State of the Union the new Bush doctrine: That it is the policy of the United States to seek and support the growth of democratic movements with the ultimate goal of ending tyranny in our world. Did Sharansky change American foreign policy?

Interesting enough, several years after that meeting, Natan Sharansky believed that the method America used to promote democracy is seriously flawed. Sharansky felt it was irresponsible for the Bush administration to push for early elections in Iraq and in Palestine. Democracy is more than holding free elections. The substance of democracy is building and protecting a free society including the rule of law, and including the rights of minorities. Sharansky argued that democratic elections should not take place until at least three years after a series of democratic reforms have been fully implemented. Elections may seem to be a milestone to get political kudos but they are irresponsible and deceiving if held too early. The result of the easy but false test of free elections brought power to Hamas, the Palestinian terrorist organization. It also gave a false appearance of a democracy in Iraq that can reach the opposite effect when it brought power to the Shiites that seemed more bent on seeking revenge on the Sunnis for suppressing them under Saddam Hussein. Sharansky goes on to argue that democracy is eventually all about "treasuring" instead of trampling on the opposition. Treasuring the opposition? Jesus could have said that.

Assuming that Mr. Bush was serious about his doctrine of spreading democracy, America's friends in the Middle East may see this as a hard slap in their face and betrayal of long standing friendship. After all, our friends in the Middle East are the dictators in Saudi Arabia, Pakistan, Egypt, the United Arab Emirates and others, and democracy will mean their downfall, literally.

It had been a longstanding American belief, that with the world's largest oil reserves in the Middle East, the region needed an iron hand to maintain stability. And if the situation in Iraq is any sign, the downfall of dictators might reduce or interrupt their oil production. In turn this could seriously interrupt a stable oil supply to the world markets, and thus would threaten the prosperity of the current world economy. American realists, including the author, would argue that while spreading democracy in the world should be the ultimate policy, implementation thereof would be far more interesting after we have made America independent from Middle East oil. In fact, the key to our foreign policy, fighting terrorism and economic stability, is the development of energy independence first. That is why foreign policy is so integrally intertwined with domestic policy.

Foreign Politics is obviously more complex than one could derive from the cheap on-the-go opinions of popular talk shows. One of the greatest dangers of our liberty today, most people would agree, is the possibility of Muslim fanatics getting their hands on nuclear weapons. However, Iran as a nation, having nuclear capability may not be that much more of a threat to the world's security. After all, once Iran has it, it'll realize that using it will result in immediate retaliation and obliteration of Iran, and while at times they may seem crazy and fanatic, they are not that crazy and fanatic. Terrorists on the other hand have no country of their own to worry about.

According to Pakistan's slain Benazir Bhutto who ran as candidate for president, the security forces in Pakistan are closely aligned with the terrorists. We also know that Pakistan's scientists clandestinely provided rogue nations with nuclear technology, including Libya, Iran, North Korea and Iraq. What we don't know is how much knowledge they provided to terrorists. In the hands of terrorists and their Middle Eastern martyr attitude, the long held belief that possession of nuclear weapons deter the use of it, may well have become obsolete. It is Pakistan and the terrorists in Pakistan that our national security policy needs to worry about.

What has been puzzling about the foreign policy under President George W. Bush is the gap between words and acts. He campaigned that rogue nations developing nuclear weapons would be in deep trouble with him, as President. Once President, he said that America has no plans to intervene preemptively in Iran or North Korea. Nor did he do much after it became known that Pakistan's scientists gave nuclear technology away unpunished. He didn't do much different when it became evident that al Qaeda had regrouped in Pakistan. The problem here is that our strong language wasn't matched by action but into bully-bluff without teeth, seriously weakening our power in the world. Bluffing is a huge weapon but only works when the world knows you mean it. Once the world knows that you are known to be just bluff; enemies loose respect.

If it is truly believed that democracy will be the most powerful way to defeat terrorism, than spreading true democracy we must. However, we are also addicted to oil, and a stable oil supply is vital to the world's economy. Democracies in the Middle East will unlikely give the world a stable oil supply. What gives? The development of alternative energies to oil and an infrastructure for distribution are paramount to world peace. Relying on free market capitalism to develop alternative energies was a serious mistake because the one obvious failure of free market capitalism is that it doesn't care about the timing but as a nation, we do.

In summary, America's economy is intertwined with the world and isolation is no longer a possibility. Mr. Bush saw that correctly but made huge mistakes in alienating the world with half-baked execution and wrong timing. We must be actively involved only using military as a last resort. Our military should be at home as a strong bluff to the world but used only as rapid punishment of any planning organization behind a perpetrator, so severely that they give up, for good.

CHAPTER 24

▼

IRAQ, TERROR AND OIL

The Iraq invasion was all about eliminating an immediate threat to the national security of the United States. The allegations included that Iraq under Saddam Hussein developed Weapons of Mass Destruction (WMD), that Saddam Hussein was about to give those WMD to his friends, the al Qaeda terrorists, that al Qaeda terrorists would smuggle disassembled nuclear bombs into our country, assemble them right on our soil and strike America's highly populated areas in the worst imaginable ways. Based on these allegations, Congress agreed to authorize the war against Iraq, as did most Americans, including the author.

The arguments, however, did not sound logical. After all, in the view of al Qaeda's fundamental beliefs, Saddam was an infidel. It seemed hard to believe that Osama bin Laden would work with an infidel. Or that Saddam would have desired to work with Osama whose stated objective was to replace secular countries, such as Iraq, with Islamic law. It seemed more logical that al Qaeda would have sought nuclear weapons from Pakistan or the breakdown of the Soviet Union. It was reported that Russia had been unable to account for all the nuclear weapons. But against all logic we believed our President's arguments about Iraq. After all, our President had information the public didn't have.

But was the alleged "immediate threat" the real reason for invading Iraq? If so, why didn't we simply apologize to Iraq and walk away after we found no weapons of mass destruction? Our President simply changed the purpose of our invasion, without Congressional objection. This was another confirmation to the world that America could no longer be trusted because it proved inconsistent in such a vital issue as invading a sovereign country.

The original purpose of the invasion was changed from "immediate threat" to "creating a democracy" and later to "fighting terrorists in Iraq". Then the President said that we shouldn't leave Iraq because the terrorists-would-come-after-us; we'd rather fight terrorists over there than on American soil. That was quite an argument telling the world, and in particular the Iraqis, that the lives of Iraqis were inferior to American lives. As if that made us popular.

Wars should always be finite and with a clear end purpose. In World War II the end purpose was clear. When the German Nazis and Japanese Imperialists were defeated, our troops came home (except for small contingents stationed strategically around the globe). When Iraq's Saddam Hussein's military was defeated, it was supposed to be the end of that war too, but our troops stayed, 130,000 of them, later we added another 30,000, in addition to some 160,000 non-Iraqi civilians that were contracted by our government.

In hindsight the Vietnam War raised an interesting question to ask some forty years later. If we had never entered that war or conversely if we had defeated the Vietcong in Vietnam, in what way would that have changed the world today? Would we have been any more or less rich, or any more or less powerful than we are today? In what way would a different outcome of that war have justified the hundreds of thousands of soldiers killed and maimed?

Likewise, if we had not attacked Iraq, in what way would the world have been different today, five years later? Saddam Hussein would still have had control over Iraq-assuming no one had assassinated him. Iraq would have continued as a stabilizing force against Iran and without UN embargo, more oil could have reached the world markets. The Iraqi economy would have been better, especially without the sanctions against them. Our world reputation would have been vastly better with the world solidly behind us helping with the destruction of al Qaeda. Al Qaeda and affiliates would not have been able to rebuild and recruited more terrorists. Above all, we would have saved the lives of more than 4,000 American soldiers, and avoided some 29,000 seriously wounded Americans through December 2007. (Source: Brookings Institution's Iraq Index-rounded). We also would have saved over 600 billion dollars going towards one trillion dollars. Fewer Iraqi people would have been killed and maimed. The number of killed Iraqis is wildly gyrating depending on the source, ranging from some 100,000 to over 1,000,000. (See Wikipedia, casualties Iraq war). Yet, the world would still have had monster Saddam and a possible threat, like Iran, of developing weapons of mass destruction, and his two brutal sons would still be terrorizing the Iraqi people. What would have been better for us?

By over-staying in Iraq and dismissing the soldiers of Iraq, we created a whole new enemy. As a result, we were no longer waging a war against a country's regime but against a new more illusive enemy, newly minted terrorists or insurgents or whatever we call them. Even though General Petraeus made a huge difference in dealing with terrorists compared to the first five years, the question is still, what now?

Terrorists have existed as long as mankind. Therefore, the War on Terror seems more akin to the War on Drugs. Nobody knows the end game. Will the War on Drugs ever be concluded? No, never, not as long as there are people in this world. Will the War on Terror ever be concluded? No, never, not as long as there are people in this world. So we struggle with this dichotomy. How can we fight infinite wars with our military?

President George W. Bush compared the War on Terror to World War II, indicating that the massive war efforts in Iraq were necessary. On November 1, 2007 in a speech at the conservative Heritage Foundation, President Bush compared Democratic leaders to people who ignored the rise of Lenin and Hitler early in the last century, saying "the world paid a terrible price" then and risks similar consequences for inaction today. "Unfortunately, on too many issues, some in Congress are behaving as if America is not at war," Bush said.

How could the President compare the Iraq war to World War II and be serious? The Nazis and Japan were on the way to conquering most countries in the world, winding up with two gigantic empires. Our own freedom was at stake. Compared to Nazi Germany and Japan, Saddam's Iraq was just a nuisance. That kind of evil didn't lurk in Iraq. That kind of latent danger, however, could lurk in the border region of Pakistan and Afghanistan, as well as in the march of the Islam across Europe and Asia. Our focus on Iraq has masked these problems as well as other international problems such as the attack on our economic power.

Some are pointing to Iraq as a religious war foreboding the Armageddon, as prophesied in the book of Revelations in the New Testament. If in any way this is a holy war, our secular nation sacrificed many Americans who may or may not share that belief. But if this is a holy war, why didn't God prevent the immense blunders our government made? We fired all Iraqi's military and government personnel (from the Baath party), consequently we asked for the anarchy that followed and we were the cause of the easy recruitment of these disgruntled cats turning into insurgents or terrorists. If this was a holy war, why did God not give our Administration the wisdom to avoid the slaughter that ensued spurred by the deep hatred between Sunnis and Shiites? The Sunnis and Shiites are all Muslims who disagree about some fundamental religious issues. When we freed the Shiites from tyranny and held elections, they were squarely put in the center of power, ready to settle a score with the Sunnis that perhaps had it coming. Apparently God stayed away from this conflict.

Why are we still there with 160,000 troops? In his book <u>The Age of Turbulence,</u> Alan Greenspan speculated that the prime reason we are in Iraq is oil. While this makes sense, the President never mentioned that. Some say we are there because Saddam was a bad man, violating human rights, and we are good Christians for disposing of him. No doubt Saddam abused human rights and no doubt his sons were monsters but we didn't blink an eye about the genocides in Cambodia or Africa, slaughtering millions of people. If Americans really cared we would have committed major troops to Africa long before Iraq. While campaigning in 2000, candidate Bush, however, criticized President Clinton for intervening in Bosnia and Serbia to stop human rights abuse. So obviously, Saddam's human rights abuses were certainly no motivation for George Bush to commit ground troops to Iraq.

Yet, another reason cited by the Bush Administration was to establish a democracy. It is a nice touch that speaks to the heart of most Americans though who would expect this to come from a conservative President? However, committing military troops to force a democracy on a dictatorship is a far-fetched strategy. First, military forces as occupier on foreign soil are unlikely to sway the occupied into a democracy, especially without infrastructure to support one. Second, military forces are trained to kill, not to build democracies. Third, we have supported dictators routinely even those who were known to abuse human rights. We even supported Saddam Hussein under the Reagan administration as a strategic ally to keep Iran at bay. (Source: The National Security Archive). Few democratic countries have been able to develop such close and long friendships with the United States as the dictators of Saudi Arabia and Egypt did. Israel and Britain come close but that depends on the prime minister running their government. Dictator Musharraf of Pakistan received our support. So did Pinochet of Chile, Franco of Spain (John Foster Dulles, Secretary of State, saw Franco as a safe bet against the spread of communism in Europe), Somoza of Nicaragua, even Batista of Cuba and Saddam Hussein (before he invaded Kuwait).

Did Alan Greenspan hit the nail on the head when he suggested that the Iraq war is about oil? Did the oil companies advise Vice President Dick Cheney that invading Iraq would be the best bet for securing a stable supply of oil to the world? After all, black gold has been considered a serious part of national security for at least the last seventy years. The combination of possible WMD, human rights, bad dictator, oil and democracy, as well as revenge for attempted murder on President #41 (the father of George W. Bush), may collectively have been convincing enough to invade. Could it be that we expected the people of Iraq to welcome us with open arms for disposing of monster Saddam Hussein, and voila, the vast oil reserves of Iraq would be in our reach to secure a stable oil supply to world markets? Having troops in a friendly country in the heart of the Middle East would have come in handy to stop a brewing violence, such as that against Israel. It may have worked if the Bush Administration hadn't butchered the execution of the plan. First by firing the entire military and its hierarchy to the unemployment line (except that Iraq doesn't have unemployment benefits). Second by destroying the country's infrastructure that was entirely run by members of the Baath Party who we also disposed of. Third, by overstaying as conqueror we created a monster with a whole new enemy of terrorists made up of ex-military and Baath party members who welcomed al Qaeda into the country.

In American business, a CEO and underlings making such fatal blunders would have been fired (with a golden parachute). In American politics, we rewarded the Bush Administration with a second term. It is more likely than not that the Bush Administration's plan for Iraq could have been a success with better management by keeping the Iraqi military and motivating them with a raise and charter to rebuild and police the country. We could have handed over power, and just minded our business by securing their oil fields and pipelines while the rest of our troops could have come home. It would have been cheap and with few losses of lives.

But now that we are still there, what should we do? Are the new Iraqi military and police forces capable of keeping the peace? Then our troops should come home while a contingent stays behind to protect the oil fields and pipelines, while keeping an eye on Iran.

Iraq produces less oil today than before our invasion but the potential of Iraq's treasure is staggering. It has 115 billion barrels of known reserves; that puts it as the third largest reserves in the world. Because Iraq has relatively few drilled wells, it is believed that it has another 200 billion barrels of undiscovered oil reserves, making Iraq possess $1/4^{th}$ of the world's oil reserves. To put this into perspective, according to the CIA's World Fact-book, in the U.S. we consume 20.73 million barrels per day; that is 7.5 billion barrels per year. Iraq's reserves may exceed 300 billion barrels. That is 40 years of American oil supply, just Iraq. The U.S. government has already been involved in getting 30-year oil contracts to BP, Shell and Exxon for large-scale explorations in Iraq.(Source: Oilempire.usa/iraqoil)

With oil reserves dwindling in Saudi Arabia, Gulf of Mexico, the North Sea, and other areas, these huge untapped reserves could be essential in stabilizing the world's economy. Further, at any time in the future, terrorists may blow up wells or refineries in Saudi Arabia, Nigeria, and Venezuela, leaving the world economy more vulnerable. Significant interruption in oil supply and the world economy could have dire consequences for us; think of the chaos we have seen in Nairobi, Kenya, after the January 2008 elections when businesses closed, unemployment rose, transportation of food supply stopped. If something like that were to happen, we'd be surprised how quickly we'd forget ideological positions.

How long would we have to stay in Iraq to protect the oil fields and pipe lines? Until we have secured sufficient alternative energy sources to eliminate dependency on foreign oil. In effect, this means that American demand for oil would have to be reduced to whatever we can get from North America such as oil sands from Canada and Colorado, and whatever is left from the Gulf of Mexico. Until that time, we may have little choice but supporting dictators. Until that time, we may have little choice but keeping troops in Iraq.

Now, here is a theory that would support why it is worth having our troops in Iraq, consistent with our past behavior. The Bush Administration deserves an F for the execution of its Iraq plans but perhaps with an oil strategy, the Bush Administration was not stupid. If oil was not the overriding reason, then the Bush Administration's Iraq policy is the most irresponsible foreign policy since Vietnam. But Bush is not stupid. We'd have to assume that oil is the overriding reason for our presence in Iraq. The Bush Administration may have tried to deceive the world but probably would defend it with "national security reasons". It is time that the Bush Administration comes clean with the world and us.

It is time to sway the world and Iraqis that by protecting and exploiting Iraq's huge oil fields everybody would be better off. A stable oil supply to the world will save the world economy. Iraq would benefit by us returning to the Iraqis all oil revenues minus military cost and the cost + profit to explore and sell. The national and world security could possibly justify the over 4,000 American military lives and nearing a trillion dollars of our tax money. We need to convince our Muslim brothers that we want a better world, not at their expense but a better world for Muslims and all children of God. If we can successfully convince the world of that, we may get NATO, South American, Chinese, Indian, Japanese and Saudi troops to replace a large percentage of our troops.

Once we have succeeded in producing sufficient alternative and renewable energy sources in encouraging quantities, we can, for the first time, make an honest attempt to improve the world though true leadership, walking the talk. We could work with our dictator friends, wherever they are, to slowly introduce a parliamentary democracy that over time may result in a true democratic freedom in the Middle East and elsewhere. The key word is "slowly", a gradual process, winning the hearts and minds of Muslims all over. With true American leadership that walks the talk, demand for terrorism should cede over time as peasants and laborers become middle class, more confident of their position as democratic voters and able to build local economies within their rule of law and property rights on their side. Our war on Islamic fascists would end!

In conclusion, nothing seems more important to the peace of the world than establishing alternative and independent energy sources. The passiveness and indifferent attitude towards development of viable and renewable alternative energies must be replaced with an active national program akin to Kennedy sending a man to the moon.

World peace and defeating terrorism depend on us first establishing independence from imported oil and other critical materials.

CHAPTER 25

▼

MEDIA

A world without moral clarity is when people in a free country come to see their fellow citizens as their enemies, and foreign dictators as their friends. Natan Sharansky

An enduring democracy cares about a free press, and the hope is that a free press cares about an enduring democracy. Yet, according to a poll by U.S. News in the fall of 2007, 52% believes that the media are too politically liberal, whereas 27% say they're too conservative. This is strange. If the press were unbiased, one would expect people to vote according to party line. Too many think that the media is too liberal. Is this true or is it another myth? A free press is vital to a true democracy as much as protection of the minority is vital to a true democracy and as much as the rule of law is to a true democracy.

No government likes objective media no matter what they say. After all, a government consists of people who like to be re-elected, and objective media loves to show shortcomings of leaders. Leaders like to suppress objective media, and some leaders in so-called democracies succeeded, such as Hugo Chavez and Vladimir Putin. Luckily our Founders drafted our Constitution with a Bill of Rights that guarantees a free press. And luckily, our Founders established independent courts that wouldn't allow our President to copy Chavez or Putin.

Even so, the reality is that American government attempted to mislead us. For example, our government loves to pre-select the media in press conferences that guarantee a friendly press. Way back, in September 2003 while John Ashcroft, our then Attorney General, was on the road to get support for the proposed Patriot Act, he refused to speak with reporters in certain cities known to write "objectively" such as Buffalo and Philadelphia. It is said that Ashcroft preferred to speak directly to audiences that had been pre-selected. In such case, even unbiased media that would pick up such news as from Ashcroft, could only report the news as received, which is biased favoring the government's view. Likewise in press conferences, President George W. Bush is said to pass over the tougher, unbiased reporters in favor of those who like him and wouldn't ask the tough questions. Additionally, the White House was accused of paying reporters to spread conservative news (paying from tax-payers money). Given that people control all media, and that all people have personal political preferences, could an unbiased, objective press even exist?

It begins with media owners understanding not only their rights of a free press but also their awesome responsibility granted them to inform the public. Of course, media owners, have a personal bias, like all of us. Yet, good media owners would not show personal bias in news reporting, demanding that reporters obtain the facts and write news without interpretation of a personal bias. These unbiased media would show their true colors only in columns, editorials or opinion articles. If most media owners would report news based on liberal bias, as the US News poll suggested, our country would not be much better off than say Russia or Venezuela.

First, let's define the word media. Webster's Unabridged Dictionary calls media: The various means of mass communications thought of as a whole, including television, radio, magazines and newspapers. This means that talk show hosts such as Rush Limbaugh and peers are an integral part of the media too. They pretend that they are not part of the media because they always talk about the media as if that is something different than they are. They pretend to be the good guys while "the media" is bad. It is a trick. Webster's definition makes it clear; they are part of the media. So, when they accuse the media of being biased, then what does that say about them?

It is clear by listening and reading web comments that most talk show media are very biased to conservative views such as Rush Limbaugh talk-show and peers such as Sean Hannity, Laura Ingraham, Glenn Beck, and numerous others, as well as notorious writers Ann Coulter and Michelle Malkin. Conservative media include Newsmax, an Internet media, which also prints a monthly magazine. In Newsmax their conservative writers consistently condemn the media for being liberal pretending that they, the writers are not biased. MoveOn.org is a very liberal biased Internet organization though they do not hide that they are liberal.

It makes political sense for political candidates to turn people against their opponent but for the media to hide that they are biased while accusing other media of bias is just inappropriate, and as a matter of fact it is unpatriotic. There is nothing wrong with being biased but say so. William Buckley Jr, one of the greatest conservative thinkers and writers of our country, wouldn't hide his bias. That is important because if media wants to genuinely provide a service to Americans, they should tell Americans where they come from and where they stand so that Americans are able to form their own opinion based on qualified news. Sadly and hypocritically, much of the media deceives the American public.

How did the public form its opinion that the media are too politically liberal? Is it based on facts or brainwashing? Logically, it would make more sense if the majority of Americans had believed that the media is biased towards conservatives. Most national newspapers, news magazines, talk shows and TV stations are in the hands of conglomerates that are owned by wealthy people. Though not all, most wealthy people are conservative and vote Republican. The larger the business, the more conservative the owner and management often are. Thus, it seems more logical that "the media" is biased towards a conservative view. Some say that working-bee reporters are often more liberal than conservative. But why? And why would conservative owners put up with that? Wouldn't they find a way to replace them with more conservative reporters? The logical explanation is that the media is too politically conservative. Logic usually wins out. Yet the public opinion says the opposite. Are they brainwashed?

Conservative talk shows have been pounding on Americans that the media is liberal. That was a smart move. Most people now believe that whatever they read in the newspaper or hear on TV is biased news, slanted towards a liberal view. The irony is that most of these people seem to trust Limbaugh and others to tell them the truth. Limbaugh is more likely to tell his version of the truth slanted towards a very biased conservative view.

After reviewing major newspapers for several years to detect a bias, here is a summary of what we found:

> The Wall Street Journal ("WSJ"): A good paper with high quality journalism. The news is unbiased, objective. The editorial page is very conservative and its editors demonstrate time and again that they loathe democrats and liberals. Yet, as news goes, this paper should not be considered biased, never mind their editorials. Regarding editorials, as long as it doesn't hide that it is conservative, and as long as they don't accuse "the media" of being biased, readers are served.

> The New York Times ("NYT"): Just like the Wall Street Journal high quality journalism and at times a somewhat brutal disregard for convention that

has made this paper a target of angry governments. Sometimes they come up with unproven allegations such as John McCain's alleged affair with a lobbyist. Their editorials show a real liberal bias. But, just like the Wall Street Journal, as long as the news is objective, the public gets it objectively and unbiased, and as long as they don't hide their liberal editorial views the public is served well.

The Financial Investors Daily: Brings detailed financial news. Its commentaries are unusually biased towards conservative views. They don't hide their true colors.

The Los Angeles Times ("LAT" or "LA Times"): Just like the Wall Street Journal and New York Times, in general good quality journalism and unbiased and objective news. Its editorials are mostly liberal but they don't hide their bias. Therefore they are objective and serve the public well.

Orange County Register: A good newspaper with unbiased news reporting. Its editorials are conservative.

The Press Enterprise: A good newspaper with unbiased news reporting. Its editorials are conservative. Same comment as Wall Street Journal.

The Daily Breeze: A fairly good paper. It reports mostly unbiased news. Editorials are very conservative while Op-Ed articles appear more conservative than liberal.

CBS, NBC News: While somewhat dull, the news appears objective.

Fox News: Brings entertaining news that attracts viewers, yet they are biased towards a conservative view while hiding that they are biased towards conservative views. It is deceiving of them to call their news Fair and Balanced. The majority of their talk shows are clearly conservative.

Rush Limbaugh show: What can we say! He is a genius for attracting many listeners to his conservative show. But Rush blames the media of being liberal while he doesn't inform the listener every day that he is extraordinarily biased himself. Therefore, he doesn't serve his listeners in a patriotic way. Reasonable intellectual listeners, even conservatives, should be annoyed with his insults to intelligence.

Besides the WSJ and NYT, all other newspapers mentioned are from the Greater Los Angeles area. As one can see, the five papers to which I have access on a daily basis are three with conservative editors and two with liberal editors. If that seems unusual in the liberal state of California, it supports the theory that most media in America have conservative owners and editors.

When examining newspapers for bias it is easy to fall in the trap of one's own bias. Because of our personal bias, say independent, liberal, conservative or libertarian, we could read the same newspaper, yet come away with different conclusion about a paper's alleged bias. A liberal might read a factual report that is not favorable to liberals; the brain might register that as political bias towards conservatives. A conservative might see news in the same paper that goes against conservatives; the brain might register that as political bias towards liberals. The key is to force oneself to look for articles that go against the opposition and weight them. If you see negative reports on the front page that goes against left as well as right, there is a good chance that the paper is not biased. If a paper is mostly negative towards just one ideology, chances are that paper is biased.

I subscribe to the LA Times, often reading the Press-Enterprise, sometimes picking up the Daily Breeze or Orange County Register and occasionally picking up the NYT at Starbucks. Often I would compare the news of liberal LAT to the news of the conservative Press-Enterprise, and I came away with the same fair feeling of unbiased reporting in both newspapers. Both the LAT and Press Enterprise with ideologically different editors deserve praise for their unbiased news reporting. At times I listen to Rush Limbaugh. I found that Rush could pick up on a news article from the LAT that went against conservatives and he would rant about that liberal LAT. Then he would talk about articles against liberals also published in the LAT, except he would not mention that the LAT reported these as well, thus giving listeners the perception that LAT only reports against conservatives.

For months leading up to the 2008 Presidential primaries, the LAT reported almost daily on its front page an updated profile of the leading candidates. Most of the time, the articles were informative and positive whether the candidate was Republican of Democratic. From their profiles one could not ascertain which would be a preferred candidate from the view of LAT editor.

Back in 2004, the LAT reported actually more articles favorable to George Bush than to John Kerry. Further back in 2000, there were more articles favorable to George Bush than to Al Gore. I also recalled that throughout the nineties, many negative Bill Clinton articles appeared even before the Monica stories broke. It seemed that the LAT was first to break news about Whitewater, Paula Jones and Jennifer Flowers. These unfavorable reports towards a Democratic President were never proven. Wealthy conservatives funded investigators to find the truth 24/7 during eight years that Bill Clinton served as President, finding nothing illegal other than the lie about Monica. After Clinton's terms ended, the Republican prosecutors dropped their harassment cases as if justice was no longer important. It amazed me that the LAT failed to report the final exoneration on the front page as if its eight year long alleged harassment against a sitting President was unimportant. That exoneration was hidden inside the paper more or less as a footnote. Apparently, this is what objective newspapers do. Scandals sell, so they get the front page. Exonerations don't sell, so they get hidden inside that few readers get to see.

What follows here are some excerpts of random articles reported on the LAT front page. To verify my conclusions, any reader can pick up the LAT and read the front page to come up with the same conclusion. With my limited review of the NYT, I couldn't make that conclusion though the days I did review it, I could not detect any bias on its front page either.

On **September 11, 2007**, there were two main front-page articles. One headline: General Petraeus urges gradual drawdown of troops (from Iraq). Considering the sensitive political nature, the news report gives a positive headline for President Bush. The other main front-page article: Hillary Clinton, returning campaign money from Norman Hsu (a long time democratic supporter). For weeks the Norman Hsu case has been front-page news in the LAT, putting Hillary Clinton's campaign in a bad light as Norman Hsu was found to be the same Hsu who in the early nineties was found guilty of a Ponzi scheme. It was great that the LAT didn't let down on this case but why, I asked, would a paper that Rush claims to be biased in favor of liberals, report front page news negative to Hillary? Why not hide it inside the paper? Anyway, two articles, one positive for Republicans, one negative for Democrats.

September 4, 2007

Two main stories on the front page; one: Bush hints at troop reductions. Cool, one up for George! The other one: Accusatory article of a non-profit organization deriving clout from their association with the Democratic Chief of Staff. I came away with the feeling that this Democratic Chief of Staff did something unsavory. Yet, after reading the full article inside, it is unlikely that she did anything wrong. So why was this front-page news? In addition to reporting real news, hints at scandals sell. Bottom line: A positive towards Bush and a negative towards Democrats.

February 21, 2004

The most contentious issue of the last decade has been the appointment of conservative judges in powerful positions such as in federal appellate courts and above them all, the Supreme Court. There was probably no hotter issue to influence the public, pitting conservatives against liberals. The LAT front-page news read: "Bush, frustrated by Democrats, again bypasses Senate on Judge." What followed was an article of factual reporting without a negative towards Bush, actually it was positively written portraying Bush as a man of action. Now, if a so-called "liberal" press wanted to condemn Bush, the headline should have slammed the brakes to cause an uproar something like: "Again Bush violates Constitution by irresponsibly appointing ultra-conservative judges who will erode our freedom and deliver us over to the hysteric ultra conservative evangelicals." Why did the LAT pass up such beautiful liberal slant? Conclusion, it reports news unbiased.

July 20, 2005

Bush picked John G Roberts Jr. to fill the vacated Supreme Court seat by Sandra O'Connor, later by Rehnquist. The front page of the LAT had only factual and positive things to say. "Bush leans right in court pick and reaffirmed his commitment to a bold stroke presidency. The nominee is low-key, smart and effective and argued cases across the spectrum." Once again, it would have been easy to use a different headline that depicted Roberts as a staunch conservative and anti-abortionist who would turn the clock back on back street allies. That would have been factual too, but the LAT chose to use the positive, in favor of Bush and Roberts.

October 5, 2003

Remember the recall election in California of the liberal Governor Davis? He wasn't a motivator, and when state coffers got hurt by the "dot.com" bust in the 2000's, Davis became very unpopular. In a very damaging article to Davis, just two days before the recall election, the LAT cried on the front page: "Davis is battling his image of aloofness. At town hall meetings the governor doggedly tries to connect with voters. But he remained true to his trappings." In the same paper on the same day, columnist Steve Lopez wrote how Davis had been the target of the conservative radio talk hosts, yet these talk show hosts called Steve Lopez part of a vast left-wing conspiracy (page B1 of LAT 10/5/03). The very unfavorable articles on the LAT front page towards Democratic Governor Davis may well have swayed enough voters for his recall. I didn't hear any praising remarks from O'Reilly or Limbaugh that the LAT effectively got Republican Schwarzenegger elected.

October 9, 2003

A short time afterwards when Governor Schwarzenegger was elected, the LAT leaked news on the front page that Schwarzenegger had groped girls on the set, the kind of news that sells newspapers. Fox News' Bill O'Reilly was furious about that liberal slant of the LAT. The LAT quoted Bill O'Reilly as saying: "Maybe Arnold is a groper but a bigger danger to our democracy is not Arnold's grabbing of buttocks but the LAT trying to destroy a politician with whom they disagree." What hypocrisy! Bill O'Reilly is so darn biased towards conservatism that he didn't expand on the fact that proved the opposite: Just before the recall election, the LAT wrote damaging news about Governor Davis while reporting only positive news about Republican Schwarzenegger, keeping the groping for after the election. The irony is that Bill O'Reilly portrays his show as a "no-spin-zone".

October 23, 2003

The LAT reported a positive front-page article "filled with action picture" brimming with hope about Republican Governor Schwarzenegger for actions to improve the state. That day, I heard no praising comments towards the LAT from Rush Limbaugh or Bill O'Reilly.

On 18 March 2004

The LAT posted a John Kerry banner cartoon and underneath Muslim and Al Queda leaders with guns, underlined: "Unidentified Foreign Leaders who want Kerry to beat Bush." This was stunning. Could a paper think of a more mean-spirited attack on liberal John Kerry in an election year? If the editors had been staunchly conservative, it would have been understandable though shameful. Coming from a liberal editor, this was bizarre.

August 28, 2007

When Alberto Gonzales resigned as Attorney General, the LAT chose to provide a full section of opinions from leading representatives in Congress in equal number of liberals and conservatives. Contrast this with conservative Newsmax that provided comments only from conservative views, lambasting liberals.

July 4, 2005

On this day of independence, the liberal editors of the LAT published in their editorial commentary a reprint of the Declaration of Independence, without comment. That was class!

The Press-Enterprise serves as leading newspaper in Riverside County. Their editorial recommendations on October 31, 2004 for the November 2004 elections: For President: Republican George Bush; For US Senate: Republican Bill Jones; For US Congress: Five Republicans, One Democrat. For the California Legislature (for the nine districts): Nine Republicans, no Democrats. Mind you, California is a Democratic state. Still, I found this newspaper unbiased in news reporting.

Compare these results of unbiased news reporting with the so-called Fair and Balanced News of Fox News. Hours long news reporting occurred when Condaleeza Rice, Secretary of State, testified in Congress about what President Bush knew before 9/11 about upcoming attacks. During the testimony, Fox News displayed a huge banner over the screen: RICE SAYS WE DIDN'T KNOW THAT 9/11 WAS COMING. This was clever and a beautiful twist of facts. Obviously, Bush or Rice didn't know that the planes would be hijacked on 9/11. If they did, they would have stopped it. That statement was not news. But by portraying with big banners as if it was news, Fox News brainwashed its viewers that Bush didn't know anything about an impending attack. It exonerated him but should it have? As came out of the testimonies, Mr. Bush was allegedly briefed a month before 9/11 that the CIA feared a terrorist suicide attack from a hijacked plane into an important American target. From the testimonies it appeared that Bush did nothing about it until the planes hit us on 9/11. Imagine for a second that Fox New would not have been biased towards conservatives but unbiased as news is supposed to be and had instead displayed the following, more truthful banner across the screen: "BUSH KNEW AN ATTACK WAS COMING BUT DID NOTHING!" Two different banners from the same testimony, both factual, but how opposite in emotional effect! A more objective TV station, such as NBC or ABC or CNN, would not have displayed such huge banner about a meaningless statement but would have let the viewer decide. From a conservative view, the Fox News banner was brilliant, but from a patriotic standpoint it wasn't, it was deceiving and un-American, not much different from a Russian state controlled TV station, in my view.

In 2004 when the war in Iraq had intensified because of insurgents, Fox News showed a banner for weeks: WAR ON TERROR each time they covered the war in Iraq. The only purpose I could ascertain was to unconsciously influence Americans that we were fighting the war on terror in Iraq. Politically, this was the view of most conservatives. In reality we had diverted the war on terror. But, it had its desired effect for conservatives as most people during the 2004 elections believed that the war in Iraq was a just war to fight terror. Never mind that our presence in Iraq bred terrorism, and that without our presence there, Iraq would have had no terrorists that were a threat against America.

Patriotism follows the Constitution, and the Constitution does not take sides. George Washington, arguably our greatest President and greatest patriot, was above politics by doing what is best for our country, not what is best for a party.

For us, Americans it is of paramount importance that we know the truth. Which media provides unbiased news and which media colors it. Without the truth we become puppets in the hands of propaganda, brainwashed as the Germans were by the Nazis propaganda machine. They were smart people. They thought they knew the truth. You can figure it out. If all you hear is negative bias towards one party or person, you should know that media is deceiving you. To heal our country, we need to know the truth; we need to stop listening to pretenders.

CHAPTER 26

▼

SOLUTIONS FOR POLITICS

Many political attitudes have changed so much that two-thirds of Americans said that today's leaders pale in comparison with those twenty years ago. It expresses the feeling of frustration that in Congress little gets done and what gets done is often not done in the interest of the majority of the American people.

The main reason for the poor results is the deep polarization in politics today. We are so polarized that representatives in Congress will not vote conscience but party line. We are so polarized that even with the enormous failures of the Bush Administration far outweighing the good, over 80% of Republican voters (some 30% off all voters) still support the President; that defies all conservative reason for a man who outspent all liberal presidents in over thirty-five years.

We can blame politicians for the polarization but the real culprit is us, the American people. We are the ones who listened to deceptive talk of most talk shows and campaign managers. We are the ones who gave confirming feedback. We are the ones, who participated in trashing the opposition party and their politicians, or read and forwarded to friends character assassinations over the Internet. Polarization is the root of the evil of our dysfunctional political system; it caused paralysis and it won't stop until we, Americans, stop ourselves from the trashing, and until we have the courage to tell our friends to stop it.

Americans, whether conservative, liberal or libertarians are trying to do the best for America. They do not deserve to be trashed. No conservative or liberal ideology is absolutely correct. We have demonstrated it. We should learn from the people that think differently. The beauty of diverse ideologies in politics is that when we work together it will result in the absolute best decisions for the country. Am I sure? Yes! This is no different than in successful business, where we work with people who are diverse in opinion. When all people think alike inside a company, it will loose out. In meetings when two people thought alike, we'd say, there is one too many. And so it should be in politics. Political ideologies should only exist for political campaigns but once elections are over, politicians must work together by taking advantage of the diversity of political opinion and then compromise. That will achieve not only results, but also the best results for America. The only good result for America is when it is good for all Americans.

To stop the polarization it must begin with us. Stop the trashing of politicians. Stop reading or forwarding the trash on the Internet. Tune-out polarizing talk shows. When we listen to lies too often, we might believe it. You know who they are, the ones who are intolerant of the opposition. If you hear nothing but positives about a political party, the information is biased. Likewise, if all you hear is negative, it is biased. They are deceiving you if they don't tell you that they are biased. Turn them off. Switch from Fox News to broadcast news or CNN. Contrary to popular belief, they are not pro-liberal, more boring perhaps but not liberal, simply because they are owned by conglomerates that are largely conservatives. Read many newspapers. These media are also not pro-liberal, simply because most papers are owned by conservatives. Listen to talk shows with diversity but not the ones I have seen on Fox News when the conservative host always wins by inviting less competent opponents. Good hosts should neither force political ideology on its guests nor constantly interrupt the guest.

Let's become politically more developed and astute. Invite political debate into homes, schools, work and golf course; seek out debate only with those who have opposing views. We must become as knowledgeable about politics as we are about golf, work, cooking or educating kids. You and the country will depend on it.

Once we get rid of polarization ourselves, we might be able to elect more competent and charismatic Presidents who will not use fear as weapon of leadership but use hope followed by substance that will lead us to prosperity. Likewise, we should vote for competent representatives who promise to work in honesty with the opposition party. Without polarization, a breath of fresh air will descend on Congress.

We need to help them in setting a limit on how much they can spend. We often listen to the trash talks of "tax and spend liberals". Now that we know the truth that a Republican President and a Republican Congress has outspent liberals, we need to help both parties. Let's demand that federal spending must be capped at 18% of GDP. No matter which party runs the government, this will avoid out-of-control spending. In addition an attempt should be made to balance the budget by us demanding from them that budget surpluses are generated in good economic times with positive growth. These surpluses would compensate lower tax receipts in bad economic times with lesser or negative growth.

Once we have done that, we must overcome the fear of terror, and fear of just about everything else. Osama bin Laden loved the fear he caused us. He must have loved it too that President Bush didn't attempt to overcome our fear. Let's demand that our new President prioritizes to get Osama bin Laden and eradicate or at least dismantle the entire al Qaeda organization currently in the border region between Afghanistan and Pakistan. We must also begin to neutralize Islamic fascist clerics through the face of consistent American values and through an effective combination of American powers of leadership, consistency in our values, public relations, education, and dialogue … without fear; a design to win the hearts and minds of Muslims. Let's also establish many Boys & Girls Clubs in Pakistan similar to the Boys & Girls Clubs in America that bring hope, character and opportunity to each individual child.

If we want to continue fighting wars with military power, we must have the guts to show solidarity with our troops on the front line. The least we can do is to sacrifice and pay for the war by temporarily raising taxes, instead of hypocritically borrowing it on the shoulders of our kids (and the youngsters in the military when they get older). If we don't want to sacrifice, then let's stop supporting the war.

For our national security it is of the utmost urgency to create a national emergency task force to develop alternative renewable energies that will make us independent of oil from the Middle East, as rapidly as possible. In the meantime, Iraq must be turned into a win-win for the world and Iraq. Let's occupy major oil fields and protect their pipelines, exploiting oil while making sure that the Iraqis get reimbursed at the prevailing world oil price. Most of our troops in Iraq should come home and even more of them when international military could replace Americans, once the world understands how vital this oil strategy will be for the world economy.

There are hundreds of very important reasons we need the world as much as they need us. Outstanding relations with the world are paramount to our success because America's economy is intertwined with the world and isolation is no longer a possibility. Let's stop antagonizing the world. After seven years the world has learned not to trust us; that must be reversed. We need to become realistic in how we see our place in the world. Even if we are the best, and I am sure certain folks will find that debatable, the best leaders always stay humble. For our sake we must begin to restore, no, improve upon our role as world leader. Without the world behind us, our efforts to eradicate Islamic terror cannot be successful. Let's recapture the American spirit of fearless freedom, lead the world morally, economically and politically, and live life to the fullest, as long as we can. Our nation shined for many decades. Let's try again.

SECTION IV:
JUSTICE

Justice is in the mind of the beholder. Justice could be based on personal morals, commonsense or for the technical minded, the administering of law.

Those who see justice in terms of certain morals, consider a lack of justice when other people do not live up to those morals. For example, for some, abortion is immoral and even though it is legal, they see it as injustice.

Others see justice less as a moral issue but more as a commonsense for people with different views to live together. Common sense provides for pragmatic, flexible laws. Common sense laws create fairness. Common sense uses the standard of what a reasonable person would have done under the circumstance. This view prevailed among the founders of our nation. Others feel that better justice is achieved with perfectly detailed laws covering each and every situation that removes the need for human judgment and the need for common sense.

Finally, there are those who see justice solely as the administering of laws. In this view, abortion couldn't be seen as an injustice as long as the law says it is legal. Practitioners of our legal profession would take this view of justice; when practicing law they would normally care less about moral issues or even commonsense. Moral issues and commonsense do not earn them a living, the wording of laws does.

What is justice? According to Webster's New Universal Unabridged: 1. Justice is the quality of being just, righteousness, moral rightness, and equitableness. 2. Administering what is just by law, deserved punishment or reward.

The first definition incorporates pretty much the moralist and commonsensical people as well as the perfectionists. The second definition incorporates the legal profession.

In the opinion of the author, personal morals should not be included in the subject of justice in this book or for that matter in any human law or any political ideology. Personal morals are linked to our personal religion or personal value system. Anything as diverse as personal is best kept out of laws and politics. If others do not share our morals, then it is up to them to justify their actions with their God, if they believe in one. If personal morals were made into human laws, adherence to it would diminish the effect on the final judgment of religious believers. It is incomprehensible why, for example, many Islamic leaders believe that by elevating, or rather demoting, the Sharia into human law, their Muslim followers could earn salvation. What value could a person achieve in the eye of Allah if a Muslim followed the Sharia to avoid human punishment? Wouldn't Allah value a Muslim more that followed the Sharia, not because it was a human law, but because of true submission from the heart, especially if temptations were legally in reach? Anyone who truly submits to God's morals because of beliefs from the heart wouldn't want these moral values incorporated into human law.

Our lives are guided by our personal morals. They determine how we live and how we raise our children. Luckily, not everybody shares the exact same moral values or the intensity thereof. It would be a boring world if they did because we'd be all "perfect". No differentiation in judgment or in earthly requirements for job characteristics. We wouldn't want everybody to have the same level of personal values. At the same time it confirms that personal values are personal and shouldn't be elevated to human law. It could be desirable to include values into law, not for the sake of such value but as sub-set to other laws. For example, the value of honesty is required by law to tell the truth under oath, not for the sake of honesty, but to determine if life or property rights were violated by an accused.

Therefore, a stand-alone moral value should not be included in human law. All society needs is laws that regulate how people in a society interact together. Rules of the road come to mind. Or murder. It is a no-brainer that murder should be punishable by human law, not because it is a personal or moral law or a moral law from God. It is simply a necessity of society because it can't function well when people murder one another on a whim without punishment. Human laws that protect property rights are likewise, not because stealing is against a moral law but because without protection of human law, we could never enjoy the fruits of our work, not for long anyway. Free market capitalism couldn't function without the guarantee of property rights. It should be merely coincidental when a human law coincides with a personal value or moral law.

Justice is best served when based on commonsense laws and administered accordingly. In <u>The Republic</u>, Socrates described justice as "doing that which is appropriate to the person and situation". Therefore, Socrates advocated common sense in laws; he didn't advocate uniformity and perfection in laws and regulations. In the next chapters we argue that our judicial system has been abused in many ways. Aside from the current abuse in tort lawsuits, overzealous lawmakers have over-regulated our society by piling up laws one upon another, perfectly detailed covering each and every situation, that have overwhelmed our nation and left little of the famous American spirit of freedom. We believe it is time to correct the judicial system by reestablishing the bases of true justice with nostalgia for common sense and America's love for freedom, doing that which is appropriate to the person and situation.

CHAPTER 27

▼

FREEDOM

O, say can you see, by the dawn's early light..,
'Tis the star-spangled banner—O long may it wave
O'er the land of the free *and the home of the brave*

With the tune on my mind I was driving the eve of July 4 from home in River-side County, California, to the Beach Cities of Redondo Beach and Hermosa Beach. Then the words that made Thomas Jefferson famous came to mind, from the Declaration of Independence:

> That all men are created equal, that they are endowed by their Creator with certain unalienable Rights, that among these are Life, Liberty and the pursuit of Happiness.

As I approached Hermosa Beach, banners welcomed its visitors:

> "Firework of any kind will not be tolerated on our beaches or anywhere."

I frowned because I remembered the traditional fun of fireworks on July 4 with my kids and friends. It seemed that as a society we were freer back then, less inundated with laws that tried to take our individual adventures away. Our fire-works never hurt anyone because as parents we were careful. Sure, I had read about some kids getting hurt but the point was to have fun and to learn not to be stupid just like anything else in life. After that first banner I saw another one, a July 4 warning.

"No alcohol will be allowed on the beaches or anywhere on public land."

July 4 parties in these beach cities were legendary. In the past, the city used quite a bit of tolerance about drinking on the boardwalk (they call it The Strand). After all, it was July 4. The ban forced fun-seeking people to put rum or beer in a coke can, violating the silly laws. In most countries, with crime rates far less than ours, no one seems to have a problem about drinking beer in public. In the United States, we are slowly seeing a new approach to Prohibition. We can't drink on the beach or outside bars or even at street parties. Adults of 18–20 are discriminated against, as they can't drink at all anymore. Some lawmakers felt that 18–21 year olds aren't responsible enough to drink a beer. Yet, we find no shame in making them responsible enough to die for our country, defending us with guns in wars that we older adults find too dangerous to handle ourselves. Why does it make sense to our conscience that we discriminate against adults from eighteen through the age of twenty? Adult is adult. If we truly think that they are not responsible enough to drink at 18, how can we have them vote or fight a war for us? It is shameful. If we truly believe that they are too young to drink at 18, then be consistent and move up the age of adulthood to 21. That means they can't vote and they can't be sent to war to fight with their lives until 21. Otherwise eliminate the discrimination against a minority group of adults because that's what 18–20 year olds are.

Early in the morning on July 4, I strolled on the beach in Redondo Beach. A man was staking out a spot at the beach while setting up a small hibachi for a little BBQ celebration. Good for you man, I thought. Within ten minutes, a patrolling guard had the hibachi removed: No barbeque allowed on the beach, not even on July 4! Why? In the meantime, the city council voted to make it illegal to smoke on the beach. I don't smoke and should have no problem with new ordinances prohibiting smoking on the beach. But I do have a problem from the standpoint of the principle of fairness. It is great that we warn smokers of the dangers to their health, and that restaurants and airplanes do not condone second hand smoke. But on the beach? Come on! Was anyone afraid that some one would sue the city for second hand smoke on the beach? Are we dealing with obsessed lawmakers that love to take all fun and liberties away from Americans? What could have been the motivation?

According to a recent CBS report, 130,000 Americans die annually of salt overdose mostly from fast food, packaged food, and restaurants. Several years ago, the food industry was asked to voluntarily reduce salt in fast food and processed food by 50% that according to the American Medical Association could have saved 130,000 lives a year. The result? Nothing happened, well actually, the salt level of packaged goods increased, not decreased. Apparently, lawmakers shrug about 130,000 unnecessary deaths. Since 9/11, that accounted for 850,000 unnecessary deaths, simply due to salt. We are told that we can't and shouldn't legislate everything we eat. I agree. Of course we shouldn't regulate everything. But if 850,000 deaths since 9/11 due to salt are not worrying us, how could an ordinance pass, banning smoking on the beach?

This chapter is not about banning fireworks, beer drinking or smoking on the beach. It is about the warped wisdom of lawmakers and the personal agendas of minority interest groups that manipulate us by fear and politics of safety at the cost of our freedom. It is about the erosion of our liberties in America, "the land of the free". Besides beer, fireworks and smoke, you and I could come up with hundreds or thousands of examples of laws, rules and regulation that are an insult to our intelligence as if we are incapable of making a choice. The point is that states and local governments have overpowered its citizens with too much legislation. Most of us have become numb to feel or even to remember the times of the fun it was to live in the spirit of that once famous American culture of freedom. I remember some of that culture of freedom when I immigrated thirty five years ago. But over the last decades, our culture slowly changed from a daredevil nation to a nation of wimps that now live a uniform life of entitlements without risks.

Lawyers love laws, the more detail the better, the more money they make. But does it serve the country? Philip Howard in "The Death of Common Sense" wrote about how our Founders abhorred regularity and sameness. The Founders and generations of Americans in America's first century thereafter glorified individualism and the frontier. The spirit of Common Law, which America inherited from England, is pragmatism. Common Law is flexible law that allows judgment based on the circumstances. Its most important standard is what a reasonable person would have done in the circumstances. Common Law invites common sense.

After World War II, our lawmakers decided to change that great American philosophy of individualism when they began to transform our legal system, by writing laws in greater details for the purpose of creating uniformity, and taking judgment away from judges and government officials. Accumulating laws after laws, Philip Howard observed that we now have a bureaucracy with vastly more details than countries in Europe that have been in existence for thousands of years. In a little over a hundred years we succeeded in becoming more over regulated than they are. Every business is in violation of some law or regulation because no sane person is capable of understanding all of them. What good do all these laws and regulations do if ordinary citizens can't understand them?

Lawmakers believed that more precision in law would ensure fairness and eliminate room for judgment at personal discretion. Precision requires uniformity, the antithesis of what this country stood for. It failed. It didn't improve fairness; to the contrary, it ignored it. It didn't reduce corruption. What it did is kill individualism, kill common sense, kill personal responsibility and accountability, delayed decision-making and vastly raised the cost of doing business. Worse, lawmakers killed America's famous spirit of freedom.

Along with the attitude of indifference, the overregulation became the prime stimulus for excessive lawsuits in our country. Behind every detail of a law or regulation lurks a potential lawsuit. The excessive regulations are a major contributor to the decline of our country. Will we have the courage and willpower to reverse the trend? Does anybody want to do anything about it?

Because every case is different, true fairness in justice requires case-by-case judgment. Uniformity in law treats every case the same; therefore it serves the opposite of fairness. When we discussed in the chapters on the economy that the fairness principle was lost in this country, we need to add that our lawmakers greatly aided in that process.

Today, most of us are living a less remarkable life, overshadowed by laws, regulations, rules and ordinances. The Declaration of Independence speaks of us as the "governed by a government that governs based on the consent of the governed". But we didn't consent, or instigate or contest the thousands and thousands of laws that were piled upon us. Who did? Usually special activist groups, active in their cause, who couldn't care less about imposing on the majority. But the fault is not theirs. The fault lies with us, the majority. We were and still are led to the slaughterhouse of captivity by more laws without putting up a fight. In this freedom loving country we are beginning to see less freedom than we'd find in any other Western democratic country. With the rate we were and still are going, countries that have been in existence for two thousand years such as Holland and France, have fewer freedom restricting laws than we do. Isn't that embarrassing, America?

We are at fault! In Europe, the constituents are more active in politics than American are, partially because our culture does not favor political discussions in company or at the dining table. In Europe, political discussions flow more freely making it more difficult for minority activists to pursue their agenda without a fight from the majority. The other reasons that special interest laws pass less easy in Europe is Europe's multi-party system and thus lesser influence from lobbyists. In America we are too easily persuaded by slogans that seem right on the surface but that make no sense when the layers of the onion are peeled. Think of overused slogans such as "if this law saves one life it is worth it". As if lives are to be lived in a bubble of safety instead of a life of exploration and freedom.

With that attitude we would never have won the Wild West; we would not have won our Independence from the British. America was about freedom, courage and sacrifice! The daredevil in us that seeks to express itself early on in our lives in its own individual way is not getting much chance to experience that unique American character of the past.

Many an old-timer-blogger has expressed dismay with today's restricting laws. If the current deluge of laws made any real sense, these old-timers over 40 said; they should be all dead by now. Kids played after school outside the house without parents knowing about their whereabouts. (Today, that could be child-neglect.) Seatbelts were not required, child car seats were voluntary, no problem drinking at eighteen, or younger if parents let them. Kids would ride their bikes to school and…. without a helmet. Riding in the back of a pick-up truck was a treat. On July 4, kids played with fireworks, their dads taught them how to use it. Kids fought with other kids, getting black and blue without parents getting involved, it was part of growing up. Kids climbed trees, sometimes one broke a leg; parents didn't think about suing the city. Teachers were allowed to discipline kids. Parents punished their kids physically too if they deemed that necessary without fear for some social agency taking their children away to an inhumane alternative of foster homes. We had crazy people like Evil Knievel who jumped canyons; well, he had to be crazy, but hey, it was his life and he could do what he wanted to do with it. If you wanted to be a daredevil, you could. Today you can't legally cross a street when your pedestrian light is on red, even if no cars are to be seen. Kids were allowed, no, encouraged to learn from their mistakes.

Most kids nowadays don't stand a chance. Even at eighteen, most of them act as if they never could live on their own. We weakened them, all for the sake of perceived safety and possible lawsuits. Before kids play together, the parents need to come to terms with other parents, worried about all the things that could go wrong, injuries and lawsuits. Should we invite our kids' friends over for a swim at the house? It would be a nervous day. "Don't jump, don't dive, don't do this or that", we'd yell, to avoid lawsuits. My stepson asked me if his high school sophomore class could come over for a study/swim party. His teacher was O.K. with it. So, I said, fine but have the parents sign a release form. The result? I killed the party; it was too much trouble.

We created a monster of laws that vastly exceeds God's laws in Leviticus that with over 600 laws already overwhelmed the Jews so much that no one could possibly live up to them. As a result, God's laws in Leviticus are mostly ignored but human laws don't give us that luxury. We are supposed to know any and all of the tens of thousands of human laws that affect our lives. No doubt, every human law was made with the best of intentions but the aggregate of laws has made America loose its unique place on earth that was guided by the special spirit of liberty. Can we gain back that special spirit of freedom? Or do we accept the overwhelming load of laws, with thousands being added annually, that have made our freedom undistinguishable (or even eroded) from other developed countries?

Philip Howard wrote his book <u>The Death of Common Sense"</u> over a decade ago. It is compelling and his message is more valid today than ever before. Yet, lawmakers paid no attention and continued feverishly writing more laws with greater details. We voted these lawmakers into office. Why aren't we appalled? Why don't we do something? Let's form a political group "Americans For Common Sense Laws" and fight lawmakers out of office until common sense and freedom return to America's system of justice.

CHAPTER 28

▼

TORT LAW

With countless laws with great detail on our books, Americans have a potentially huge arsenal for tort lawsuits. In 1977, when the Supreme Court decided to allow lawyers the right to advertise their legal services as a form of free speech, it seemed as if free reigns were given for greed to break through the barrier of American decency, to take advantage of a smorgasbord of laws in court. By itself, this Supreme Court decision seemed relatively innocent. But in combination with other collaborators, the effects became very damaging for our society as the most litigious country in the world. There were collaborators galore! One was Wall Street's obsession with short-term earnings. Another one was the fading of personal responsibility and social responsibility as well as a growing fiction that we are entitled to the rights of life. Yet another was the growing unfairness in workers' wages as well as the growing disappearance of job security. Combined with a perceived unfairness in the tax system they caused a trend of growing indifference among Americans. Indifference about fairness blew the tort system wide open.

Right after the 1977 Supreme Court decision, only the ethically challenged lawyers sought out clients to pursue fortunes in court but as judges and juries began to accept one outrageous decision after another, the gates opened widely. The rest is history. Lawsuits grew almost exponentially to the point where today it has not only overwhelmed the court system but also how we live from day to day.

Towers Perrin, a global professional services firm, headquartered in Stamford, CT, released a report that the nation's tort cost in 1970 amounted to $13.9 billion, or $68 per capita. In 2004, the tort cost reached $260 billion, or $886 per capita. Adjusting the 1970 cost for inflation to $329 per capita, the tort cost in 2004 was almost a huge three times the tort cost in 1970. As a consequence, tort lawsuits have pushed up liability risks, and insurance premiums, a big concern of business, local governments and wealthy individuals. "What's the risk" is often one of the first questions from the tongues of council members, board members, teachers and parents.

For tens of thousands of years, men accepted that life was fragile and temporary. Anything could happen in life, and people accepted that. But in the last thirty years, we changed our mind. If something happens to our lives or relatives today, someone is going to pay-as if money would return lost happiness. Today, from birth we can expect to live to 77.9 years (Source: Economist 2006). In comparison, other parts of the world aren't so lucky. In Swaziland, life expectance is a mere 29.9 years. Who are they going to sue? Life expectancy in many countries in Africa is still no higher than around the 40s and 50s. (Source: Economist 2006). These people know that life isn't an entitlement and when things go wrong they don't sue.

In America, life expectancy in 1900 for a white male was just 48 years. Non-white males lived to 34. In 1850, an American white male's life expectancy was 38 years (Source: infoplease.com). A hundred or so years ago we didn't sue as a rule. Compared to African countries today, we should be so grateful for our extended life afforded by modern medicine, clean water and standard of living with balanced diets. Yet, we expect that extended life as an entitlement and will sue anyone who'd contributed to making it shorter or less pleasant.

Life never was and, of course, never will be an entitlement, but in the spirit of tort lawsuits we pretend it is. Universally when a person is injured or dies as a result of gross negligence or intent by a third party, the descendents usually find satisfaction when the perpetrator is put away in jail. A dependent from the dead or injured should sue for lost income. But in America today just about anyone related would try to sue for personal gain. Why did our system of justice accept tort suits unless it came from a dependent? Why did the system accept the excessive awards from the principle of emotional distress? Emotional juries took that principle out of proportion. Life is full of emotions. God made it so. In case a compelling reason exists to award money for emotional distress, why didn't we use common sense and cap it to a lifetime of psychological counseling. Likewise monetary punishment has been abused. Why did the system allow awards of monetary punishments to go to the plaintiff? It should go the jurisdiction of tax-payers, not to the plaintiff. There is no justice in giving it to the plaintiff. Both emotional distress and punitive damages were huge motivators for the out-of-control lawsuits today.

Why did the system accept the suits against tobacco companies for the death of an addicted smoker? Of course, we understand that a dependent seeks loss of income. But why do we call it justice to see jury verdicts of fifty million dollars for a dead smoker of sixty-five years or seventy years old? In Africa, one would be lucky to live that long.

Why did the system accept that "bystanders" could be sued? Almost any American finds it now completely normal to sue deep pockets if they can be linked to a wrong committed against us. A good plaintiff lawyer is trained to per-suade a jury to find neglect with a deep pocket, who may have done nothing wrong, yet his wealth is a magnet when he/she is facing the "little victimized per-son", represented by "altruistic" lawyers seeking only justice for the little man. On the TV series Boston Legal altruism frequently dominates the law firm of Crane, Pool and Schmidt but try to find top notch lawyers in the real world with-out deep pockets on either side of the aisle. If a deep pocket can be connected to a case, finding a lawyer is easy. Did a rich uncle pay for his poor niece's new car that subsequently got involved in an accident with you? No problem, he'll be named in the suit and will pay big bucks.

Did your kid fall from the top of the swing equipment he climbed on at an amusement park? Sue the park. Did your kid get hurt when making daring dives from your neighbor's diving board? Sue the neighbor. Did your child put a plas-tic bag over her head without a warning label? Sue the bag maker. Did a ladder collapse because you forgot to set it up correctly? Sue the ladder maker. Was the coffee at McDonald's too hot? Sue McDonalds. Did a doctor not save your mama? Sue the doctor. Did you enter a house, unauthorized, but you fell from an unstable ladder that the owner had left outside below a window? Sue the home-owner. Was there a pothole in the road? Sue the city.

The joke of our tort system reached far across our borders. At one time, I hired a PhD in Physics from Europe. He brought his family over. One day, his kid climbed on a shed that didn't look safe. The kid had no business climbing on it. He fell, broke his leg. In Europe they would have shrugged it off with a he-needs-to-learn-grin. Being in the U.S., the dad's reaction was a different kind of grin when he said: Let's participate in this joke of American tort and do what Americans do, let's sue the owner and get some money for pain and suffering including emotional distress. He pursued the case in court and won big. He knew that this was not about justice but about manipulating a dysfunctional justice system.

Even "acts of God", a bus skidding on an unexpected icy road, are no longer shielded from lawsuits. Nothing is supposed to go wrong in our lives. Once upon a time, a victim sought remedy in court only for a serious breach. Otherwise we accepted an apology for an inadvertent wrong, as part of life. Apologies can't be given anymore. That might be seen as admission of guilt and would advance a possible lawsuit. Thus, we suppress the decency to act on the feeling of personal responsibility. It is too dangerous, our lawyer will advise against it. And so, personal responsibility slowly disappeared in our nation. Sure, management books still talk about taking personal responsibility, and psychologists still do but it just doesn't fit our new culture.

For the legal profession, our nation's growing indifference to justice has been a bonanza. No doubt it was a golden day for those in the profession who pursued the gold mine of class action suits. The players in class action lawsuits are deep pockets on the defense side and lots and lots of "little men" on the plaintiff side, the losses of which are too small to seek a personal lawyer. Stockholder Class action lawsuits are a prime example of how the system ran amok. In most cases, the ones that get noticeably better are the plaintiff lawyers. The pittance of settlement that is spread over the class members is a joke compared to the losses incurred by small investors. The legal profession argues that these suits are the only vehicles for the little man to seek remedy. Altruism rules! Lawyers also argue that they take all the risks in class action lawsuits because they don't charge legal fees unless there is a settlement. Yet, when checking into these suits, I have not seen a class action case that didn't result in financially rewarding payments for the lawyers. In fact, these lawsuits are so "risky" that lawyers have sought out "victims" to play the role of plaintiff. Some partners of law firms such as at Milberg Weiss found creative, though illegal, ways to become lead partners in class action lawsuits by having so-called victims waiting in the wings for a stock to go down, then quickly file a suit with these "victims" as plaintiffs. The stock price of many high-tech companies got hit after the dotcom bust. Subsequently, many of these companies flush with cash from rich IPOs got hit with class action suits, even though every common sense investor knew that the market was over-hyped by analysts, media, shoe-shiners.

Class-action suits are often akin to "robbing a bank" legally. Some cases deserve a class action lawsuit (Enron, WorldCom). Yet class action suits against companies do not serve justice. Besides lining the pockets of attorneys and disrupting business, they are intrinsically grossly unfair. After all, the people that are paying the settlements are the owners of the company, the shareholders. They are not guilty of any crime nor did they gain from an alleged fraud. These current shareholders can be one of two possible types. They were not an investor at the time of the alleged sins of management, so why should they have to pay? Or they are long-time investors that bought the stock perhaps at high prices before the crime was exposed, and thus before the stock price dropped; they didn't gain from any fraud; possibly they are in the group of plaintiffs suing themselves. Who were the real winners that are not targeted as defendant? First, that could be the CEO, and some officers, who committed the alleged crime and profited from it. Second, they are investors who sold out at high prices just before the crime was exposed and laughed all the way to the bank, yet they are not targeted in these lawsuits. Most companies, even those without guilt, settle these lawsuits to avoid a time-consuming process in court and the fact that juries are often persuaded to make deep pockets pay anyway for the losses of the little men.

As it is, justice doesn't exist in class action lawsuits. Because the current owners are not at fault nor got the better of it, the company should not be sued. Justice could be found by allowing class action lawsuits for intent or gross negligence by the CEO or other officer that was involved in the alleged crime, as well as any board member involved with proven intent to mislead. A lawsuit should be thrown out unless prior to allowing a lawsuit sufficient evidence of intent or gross negligence by the CEO or officer should be demonstrated to the judge. As it stands now, plaintiffs can go on a fishing trip through a company's email system or notes to find some out-of-context incriminating document that might sway a jury. Once a CEO, officer or director is found guilty, the company should not be allowed to reimburse CEO, officer or director. Innocent shareholders should not have to pay. This true proposal of justice would not be as lucrative for the lawyers, so they will cry that the little investor would have no remedy if they can't sue the big bad corporation. But that doesn't justify imposing injustice on someone else.

Tort lawsuits by individuals have gotten out of hand because the courts allowed too many secondary actors to be held liable. A police officer that beats up a citizen, who was of no threat to him, deserves to be sued, perhaps serve time in jail too, but why should his/her employer pay? Why should taxpayers, that fund the city or county, be responsible for the criminal acts of an officer? Unless the city was directly involved, for example by commanding the officer to beat up the victim, it is great injustice to punish the city and thus the taxpayer. Unless an employer's intent was to cause harm through his employee, there is no justice when we sue the employer! We understand the motivation of lawyers to seek out deep pockets but something went wrong when our system of justice began to accept that employers are responsible for wrong actions of employees that are not condoned or promoted by the employer. Often deep pockets are targeted because our system accepts low levels of responsibilities that could make them cough up for the damages. No suit should win against anyone unless the intent to cause harm was proved or gross negligence that was directly responsible for the harm.

A great victory of sorts for justice came on January 15, 2008 when the Supreme Court threw out a lawsuit, it ruled that, in the words of Justice Anthony Kennedy, "secondary actors are too remote for liability". This was the case of Stone Ridge Investment Partners versus Scientific Atlanta, a subsidiary of Cisco. At issue was whether Scientific Atlanta could be held liable for its involvement with Charter Communications, which was found liable in a stock fraud case. It seems that Cisco's deep pockets were attractive to Stone Ridge and its lawyers.

Our system of justice is in its roots a good system but it has become increasingly abused for personal gain that has not served justice. In our world today, the drive to win trumps the legal search for justice by making it a perpetual open hunting season on deep pockets. The only defense they have is to buy more insurance and place more and more laws and regulations on their citizens. It has induced stress, impaired happiness and reduced freedom. This in turn will affect America's ability to compete on the world scene.

It is doubtful that our founding fathers had an American Dream in mind of pursuing that dream through the courts. Of course, there are many profound reasons for tort lawsuits that should be filed but the system got out of hand. For too long now, our legal system has encouraged legal stealing from so-called deep pockets. Making our judicial system a lottery for relatives of victims serves little benefit to society. It is in fact an unfair redistribution of income.

We must restore the tort system to serving true justice. This requires specific steps for lawmakers to enact:

- Americans must once again learn to accept personal responsibility. To foster the taking of personal responsibilities, we need to legally encourage apologies for wrongs committed or wrongs caused without intent. To foster apologies, the making of apologies should become inadmissible in court; except during the deliberation of sentencing when apologies should get consideration for a lesser financial verdict.

- The tort system should remedy only wrongs for intentional or gross negligence; you shouldn't be liable for negligence by association.

- "Secondary actors" should be shielded from liability. Everyone is a secondary actor unless they instigated or promoted a wrong through the person who committed the wrong.

- Tort lawsuits should be rejected unless the plaintiff is the victim or the victim's dependents who became deprived of income or wealth or suffered emotional distress.

- Emotional distress should be capped, not to exceed the reasonable cost of a lifetime of psychological counseling.

- Punitive damages should be awarded to the jurisdiction of the court, not to the victim or victim's lawyer

True justice in America will not return unless voters insist that lawmakers enact these proposed changes. Many trial lawyers and politicians could vehemently fight to avoid changes to a system that has served them well. They might cry: "The little man would loose the privilege to pursue their rights under the Constitution." Since when do politicians genuinely care about the "little man"?

CHAPTER 29

▼

COMMON SENSE

Thomas Payne first published <u>Common Sense</u> in January 1776. It helped the colonists make their case for independence. Common sense prevailed and our nation's legal framework was founded upon it. The American Constitution breathes common sense. America inherited the legal framework of England, called Common Law. It is based on common sense because it looks for human judgment based on the circumstances. Therefore, American law today should be all about common sense. Yet, it isn't.

<u>The Death of Common Sense</u>, by Philip K. Howard, describes with many examples why America's regulatory laws of the last decades are ill conceived, a bonanza for lawyers, but removed from common sense.

This chapter muses over two American obsessions of the last decades that concern extensive child and animal protection, both of which defy common sense.

In January 2008, two staff writers of the Times, Jack Leonard and Richard Winton, covered a story about a homeless man in Los Angeles County that in a discussion with social workers appeared eager to take care of his well-fed, healthy baby, abandoned by his wife. Apparently because of compassion, county social workers let him have his baby and dropped him off at a cheap motel. This is common sense. Unfortunately, the baby died, apparently killed (in November 2005). County Supervisor, Gloria Molina, apparently went ballistic. For months she grilled county managers about what went wrong. She used the death as a rallying cry that led to sweeping changes in how social workers deal with homeless children and she personally intervened, now pressing sheriffs to double their efforts to bring justice to that child. No doubt, they'll find distant relatives who could now sue the county and make a fortune. The taxpayer pays. Gloria Molina's spending of taxpayer funded time and money defies common sense.

According to the United Nations Children's Fund, worldwide deaths of children younger than five years was last year a "low" 9.7 million of which 7.9 million in sub-Sahara Africa and South Asia. Most of these deaths are caused by HIV/AIDS, poor sanitation, diarrhea, malnutrition and conflict. When we look at Molina's effort to change practices of and chastise social workers for using common sense and being compassionate, one can only wonder. Why do we get so obsessed and emotional about loosing one baby's life? Shouldn't we really use common sense and use our energy to avoid a repeat of the annual deaths of about 9.7 million young children that die unnecessarily? Or if deaths in the US concern us more, shouldn't Gloria use taxpayer's money to care about the main causes of the deaths of 16,000,000 people that died in America since 9/11?

A single child dies and it takes Gloria months to upset the little common sense that county workers still had. This brings us to the well-intentioned child protection laws of today. Physical punishment by parents or teachers could be interpreted as abusive, depending on what agency gets involved. Today, when dad pulls out his belt, just about any modern child of school age knows to call 911, and would be "saved" from his "abusive" parent. Parents might be humiliated in the eyes of neighbors, peers at work and school or sports teams. Unlike in a court of law, the net effect here is that the parent is treated guilty before the facts are out while the kid laughs his head off, uncorrected, heading with a wrong attitude into adulthood.

An account by Tracey Weber, a Times Staff reporter, described the tragedy of the Udvardi family in Southern California when social workers took their four children (between 6 and 16) on allegations that the mother subjected the kids to unnecessary and often painful medical procedures. Without any sympathy for father, mother or children, the family was torn apart. Eventually a judge dismissed the charges because the children did have rare medical problems. Yet the stigma of an abusive mother remained among teachers, neighbors and others. The Udvardis were caring parents. Perhaps a bit too caring, this wasn't clear. But why do we, the People, tolerate that the state can take kids from their parents under immunity? A state law gives absolute immunity to professionals who report suspicions of child abuse, founded or not. Have we gone insane? Or are we just indifferent? Anyone can utter the word abuse, and state employees take kids away from parents, overthrowing God's system that let parents raise kids no matter what. The state should have no right to take children from their parents, unless the lives of children are in immediate and obvious danger.

In Jesus' days, polygamy was normal and he didn't seem to have a problem with it, as long as kids and women were cared for. Our society doesn't condone polygamy. Understandably, the state took action and convicted the leaders of the YWZ Ranch run by the fundamentalist Church of Jesus Christ of Latter Day Saints in Texas. But was it really necessary to tear over 400 children from their mothers? Do we really believe that the state, not even having enough places to put these kids, will be more loving and caring than their mothers? A phone call of accusations gave enough impetus to dislodge over 400 children from their homes? "Any child from that environment cannot be safe", said Child Welfare Supervisor Angie Voss. Safe from what? What happened to innocent until proven guilty! Come to find out the townspeople saw the ranch as a "mystery" so now journalists have the chance to "uncover the mysteries of the ranch". Just so the media has something to do and ugly people have something to tickle their ears they take 400 kids from their mothers and traumatize them! What would common sense have dictated? What would Jesus have done?

Child protection laws have gone too far. Whereas a hundred years ago, children worked in mines as young as ten years old while nobody gave a darn what happened to them. Today, the pendulum swung to the other extreme. The pendulum should have stopped where it was some forty years ago but it didn't. Laws are usually well intentioned, but they keep piling up towards a so-called more perfect world, a utopia, removed from common sense, from nature, from God's world.

The net results of all these child protection laws have made the situation worse for society. Today, the indispensable hug that especially younger children need to social adaptation-ask any child psychologist-is banned in most schools for fear of possible sexual connotation. Only the very good but daring teachers still hug but they risk lawsuits and dismissal from their job.

In the last few decades, we are breeding a vastly different child than naturally happened for over 12,000 years when parents were in charge until adulthood. Today, kids are vastly different from those who grew up just thirty to forty years ago. Deprived of lots of hugs, and an occasional physical punishment, many of these children have little feelings of care for others, turning more and more of them into psychopathic characters. The increasing stress of higher expectations didn't help as the pursuit of happiness is increasingly measured in terms of materialism. For kids it is now mostly about winning, getting highest grades and getting into the best colleges. Modern children show little respect for adults, especially older people or pregnant women, even for experience or wisdom. It is a rare kid that would stand up for a pregnant woman in a crowded bus or waiting room. Elderly people are routinely harassed. The stress on kids nowadays is enormous and no doubt some of them can't handle it anymore and flip. Thirty years ago who would have thought about the possibility of kids buying guns and blowing away students and teachers in school? The big difference thirty five years ago was that parents and other caring adults used the combination of hugging, affection and discipline to bring kids into adulthood, without social agencies and school principals watching every move. No doubt, there were cases of excessive child abuse, a confirmation that this is not a perfect world and never will be. Why do we try to legislate this imperfect world into a perfect one? Child abuse will happen, laws or not. Creating more and more child protection laws won't prevent excessive cases usually caused by psychopaths or the mentally ill. There were enough laws on the books already to punish them. Normal parents would never intentionally harm their child. Yet, the consequence of certain well-intentioned child protection laws swung the pendulum too far; they made normal parents and teachers too cautious. Indirectly, these laws will create more psychopaths in our future.

We are a stressed nation. A recent study found Americans low on the "happiness" scale compared to many civilized countries. It turns out that people in Denmark are the happiest people in the world. Scientists are puzzled. Denmark is a cold country with bad weather. The secret seems to be that people in Denmark are less stressed compared specifically with the United States. The income gap is low, while ours is high. The Danes are assured of free college education, free healthcare and a pension, as well as six weeks of vacation. They don't see the point of chasing materialism. In the U.S. materialism trumps everything and it has gotten much worse over the last decades. Our children are especially showing the signs of stress, which doesn't bode well for their future. Let's get back into hugging and get rid of laws that we enacted when we were lulled asleep with "if it saves one child's life it is worth it".

Animal rights are fashionable nowadays. Many supporters seem to have lost all common sense. For thousands of years, men ruled over animals as they pleased. People for the Ethical treatment of Animals (PETA), is an animal rights movement seeking social justice for animals. Eventually, as Larry Copeland wrote in USA Today, they are trying to win the same rights for animals as humans. PETA supported a measure to ban carriage horses that haul tourists around in New York. From history we remember that in 1891 electric trolleys replaced the mass transit of those days: the horse carriage. PETA may find it unbelievable but for centuries horses were actually used for mass-transit. That was the place of a horse. These horses were and are well-fed and taken care of if the owners want a good business. But now, thanks to PETA's warped common sense, the fun of horse-carriage nostalgia may soon be history. What's left for fun? In China, people pull carts; heck, in most beach cities people drive bicycle taxis—shouldn't we ban that too?

One wonders if PETA is an outgrowth of bored city dwellers in this rich country, having too much time on their hands. I have no problem with animal lovers. I love my animals. But where is PETA's common sense? In a world, that God created, coyotes tear apart rabbits-alive. Actually most carnivores eat animals alive causing agonizing deaths. Snakes do. Tigers, lions do. So do birds that eat worms or insects. Yet, these animal lovers think that in their 78 years of average life they can take on the design of nature. I have no problem with basic common sense laws that prohibit animal cruelty with sadistic intent. The Humane Society that I know has fulfilled a very useful role. However, common sense dictates that animals aren't human and shouldn't be treated as such. How soon before we go to jail for killing mosquitoes or flies or poisoning ants? If we allow common sense to die, there will be no limit to the lengths this insanity will go.

Anyone who has ever tried goose liver pate, as only the French in the province of Perigord know how to make, would swear it is "divine", exquisite. The naughty French are known to force-feed their geese so that the livers grow fatter. When driving through the Perigord Province in France, one can see geese roaming in open meadows, apparently leading a much happier life than the caged American chicken or cows that are destined for slaughter. Yet, in their great wisdom, American lawmakers were persuaded by animal lovers to ban the goose pate from France. What hypocrisy! Where is the common sense? When we don't find it necessary to ban human foods containing excessive salt that has killed 850,000 Americans since 9/11, we find it necessary to ban force-fed goose liver? In the warped common sense of American lawmakers, the practice of force-feeding geese trumps the lives of 850,000 human Americans. Go figure. We need more laws, to lock up lawmakers that limit our freedom. Of course, these lawmakers see a personal common sense in it all; in the re-election they'd be practically guaranteed the votes of special activist groups who otherwise would publicly derail re-election by labeling them animal abusers.

Bottom line is, we need to accept an "imperfect" world as created by God. We realize that many laws have good intentions behind them but the aggregate of all these well-intentioned laws pursues a utopia of a perfect world that doesn't and will never exist. The only hope we have is that we learn to live with the world we have, and that America returns to a world of common sense.

CHAPTER 30

▼

A FLAWED JURY SYSTEM

One of the original Amendments to the Constitution, #VI, ratified in 1791, states that

> "... the accused shall enjoy the right to a speedy and public trial, by an impartial jury of the State and district wherein the crimes shall have been committed;"

Amendment #VII states:

> "In suits of common law ... the right of trial by jury shall be preserved ..."

Apparently our founders distrusted judges to decide on guilt, and believed that juries would be capable of assessing true guilt or innocence better than a judge could. In their days, the legal system of the United States was rather unsophisticated. Psychology was not even a serious field of study until 1879 when in Germany Wilhelm Wundt began the first laboratory dedicated to psychological research. Since our founders wrote the Constitution, the sophistication of all professional players in a court case dramatically changed.... except the ones the Founders counted on the most to render an unbiased verdict, the jury. They are still as unsophisticated as the first juries were in the late 18th Century, no match for today's sophistication in court.

How could the founders have envisioned the effects of modern psychology, especial behavioral psychology, and the deluge of laws and detailed complexities?

Reading up on the days of our founders, we can easily understand our founder's decicion to trust the ability of a jury of any 12 men. But in today's world? Would you hire any 12 men off the street to decide on ever more complex business decisions that would determine your financial future? Would you think that 12 men picked off the street could be capable to decide on one's life or wealth in today's complex society? Never!

In the age of our Founders law schools didn't exist. Few colleges offered legal classes. Those interested in becoming a lawyer usually became an apprentice in a law office. (Source: Albert James Harno in <u>Legal Education in the United States</u>)

Today, many of our plaintiff trial lawyers and defense lawyers are trained to outsmart juries. This doesn't mean that all jury cases result in a travesty of justice. Even if trial by jury were a total crapshoot, then the large numbers would still suggest that 50% of the cases would result in a correct verdict and the other 50% in a wrong verdict. Justice shouldn't be about a crapshoot. Justice should be more important than the desire of maintaining the current system of a jury system.

Juries are expected to perform well in simple cases. But in complex cases, a jury's decision is likely more a 50/50 game. Examples are plentiful. The criminal trial against O.J. Simpson in the murder case of his estranged wife, Nicole, was resolved in acquittal. Was the O.J. Simpson jury competent? Did all twelve have full intent to find justice or did drama, psychology or race play a role to obscure justice? In our long history of justice with juries, many cases were recorded in which juries were suspected of letting white defendants off the hook too easily. Similarly, many white juries found black defendants guilty with scant evidence.

Emotions of a jury could trump justice. We can't blame the lawyers. Perhaps not all would allow injustice to trump, but in the end lawyers do represent the interest of the client, and that may not necessarily be compatible with justice. Power, money and fame are also strong motivators for lawyers to win irrespective of justice. If this were a wrong statement, you would see the brightest and best of our trial lawyers taking more cases out of compassion, cases that cry for justice without money and fame to be gained.

Our infatuation with the jury system is amazing. In polls the American people seem to love the jury system. In theory, the jury system makes us part of the judicial process, the only time we can participate in governing. It is a romantic feeling that we, the People, are asked to serve justice. In a Harris poll taken in 2004, as reported by the American Bar Association, 75% of those polled rejected the notion that jury duty is a burden to be avoided. Americans strongly believe that jury service is important, while 58% said that jury duty is a privilege.

The infatuation of America with the jury system seems odd. In my business experience for over thirty years, all Americans that were served for duty tried to get out of it and those with the most talent to serve always got out of it. The most talented working professionals are too busy to serve on a jury. Often the joke goes that those serving in a jury were too dumb to get out of it. Obviously, this is unfair to many patriotic jurors who truly feel that it is a duty and privilege to serve. But those patriotic jurors do not make the whole jury, nor are they competent enough to be un-swayed by the savvy players in court. And if there are a few competent members on the jury, they are likely outnumbered.

In an earlier poll the American Bar Association commissioned a study to seek the public's opinion about the jury system. Some 80 percent of the American citizens surveyed agreed or strongly agreed with the statement that the United States justice system is the best in the world. And the root of that perception is the jury system. Seventy-eight percent of the survey respondents believed the jury system to be the fairest way to determine guilt or innocence, and more than two-thirds replied that the jury was the most important component of our justice system.

Why did 80% of the American people agree that the American jury system is the best there is? Didn't these 80% of American citizens watch the O.J. Simpson trial? Where were they during Michael Jackson's trial? Were they on vacation during the Robert Blake trial for the murder of his wife Bakley? Where were they when a jury awarded Kathleen Robertson of Austin, Texas $780,000 because she broke her ankle when she tripped over her own toddler who ran amuck in a furniture store? Or the jury who awarded $74,000 to Carl Truman of Los Angeles, when a neighbor ran over his hand as he was trying to steal the neighbor's hubcaps? Or Terrence Dickson of Bristol, Pa who got awarded a half million dollars when after he robbed a house, he couldn't get out and had to spend seven days eating only dog food as the family was on vacation? How could 78% believe that trial by jury is the best in the world to determine justice? Juries today cannot be on the same page intellectually as trial lawyers whereas in the days of our founders, they were. All a juror can trust today is emotions along with a simple legal common sense; these are no matches for sophisticated trial lawyers along with the reams of paper documents that prosecutors and defense lawyers have prepared.

> What is a jury? A Jury is *a group of persons sworn to give a true answer to the question put before it in a court of law, that is, "is the defendant guilty or not?" or "is a party at fault or not?"*

The issue here is if a jury today is capable of giving a true answer? Most ignore that question and give juries their full support. Observed H.Thomas Wells, Jr: This straightforward definition fails to give sufficient credit to the American system of trial by jury. The jury trial—both civil and criminal—is the heart and soul of the American judicial system; it is also the heart and soul of the Section of Litigation. While the Section embraces all types of dispute resolution—from mediation and other forms of alternative dispute resolution to administrative hearings to non-jury trials—trials by jury remain, as one of our Task Forces indicates, "The Lawyer's Art."

Jury trials, and juries themselves, have hardly been stagnant over time. Historically, the jury has evolved from a group of citizens specifically selected from the community because they were already knowledgeable about the facts and circumstances of the dispute at hand, to "twelve total virgins of fact." (Source: Lawrence M. Friedman, "Some Notes on the Civil Jury in Historical Perspective.")

The law presumes that a jury will decide rationally; it should resolve each disputed issue on the basis of a fair and reasonable assessment of the evidence and a fair and reasonable application of relevant rules. We conclude that due process precludes trial by jury when a jury is unable to perform this task with a reasonable understanding of the evidence and the legal rules. (Source: *Japanese Electronic Products Antitrust Litigation.*)

Understandably, most defense and plaintiff lawyers alike favor a trial by jury because in their minds the odds of winning increase (they assume they can beat the opposition). Especially the rich and famous that can afford the best defense lawyers favor trial by jury. But in class action suits, corporations have little chance of a fair defense in a jury trial because lawyers are devilishly good in playing to the jury the stigma of the ugly corporation against the little man that lost his savings. Someone has to compensate the little man and who else is better suited to do so than the deep pockets?

My over-the-counter medicine says: packing not suitable for households with minor kids. Why is this printed? Does anyone read it? No, but lawyers got juries to agree that the failure of disclosing this nonsense caused a child's injury. Why is there a sign at McDonalds that the coffee can be hot and thus cause injury unless you are careful? Isn't coffee supposed to be hot? Yes, but lawyers extracted $2.6 Million awarded to Stella Liebeck because she spilled hot McDonald coffee on her crotch. Why did a Los Angeles jury award Richard Boeken a $3 billion (yes, billion) punitive award in addition to $5.5 million in compensatory damages against a tobacco company? Boeken, a lifelong smoker with lung cancer, claimed in his lawsuit that he was the victim of a tobacco industry campaign that portrayed smoking as "cool" but concealed its dangers. Didn't the text on the package clearly say smoking is dangerous to your health? Yes, but personal responsibility doesn't count much when juries take up the case. Many of these awards were later reduced on appeal but it proves the point that the jury was not competent in arriving at a just award.

Rudolph, the "Christian" killer who targeted abortion clinics (as well as at the Atlanta Olympics) pleaded guilty in a moment of honesty. He did so even though he knew that he might have been acquitted in a jury trial thanks to anti-abortion jurors who would consider the bombing of abortion clinics morally justified. This was corroborated in a book co-authored by Emily Lyons, one of his victims at the clinic he bombed in Alabama: Federal prosecutors staged four mock trials but Rudolph was acquitted in three of them because jurors felt that victims got what they deserved. In 2005, Michael Jackson got acquitted of child molestation. It baffled not only the prosecution who thought to have an iron clad case but also most legal experts. Jurors seem to have been swayed by star power. O.J. Simpson was acquitted because "if it doesn't fit you must acquit" as the late Johnny Cochran spoke over the gloves that shrunk after being wet. The world thought that the evidence presented was overwhelming, as did the jury in a tort case that set a large wrongful death award against OJ Simpson. Robert Blake's (Beretta) acquittal was called miraculous by many legal observers. But is it miraculous? Not when we realize that juries are per definition incompetent in complex trials.

In 2005, Richard Scrushy, the founder and former CEO of HealthSouth Corp., was found not guilty on all charges in the $2.7 billion accounting fraud at the hospital chain. Yet all five former CFOs pleaded guilty, testifying that Scrushy led a scheme to inflate earnings by $2.7 billion. "I'm surprised," said Stanley Twardy, a former U.S. Attorney for Connecticut who is now in private practice at Day, Berry & Howard. "This is probably the first time that the defense of 'I didn't know' denials has worked for a former chairman or CEO." A corporate law specialist, Soderquist, who had followed Scrushy's trial, was stunned at the verdict. "There was a mass of evidence against him. I certainly expected the jury to convict. If you look at the evidence and the firepower that the government lined up for this case, the outcome is astounding." Soderquist noted that the defense appeared to appeal throughout the trial to the sympathies of the jury, composed of seven blacks and five whites. Soderquist said Scrushy, a white businessman, has "a very high reputation in the African-American community" as he took on a more visible role [as a minister] at black churches in the months after his indictment.…

Merck pulled the drug Vioxx from the market because there were more heart attacks among the users than those who used similar drugs. In August 2005, a Texas jury awarded $253 Million to a dead man's wife. In October 2005, a jury in New Jersey found that the drug maker properly warned users about the increased possibility of heart attacks. The Texas jury saw the law in the same case different than the New Jersey jury; one of them had to be wrong. But even in the case of guilt as the Texas jury saw it, did the widow deserve $253 Million?

As retired CEO, I have had much exposure to contract and securities laws. Yet, in the case of Merck with expert (paid) witnesses and the technicalities and drama of the courtroom, I couldn't possibly be qualified to make a guilty or not-guilty judgment. The sophistication of lawyers to master the technicalities of the law and to manipulate jurors could lead jurors easily off the track in the search for justice.

The current jury system is prone to errors, and while it is a wonderful idea, the pursuit for true justice should trump a flawed concept.

The ABA and law firms have submitted ideas to improve the juror system that might help a little bit but certainly would not solve the problem. For example they proposed: "Experiments with pre-instructing juries on the law likely to be applicable to the particular case they are about to hear and giving jurors written charges in plain English rather than legalese work to make the jury experience more understandable. And jurors themselves would be allowed to become active participants in court in taking notes and submitting questions to witnesses." This is certainly an improvement but do they really think that some pre-instructions in law will make the average juror competent in law? Don't they know that successful trial lawyers are the smartest people around who studied law at Harvard, Yale or Stanford for at least four full years and then shadowed the pros for a decade or so? Likewise, the proposal allowing jurors to be more active is a good one but does nothing to increase competence. It is time to stop the charade of zigzagging around incompetent juries. Juries must become made up of professional jurors.

According to the Sixth and Seventh Amendment to the Constitution the right of trial by jury shall be preserved. These Amendments do not specify that this jury must consist of peers, incompetent or competent people. The Constitution does require that in criminal prosecutions the accused shall have the assistance of counsel but nowhere does it say that they have to be graduates in law from universities and passed the bar. In other words, the founders never expected the sophistication by which lawyers today have mastered complex laws and mastered the psychology to manipulate jurors. It is not that long ago that we required attorneys to pass the state bar. Why not go one step further and require jurors to pass a bar too? A special jury bar! Within the words as framed by the Constitution, we could maintain the right to a jury but of a jury of much more competent jurors, especially in the field of court psychology. We could create a new profession of ABA Jurors with a minimum of a Bachelors Degree majoring in "Law of Jurors". A Juror would then become a professional occupation. They apply for cases or could be called based on an on-line availability calendar and would be hired by the state while adequately compensated from the savings of eliminating jury enrollment and waste of productivity in the process of jury selection and actual trial. Further, the time of a court case should be significantly curtailed when trial lawyers discover that theatrics won't sway jurors and that it is best to cut to the chase. Above all, justice would prevail.

Changing the jury system to obtain more than a crapshoot in jury trials is vital for our country. You the voter are instrumental in making it happen.

CHAPTER 31

▼

THE CONSTITUTION

The media attacked the Bush Administration for curbing our rights that were supposed to be guaranteed by the Constitution. The President says that the Constitution requires him to keep America safe. Both sides of the political spectrum have used the Constitution to attack the other side. Conservatives believe that progressive judges misused the Constitution to advance liberal ideas. The Christian Right believes that the Supreme Courts' interpretations undermined the morals of our society. Liberals accuse conservative judges of turning the clock back on our rights under the banner of national security.

Most Americans would agree that our Constitution, along with the Declaration of Independence, is the most important document of this republic. Not surprising then, the interpretations of the Constitution have caused heated arguments. Liberals gripe that the cards are now stacked up against them because most judges on the federal bench and particularly on the Supreme Court are Republican appointees, the logical outcome of five Republican Presidents and only two Democrats since the nineteen seventies. Yet, despite liberal gripes, not all these conservative judges were from the extreme ideological conservative wing. The reason is that Republican Presidents sought a political balance of conservative ideology on the federal judicial bench. Likewise, the Democratic Carter and Clinton Administrations honored this practice by avoiding that flaming liberals would sit on the federal bench.

However, in the last seven years, the George W. Bush Administration ignored the practice of his predecessors. Mr. Bush appointed only very conservative judges thus distorting the ideological balance sought by his predecessors. His appointees will have a profound ideological conservative influence on legal interpretations for generations to come. Popularly, Mr. Bush used the term strict-constructionists for his appointees. That term is naïvely misleading or more appropriately, insulting for any judge, because it implies that judges should use all legal texts as written, without drawing any inference. Well, if the legal texts were that simple, why would we need judges in the first place? Why did the Founders even find it necessary to include Article III of the Constitution that established the judiciary branch? Obviously, strict-constructionism is nonsensical. One of our ideologically most conservative Supreme Court Justices, Antonio Scalia, would not call himself a constructionist.

Article III of the United States Constitution established the judicial as one of three separate branches of our federal government. The federal courts are the guardians of our Constitution. Their rulings should protect the rights and liberties as guaranteed by our Constitution. But judges have struggled how to interpret the Constitution. There are two diverse opinions. One is to interpret the Constitution in any legal case brought before the court as the Founders would have interpreted it based on what is known from them such as in the Federalist papers; this interpretation says that the Constitution is 'dead'. The other view is to interpret court cases based on the Constitution as what the Founders would have interpreted it, had they lived in today's culture and complex society. This requires an understanding of the motives or intentions of the Founders decisions based on the culture of their days and how that likely would have influenced them based on the culture of today; this interpretation says that the Constitution "lives".

It is not hard to imagine that the culture in the 1700s was vastly different from today. Today we talk about a vast difference in culture compared to just thirty years ago, let alone 230 years ago. It is hard to imagine how different the situation was back then. It could take weeks or months to travel from one state to another. Slavery was acceptable to our founders. Most of our founders had slaves. Women were second-class citizens without voting rights. But as the American culture changed, our forefathers, those who came after our founders, had the vision to amend the Constitution with new rights that had not been acceptable among earlier mainstream Americans in the culture of their time. Were they wrong to alter the thoughts of our founders that women should not vote and that there was no need to give black slaves the rights of free men? In today's society could we accept such situations?

The fact that Amendments were made proved that changes in culture over time required a new interpretation. Some of those changes necessitated amendments to the Constitution. Had the founders lived in the culture that existed in the early 20th Century, would they have approved of the landmark XIXth Amendment that was ratified in 1920, allowing women to vote? The biographies of our most influential founders indicate a spirit of compromise, a great common sense driven by their overriding desire to give power to the people. They were not overpowered by conservative or liberal ideology, and based on their biographies, it seems only common sense that our founders would have voted for women voting rights in the 20th Century, and would have abandoned ethnical bias had they lived in today's culture and complex society.

A most interesting observation is that the Amendments never took away rights; it always added rights (except in one case, the Prohibition which was later repealed). This is quite telling that the motivation for amendments was the expansion of rights. The American people didn't approve the Constitution to be used by certain interest groups to limit the freedom of others. It is not that certain interest groups didn't try. Jerome Agel in <u>Words that Make America Great</u> described that over time Congress proposed over 10,000 Constitutional amendments. But only 27 were adopted, known as the 27 Amendments to our Constitution since its ratification in 1788. In this light, it is inconceivable that any proposed amendment to limit the rights of certain people should or would become ratified. Opponents of abortion, or gay marriage, are swayed by promises of Constitutional Amendments by eager politicians to get their votes, but in light of the past, their chances for these Amendments that limit rights are next to zero.

Let's examine a few famous legal cases that demonstrate that significant changes in our culture had a profound effect on the interpretations of our Constitution.

Lawrence Friedman in his fascinating book <u>American Law in the 20th Century</u>, described the famous Lochner vs New York case in 1905. New York State had passed a law, regulating bakeries by setting certain conditions for employees such as; no employee could work more than sixty hours a week in the inferno of bakery heat and flour dust. It also included sanitary conditions: requiring a toilet (hmmm); and no dogs were allowed in the bakery although cats were OK to catch mice. Well, the owner of a bakery, Mr. Lochner, sued all the way to the Supreme Court. The Court ruled that the New York law was unconstitutional. The law, the Court said, interfered with the freedom and rights of bosses and workers to enter (or shall we say coerce) into any agreements of labor they chose. The judges said that this right was protected by the 14th Amendment of the Constitution, which said that no state should deprive its people of life, liberty or property without due process of law.

Thus, just one hundred years ago based on the culture of the United States, the court used the 14th Amendment rights to defend the position that workers were not protected by the law, they should be glad to have a job, inferno and rats included.

In another case Congress passed a law in 1916 trying to get children under 16 to limit their work in mines or factories to no more than eight hours per day. Imagine that today, children working "only" eight hours a day, seven days a week! The federal law's only muscle was to forbid interstate commerce of goods that were produced by children under 16. The Supreme Court struck that law down in 1918 saying that Congress went too far; if Congress could forbid this interstate commerce it could restrict anything and that would destroy the state's authority over local matters.

Children had no rights and apparently the culture back then was that Congress shouldn't bother with children's rights and that the mines were a good place for kids to work. Would there be any judge on the Supreme Court today agreeing with the interpretations of Supreme Court Justices back in 1905 or 1916? Of course not! Yet, a hundred years ago people didn't seem to think that the Supreme Court was out of line.

Women couldn't vote until the XIXth Amendment, a groundbreaking change. Thomas Jefferson spoke of equal rights for all men. All men? No, in Jefferson's days that word meant exclusively "white men". In 1920 the word 'men' came to include women. Yet, how equal were women after 1920? It took more than fifty years to attain true equality. In the case of rape, women would not normally report them. If they did, justice was rarely achieved. In a 1960 study, Harry Kalven and Hans Zeisel found that juries didn't take rape seriously. Unless the rape was very violent, the woman had no chance in court. Juries believed that women asked for it. For example a short skirt could legitimately set off a man's impulse to commit rape. Hmmm, isn't this what we see today in Pakistan and in African Islamic countries? Perhaps Muslims are only fifty years or so behind us in social, cultural evolution! With a dead Constitution, America today could have been similar to Islamic countries that treat women as second-rate citizens and that subordinate infidels.

The founders that drafted the original ten rights (in the Bill of Rights) had no intention to apply them to the states, just to the federal government. However, the XIVth Amendment, ratified on July 9, 1868, guaranteed that no state could deprive any person of life, liberty or property without due process. In effect, it extended the Vth Amendment to all the states. The other original nine rights were still applicable to the federal government only. Beginning in a 1961 case, however, the Warren Supreme Court began to re-interpret the Constitution (Earl Warren was appointed by President Eisenhower in 1953 as Chief Justice.) The Fourteenth Amendment hadn't changed, yet miraculously most of the other nine original Bill of Rights began to apply to every state. Therefore, only since the Warren Court are states prohibited from limiting our right to free speech, free press etcetera.

Today every income earner is used to paying income taxes either via payroll withholding taxes or by filing tax returns. Few realize that it wasn't until 1913 that Congress enacted the first income tax law. In prior attempts, the federal courts declared income taxes unconstitutional. It required a Constitutional Amendment (in 1913) to overcome the Court's rulings. Did you know that the top marginal rate was 6% and that only 2% of the population needed to file tax returns? What good old days! Except that these low rates of the early 20th Century couldn't have paid for the early 21st Century commonly accepted government needs from a huge national defense to infrastructure (roads, bridges, airports) and safety of clean water, safe food and drugs, etcetera.

The founders never conceived of the idea of an income tax nor could they anticipate the enormous growth of government that would require a large source of income. It may be abolished some day, but the point here again is that cultural changes necessitated a change in interpretation of the Constitution.

After the last Constitutional Amendment was ratified in 1971, the Constitution hasn't changed. But interpretations and reinterpretations of the Constitution continue to change the laws of the land. Does this prove that the Constitution is alive? Yet, the word alive is dangerous because it could open the gate too far for farfetched ideas of which our founders would not have approved. How would we know? Only a panel of scholars of history with moderate political views from both right and left ideologies should judge what our founders would have approved in today's culture. It is hoped that our Appellate Courts and the Supreme Court would contain not only brilliant legal scholars but also scholars of history that represent both sides of the spectrum of ideologies in moderate terms. For that reason, we decry the current President's departure from his predecessors to assure a political balance on the federal judicial bench.

Supreme Court Judges Scalia and Thomas, and likely Alito and Roberts, called themselves proudly "originalists" based on "textualism". David Savage, a

Times Staff Writer, wrote on 9/15/05 that their approach is to be faithful to the Constitution as it was written in 1787 along with its Amendments. Textualism holds that the words of the Constitution mean only what the framers understood by them, and is strictly based on the literal words and its original history; the Constitution should not have evolved over time. However, by accepting the 27 Amendments, didn't Scalia c.s. implicitly admit that the Constitution is alive? After all, the amendments were the result of accepted changes in culture. Even Scalia would like women to vote or wouldn't condone slavery or an occasional rape to go with it or have eight year old kids working in the mines, would he? Logically, this seems to say that the Constitution is not dead, yet Scalia indicated it is. Supreme Court Justice Breyers argued in <u>Active Liberty</u> that the framers never meant that in centuries ahead justices should guess on contemporary issues as to how the framers would have resolved them based on the culture of the 1700s. Many of our rights we take for granted today weren't considered rights under state laws before the Warren Supreme Court. Yet, let's not get too comfortable because the "originalists" view is that right to privacy for American citizens was not implicit in the Constitution. In other words, in this day and age, we may have a new Supreme Court majority of originalists that could turn the clock back on the right to privacy in our own home.

Without the Amendments made much later, and the re-interpretations of the Courts, the original Constitution wasn't all that good to many American people. The founders allowed slavery and did not consider voting rights for women or even to blacks that were free. While Lincoln abolished slavery, in the South the continued inhumane treatment of blacks, for example lynching, was not uncommon. Even less than fifty years ago blacks weren't allowed to be in white schools, buses, public parks, shops, hotels, etcetera.

Our culture changed, some for the better, some for the worse. A fact is that over time we change the way we see the Constitution.

CHAPTER 32

▼

HEALTH CARE

The Health Care industry is big business. According to the National Coalition on Healthcare it was worth about Two Trillion Dollars in 2005, or 16% of our Gross Domestic product (GDP). This makes it the largest industry in the U.S. It is also one of the fastest growing ones. This enormous amount of two trillion dollars in the U.S. comes down to about $6,700 annually per every American (whether insured or not).

A Gallup Poll found that half of our population is worried to very-worried about paying medical costs that would occur if they become seriously ill or have an accident. [Gallup Poll of 10,078 adults, April 2 5, 2007 as reported by AARP July-August 2007, page 31]. This is huge! Considering that usually the healthy, younger workers aren't very concerned about healthcare, that's almost suggesting that all middle aged and older people are worried. That's putting a lot of stress on Americans. And too much stress can kill you.

Democrats pushed health care to one of the top issues in the 2008 presidential campaigns. Some Democrats believe that all citizens should take out healthcare insurance, and that an existing insurance may not be canceled. The policy of Republicans is more captured by the statement that healthcare is a service that should be provided only to those who can afford it.

Is healthcare like an automobile industry? You get the car with liability insurance that fits your wallet. The more money you can pay, the more car you can get? And if your wallet is empty, you walk, or in the same analogy in healthcare, you die. Others see healthcare as an unalienable right of all Americans. They could derive this from the Constitution, which begins as follows:

We the People of the United States, in Order to form a more perfect Union, establish Justice, insure domestic Tranquility, promote for the common defense, promote the general Welfare, and secure the Blessings of Liberty to ourselves and our Posterity, do ordain and establish this Constitution for the United Sates of America.

Thus welfare is one reason the Constitution was established. Welfare includes health, according to the Webster's Unabridged Dictionary. Further, according to Webster, in welfare states, the government takes care of the welfare of people such as matters of social security, health, education, and working conditions.

Even though for conservative Americans the words "welfare state" are a red flag, our founders expected government to promote welfare. Just as welfare states do, our government today already provides social security, public education, and partial health through Medicare. That would pretty much label us as a welfare state, no matter how awful that may sound to some. Conservative pundits like to label national healthcare as "socialized" healthcare because that sounds even worse to the American ear. Funny that they label anything government they don't like 'socialized'. But we could call all government's work socialized. We could call the government's work on roads and bridges and airports as socialized infrastructure. Or the Homeland Security, we should call socialized security. The foreign diplomatic corps we should call socialized ambassadors, and the IRS is socialized tax-collection. How about the military? Socialized defense and the judicial system, socialized justice. See how socialized isn't necessarily bad! America deserves a more serious debate.

Given that all middle aged and older Americans are worried sick about getting the healthcare when needed, the Republican policy (that healthcare is a service that should be provided only to those who can afford it) is at odds with what most American want. Given that the younger Americans who don't care yet about healthcare will become middle aged some day, it follows that justice is not served until all Americans, or at least those who want to be insured, must be assured of healthcare when they need it. How should this be accomplished?

Private healthcare believes it is best equipped to provide Americans with the healthcare they need. Yet, we have read too many scary reports about dropped insurance policies when the insured needed healthcare the most. Perhaps it is time to review the advantages and disadvantages of healthcare insurance by the private industry or by the government.

We should consider five criteria of healthcare:

1. Cost

2. Quality of health-care

3. Providing health-care when needed

4. Stress on the American people

5. Competitiveness of American business.

Cost.

The two trillion dollar cost of U.S. healthcare in 2005 amounts to about $6,700 annually per every American (whether insured or not). If this seems ridiculously high, it is. This becomes evident when we compare national healthcare systems of civilized Western countries. The Common Wealth Fund compared the cost per capita of six major countries including the United States, 2003 data (rounded up).

- Australia spends a little less than $3,000 per person

- Canada spends a little over $3,000 per person

- Germany spends a little over $3,000 per person

- Britain is at only $2,600 per person

- New Zealand spends just a little over $2,000.

The private industry works best when there is sufficient competition in the market place. In healthcare insurance there is little to no competition. Unless an insured is young or has no medical history, an insured isn't able to leave his insurance. When you need a treatment, you have no choice but to deal with your insurer. If you need open-heart surgery and it is denied by your insurer, you can't call another insurance company the next day; it would be laughable to assume that competition exists. Without competition, we know that business is less efficient than government. National health care will remove enormous costs from the system such as the profits, the marketing, the lobbying, cost of negotiations, administrative paperwork etcetera.

The United States spends at least twice as much per person in health care than the other well-developed countries surveyed while it doesn't even insure 45 million or 15% of all Americans. Now, if our care would be at least twice as good as in those countries surveyed, perhaps the cost would be justified. But, sorry … that isn't so either. Would nationalizing American healthcare insurance result in reducing the nation's cost without sacrifice of quality of service? If other countries can do it why couldn't we? But how good is their quality of healthcare?

Quality of Care:

According to the Common Wealth Fund, among the six countries surveyed, the United States ranked #6, or the worst, in providing overall healthcare. In the five sub-categories, the United States was ranked:

Quality of care:	#5
Access:	#6
Efficiency:	#6
Equity:	#6
Healthy Lives:	#6

Wow, this came as a big shock. Could that be the answer to the question as to why Americans don't live as long as people in other developed countries? According to the Organization for Economic Cooperation and Development, people can expect to live an average of 80.3 years in France, 79.9 years in Canada, and 78.5 years in England. The comparable number for the United States is 77.5 years. Based on statistics provided by the Census Bureau and the National Center for Health Statistics, the U.S. ranks 42nd in average years we live. Thus 41 countries are ahead of us despite the fact that people in those countries smoke much more than we do. Said Christopher Murray, head of the Institute for Health Metrics and Evaluation at the University of Washington: Something is wrong here when one of the richest countries in the world, the one that spends most on health care, is not able to keep up with other countries.

So far, we concluded that America's private healthcare industry spends twice as much as other civilized countries but ranks last in providing care, and they live the shortest lives. What's wrong with that picture? It sounds embarrassing. These statistics kill the myth spread by conservatives that the private sector is always more efficient than the government, or by the healthcare industry that nationalized insurance would be inferior. Statistics don't lie. Collaborating these findings, in the Journal of the American Medical Association, a spokesman of the National Institute of Health wrote that the U.S. Healthcare system is a dysfunctional mess. The conclusion that the American quality of service is at the bottom is counter intuitive. Perhaps the growing indifference in our nation did not leave the medical profession unaffected. While we may have the best tools, indifference in the health profession may have tipped the comparable scale from care for patients to care for personal well-being.

Of course, not every service in the U.S. provides sub-par healthcare. As a matter of fact, there are pockets of excellence in the U.S., better than anywhere in the world. For example, the Mayo Clinic is considered one of the world's best hospitals. So is Johns Hopkins Hospital and a few other well-known hospitals of excellence. The rich and famous come from all over the world to the U.S. for the best treatment, but they go to these pockets of excellence. In addition some of the best prescription drugs come from the U.S.

The average Martha and Joe don't get into John Hopkins or the Mayo Clinic because their insurance wouldn't pay for it. They must do with, on average, sub-par healthcare service, the worst healthcare service among the six countries surveyed.

Private sector advocates have spread myths about terrible service in national healthcare in Canada, England and other European countries. They speak with contempt about patients in Canada waiting for three-month for an MRI. It appears that these stories are pulled out of context to scare Americans of approving a radical improvement in our healthcare system. The healthcare industry, their investors, politicians who derive huge amounts of lobbying money from the healthcare industry will do everything to save their industry. We should not expect much patriotism, compassion, or straight talk from them when money is involved.

Recently I experienced healthcare services in both America and Europe. While individual experiences do not tell much about a system overall, my experiences collaborate the results of the Common Wealth Fund and other organizations.

On a recent trip to Europe, I developed a terrible and painful bladder infection. Unfortunately, it was on a Saturday! As in the U.S., doctors in Europe don't have scheduled hours on weekends. Based on U.S. experience, I expected hours and hours of waiting time in a dispassionate emergency room among many sick people, and finally an overworked doctor or intern may help you. At 9:45 a.m. I called an emergency center in this nationalized healthcare country of Holland. They made an appointment for 10:45 a.m. at a special office, within a mile with a medical doctor on-call. Apparently, doctors are required to rotate on weekends for emergencies. At 10:55 am, ten minutes, no kidding, a man in a white coat called me. It was the doctor himself. He shook hands, brought me into his office, put my personal information in a computer while listening patiently. He asked relevant questions about my past, and examined me. 30 minutes later I was back at the reception desk where the bill was waiting for me as uninsured: 56 euros (about $75), along with a prescription drug for anti-biotic. I was dumbfounded because I had not experienced this kind of excellent service in the U.S. In California earlier that year, I had an emergency during a weekday. When I called my own internist he was too busy. I had to wait hours for someone else.

During the same European trip, this time in Germany, I ran out of one of my prescription medicines. I assumed that I needed to see a doctor to get a prescription but being on the road I didn't know how to find one. In the first town we saw we walked into a pharmacy. I explained my problem, showed my empty carton. In ten minutes I was out the door with a new package of the same prescription medicine for fifteen Euros (that was about one third of what I would have paid in the U.S. net after insurance payment). A year before, while traveling through Spain, I had lost a medicine prescribed by one of my doctors in California. I walked into a pharmacy in Barcelona, explained my problem to the pharmacist; he asked me a few questions. In fifteen minutes I got an equivalent prescription for ten Euros.

With these pleasant experiences we wanted to know more and asked Europeans how they rated their healthcare system. Surprising, there were no complaints. The answers ranged from 'satisfied to great' depending on who we asked. With serious heart problems, my brother in Holland had several invasive treatments; he was pleased with the care and the results.

Months later in California, recurrences of a bladder infection made my doctor schedule a bladder cystocopy. The earliest date I could get in? Six weeks out! After this cystocopy, my doctor recommended a surgical procedure. This was scheduled at the earliest possible date. Seven weeks out! Delays are everywhere.

Healthcare when needed.

Can private health insurance be relied upon to provide services when needed?

The nation's healthcare business is a for-profit business. It deals with two distinct different parts of healthcare. Both parts are combined in the single insurance premium it collects. The first part is for reimbursement of regular healthcare services such as office visits, prescription drugs, and outpatient surgeries. The second part is quite different, more akin to catastrophes in earthquake, flood or fire insurance. In the healthcare business, catastrophes occur when serious health-conditions require major treatments or expensive surgeries such as cancer treatment, heart transplant or kidney dialysis. The healthcare insurance business has done a good job in reimbursing the first part of the insurance for regular healthcare service, which in terms of volume far exceeds the volume of catastrophic cases; their record of prompt pay out looks good. However, the jury is out on the catastrophic part. The insurance company stands to make the most profit if it were able to finagle on expensive catastrophic service, just when as patient you need it the most. It would be even more profitable if the company could find a way to cancel the policy when catastrophe strikes. The same principle holds true in case of other catastrophes such as earthquake or flood, and indeed, many victims who thought they had flood insurance, found that the flood that hit them wasn't covered. Yet, in pure catastrophe business, it is much harder to deny insurance when the nation's visibility on catastrophes is higher than it is with individual patients. How big is that problem with the private healthcare business?

Lisa Girion, staff-writer LA Times, reported that the Los Angeles City Attorney filed a lawsuit in February 2008 against one of California's largest insurers, Health Net Inc, for selling individual policies with the promise of medical coverage while engaging in a secret and illegal scheme to drop patients if they needed expensive treatment. Girion also reported that Health Net paid employees bonuses based in part on canceling policies of people who have submitted substantial health claims. Girion further reported that another company, BC Life & Health, was accused by the Department of Health in California for mishandling half of the cases the Department reviewed.

Would a mandate that policies cannot be canceled work satisfactorily for the private health care sector? Is there a precedent to provide service? In the telephone industry there is a federal mandate that all citizens, no matter where they live, have access to affordable telephone service so that every citizen can make emergency calls from their home. The telephone companies were required to install central offices and bring phone lines to every house in the nation even outside urban areas, yet to provide services at affordable cost. Obviously, it was not very lucrative for phone companies to bring central offices and phone lines to remote rural areas where just a few customers shared the high expense of central office and extensive delivery systems but they had to. Could these phone companies have finagled on mandated services? No, because the cost of providing telephone services was essentially all up-front, in the installation. It was easily verifiable that the service was provided in remote areas. Once the telephone lines were installed, it was only in the interest of the phone company to provide service when needed.

If it was made mandatory for the healthcare insurance industry to provide adequate and timely services, could that be guaranteed just as the telephone companies did? It couldn't be guaranteed. Unlike in the telephone industry where the bulk of cost was upfront and easily verifiable, the cost in the healthcare business is not up front; it is unforeseen that at some time in the future a serious illness may strike an individual. Nothing would be verifiable. Every illness could be unique and subject to interpretation offering plenty of room to maneuver for an unscrupulous insurer. The healthcare treatment that would be approved could be quite disappointing to the patient. Any service finagled upon or delayed by the healthcare industry would increase profits while critical to the patient's health. Even a patient with the most expensive coverage would still not be assured that health care would be available when expected. In business, there is little consideration for honor and compassion. Business is about making more money every quarter. Shareholders expect it. Wall Street expects it. Nationalized healthcare insurance would have no such motive to delay or finagle.

Stress

What's coming back in the polls is that people are worried sick about getting healthcare when they need it the most. They are worried that they might be kicked out of insurance or that treatments might exceed the maximum dollar amount that insurance companies will pay over a lifetime or that they can't afford the steep rising premiums with age (especially over 50). Excessive co-payments or the cost of non-preferred providers that may significantly exceed the insurer's maximum treatment payments is a huge concern. Their worries are legitimate. What about those with a medical history? The for-profit healthcare industry refuses to accept them or if they do it's at very high premiums. Or they might get canceled, for example, say five years before you took out a new policy you went to a doctor because of chest pain but the doctor dismissed it when the pain went away. You didn't even think about the incident when you applied for a new policy. Later, boom, a heart attack, but the insurance company refuses to pay, canceling your policy because you concealed prior history. The stress of Americans caught in the private healthcare industry is justified!

An enormous stress would be lifted on half of the population if they knew that healthcare would be available and affordable when needed the most. National healthcare will reduce stress.

The case for keeping healthcare limited to those who can afford it was put well by Dr. Prem Reddy from California who controls a number of hospitals in the state. In an interview with the LA Times (July 8, 2007), he wonders why people expect to get the same healthcare service as everybody else. It is an entitlement mentality, he says. Why aren't the same people asking why everybody shouldn't be eating the same foods, or have the same clothes or the same homes? In the interview with Dr. Reddy, it was also revealed that his hospitals had suspended services such as chemotherapy, mental healthcare and birthing centers-because they aren't lucrative. And as any business would do, it has cut out non-lucrative cost centers that otherwise would have provided critical health services. Added Dr. Reddy: Patients may simply deserve only the amount of care that they can afford. Dr. Reddy, like many successful, rich businessmen, has donated millions of dollars to charities.

He is a typical businessman, doing what needs to be done to maximize profits within the law, perhaps the stereotype American businessman. There is nothing wrong with his approach if Americans were to continue to view healthcare for those who can afford it, not as a right. After all, eating lots of fresh fruit is good for your health but fruit is expensive; the poor people can't afford to have everyone in their family eat fruit everyday, so their health is affected. And nobody suggested that we should provide fruit to everybody in equal amounts.

And yet, when all Americans are stressed once they are middle aged or beyond, how could we as a nation ignore that stress? Good stress motivates us to exercise; bad stress paralyzes us. This is not the good kind of stress that motivates us; it is a bad stress that eats on us like a cancer, and could cause cancer, heart disease and strokes. Just by removing the bad stress of not knowing if your healthcare will be there when you need it is enough argument to consider national health care insurance. If cost and quality and access would further improve through nationalized healthcare, why are we even arguing instead of doing it?

Business

Paul Ginsberg, President of the Center for Studying Health System Change, a nonpartisan Washington think tank was quoted "Everyone knows that GM and other automakers are looking for universal healthcare". General Motors was regarded non-competitive because of its enormous healthcare obligations. Eventually, GM succeeded to unload all its healthcare obligations of retirees to the unions.

Matt Miller, Senior Fellow at the Center for American Progress observed in Fortune "By shifting the financial burden to the population via the government, we would free business from the burden of financing healthcare. The boon for competitiveness, not to mention shareholder value and stock market, is obvious. Miller also observed a major myth in the airline industry that the model of major airlines was non-competitive with the likes of JetBlue. One of the airlines did a study that if all their employees were as young as say JetBlue and thus with lower cost for health care and other benefits, the loss of that airline at $388 million would swing to a profit of $420 million. "If we could fire all workers every five years, and hire younger ones, our model would look good." The point, of course, is that a company's financial success shouldn't depend on the age of its work-force.

National healthcare would remove this temptation of business to fire older employees. With national healthcare American businesses would also be relieved from an unfair cost disadvantage compared to businesses in other countries.

Solution:

We concluded that national healthcare insurance will remove bad stress from all Americans of middle age and older. It should cost less; provide better quality and access. Further, business would love to get the monkey of their back. If every-thing points to nationalizing healthcare insurance as the solution, what are we waiting for?

In a national healthcare insurance, the providers of the services would still be private. So would the equipment and other medical supply businesses. Manufac-turers of MRI or surgical equipment would still work with private hospitals and private doctors. The private providers would bill their services, provided to patients, to the government, and the government would pay them-without the profit motive of insurance companies. A peak at other countries does not indicate that medical doctors are starving there or that their hospital maintenance is ignored, to the contrary.

Who pays? An excellent article by Matt Miller in Fortune "Opening the Capi-talist Mind", argues that we need to raise taxes to pay for National Healthcare. But he points out that these taxes shouldn't be higher than the current cost we pay of premiums and out-of-pocket health care expenses. And if our healthcare cost will drop to the levels of other countries, those taxes will be far less than we pay on healthcare today.

Andy Grove, legendary and retired CEO of Intel Corporation, offered an interim solution. In an open letter to the Presidential Candidates, also published in Fortune, he proposed among others that the government should cover the cat-astrophic healthcare related expenditures, while private insurers could still cover the non-catastrophic part. His proposal would relieve about two of the five crite-ria. In addition, his proposal would also make the industry more competitive as the insured would be freer to move without worries about medical history. Andy's proposals will remove the profit incentive from finagling in catastrophic cases, and thus would remove the serious stress level on Americans.

National Healthcare Insurance or at a minimum Andy Grove's proposal would do much to bring justice to our nation's healthcare system.

CHAPTER 33

▼

MORE EFFECTIVE WEAPON
THAN LAWS

We observed that our famous American freedom has suffered as it buckles under the enormous amount of laws that have been written and continue to be written. With the rate of writing laws and ordinances by Congress, states, counties, cities and localities, we have become the most regulated country even among developed countries that have had lawmakers for a thousand years longer than we have. Our founders would have rolled over in their grave if they knew how we are killing that treasured freedom. They fought for freedom from the British and their hated laws. Yes, we are free from other nations but we have become enslaved to gazillions of laws of our own doing. All laws and ordinances were no doubt well intentioned but in the aggregate have killed a free America.

Many, many laws were imposed because politicians and interest groups, through lobbying money or votes, have manipulated our emotions. The argument: "If just one child is saved by this law, it is worth the restriction of freedom" is political hogwash that manipulates emotions falsely. There are more effective ways than laws to achieve the desired effectiveness without the need to impede freedom. Instead of prohibiting smoking by law, the anti-smoking campaign has been very successful. Remember the seventies when everybody used to smoke everywhere, in offices, restaurants, at home, in bars, buses and airplanes, you name it. Today, it is remarkable to see the difference. In the seventies smoking was cool. Today smokers are outcast! Yet, laws didn't achieve this, psychological campaigns designed to alter behavior achieved this success.

A long time ago, in 1919, Christian conservatives rammed through Congress and state legislatures the prohibition of alcohol. People wanted to drink nonetheless law or no law. It created major illegal operations, the mafia was flourishing, and it caused deaths and dismemberment of citizens who had their own little home distilleries exploding in their face. Shootouts between law enforcers and illegal traders were common. The Prohibition affected too many people negatively. Consequently Constitutional Amendment XXI repealed it in 1933. Comparatively, the anti-smoking method worked much better against abusive, harmful behavior. Did lawmakers learn? No, lawmakers can't help themselves. We know that they made laws discriminating against a minority of adults, the 18–21 year olds who are prohibited to drink. Does it help? Of course not. Without statistics to back it up, it seems that this age group drinks more because of these laws. Kids and especially young adults like to do what is forbidden; that's cool! Kids are much more inclined to follow behavioral psychology than laws that restrict their choices.

Smoking habits changed from cool to "uncool" in perhaps twenty-five years. It was a remarkable success that laws could never achieve. Sure, to avoid the immediate danger of second hand smoke, legal restrictions made it illegal to smoke in confined areas such as government offices, and public places such as restaurants and airplanes. However, lawmakers couldn't help themselves again. They kept piling up unreasonable additions to smoking laws that had little purpose but harassing adults and robbing them of their freedom to make a choice. The recent additions to smoking laws near buildings, in private cars, in parks, on beaches are examples of these maddening out-of-control laws that should have no place in a free American society. Common sense is lost among lawmakers. It might be useful to remind them that despite our anti-smoking efforts since the eighties, the American life expectancy is still well below those in Europe where people smoke like chimneys in every possible confined place. (It is only in the last few years that Europe began to place some limitations on smoking in restaurants).

Lawmakers' first job should be to protect our freedom and our founders' common sense. Perhaps we should change the name from lawmakers to law busters. Perhaps that would motivate them to reduce the number of laws on the books. Some argue that laws are cheaper than costly campaigns to alter behavior. They forget that nothing is more expensive to a free people than limiting their freedom. Besides, the consequences of laws are extremely expensive. Law enforcement and Social workers prove that. Lawsuits prove that. Court cases prove that. And the penal system proves that. In the end, bringing about change in attitudes is much cheaper than laws. We understand that the long process of behavioral change may require a law that alleviates immediate and serious concerns for safety. For this reason, smoking bans in confined places such as bars, office, airplanes, avoid that second hand smoke affects others in that confined area. Lawmakers should have stopped there.

Behavioral change by education does not impede freedom and should be ultimately preferred over laws. When baseball commissioner Bud Selig announced a contribution of one million to a non-profit that educates youngsters on the risks of performance enhancing drugs, he got it right.

To care about our freedom is to accept the choices other people make in their own lives even if that may make them less healthy. Or are we going to make laws against eating too much salt or eating at fast-food places? Smoking and other unhealthy habits are choices that people should be free to make as long as those choices do not violate the freedom of others. This may sound too much of a libertarian touch but what alternatives are preferable? To continue with more laws that eventually will put us all in a bubble? Lawmakers should begin to pay attention to the big picture of the inalienable right of freedom of the individual in the pursuit of happiness as they see it for themselves. Isn't this what our founders had in mind?

Teaching passion for freedom, especially of others should be one of the upper most important requirements in a school curriculum. Kids need to learn that freedom is the highest treasure for all adults and that the right to personal freedom goes hand in hand with a personal accountability for our actions, rejecting the pointing of fingers to others. They also need to learn that education is the strongest, most effective weapon to alter social behavior, occasionally aided by laws or other methods for immediate and serious concerns, but not to be superseded by them.

CHAPTER 34

▼

SOLUTIONS FOR JUSTICE

Our changing attitudes have affected our justice system. True justice got side-tracked more and more. Politicians have played callously to interest groups and their re-election campaigns by piling up laws upon laws without regard to the erosion of our freedom. Their callous attitude was influenced by an increasingly polarized political climate that lacked care for America and Americans born from a stubborn craving for extreme ideology.

It is vital that we return to two principles, America's treasured freedom and common sense to achieve fairness. These two principles should override political pet projects. We need to accept an "imperfect" world as created by God while pursuing the highest values of our nation, the pursuit of freedom, the original American Spirit, and fairness with common sense for all Americans.

The Civil Rights Act of 1964 was necessary. But subsequently handing out special, uniform rights by Congress and Supreme Court to every American (except white males between 18 and 40) was insane. Common sense was thrown out by Congress gone wild. It is nearly impossible to fire a female underperformer in government. Even in business it is difficult. We give rights to disabled people but don't care about the rights of small businesses. A small eatery on the second floor must install an elevator to accommodate wheelchairs and provide ramps. It makes no sense. But it does make sense to provide ramps and an elevator in large eateries where the cost would not be prohibitive. Common sense and judgment doesn't exist. Everything nowadays must go by the book, uniformly. This is not the American way.

In order to consistently achieve the highest values of our nation, it is vital that we change attitudes gone wrong over the last thirty years. First, the attitude of polarization in politics must make place for a willingness to work with political diversity. Second, the attitude of indifference must be changed by reintroducing the principle of fairness that will result in an attitude of care. Indifference is a killer that has caused the age of consumerism, excessive tort lawsuits, unbridled greed, unfair tax system, loss of social responsibility and job security as well as personal responsibility.

As long as these attitudes remain unchanged, how could we, for example, expect MADD, mothers against drunken drivers, to understand that their fight to prohibit young adults from drinking is causing more harm to society than good? It breeds indifference among our young adults because of the serious hypocrisy and discrimination by declaring them unfit to drink but fit to die for us in war. It attacked the freedom and fairness of a minority group of adults. MADD would need to be convinced that the importance of the principles of freedom and fairness overrides their relatively pettiness of "saving a few lives". Saving lives is important, of course, but not more important than the principles of freedom and fairness. Relative to those 850,000 Americans killed since 9/11 because of excessive salt in food, the savings of MADD are petty. Yet, neither MADD nor anybody else suggested laws against excessive salt. How would MADD understand that their noble fight for keeping drunken drivers off the road can be better fought through education, similar to the successes in anti smoking campaigns? Laws encourage kids to do what is forbidden? Education sticks.

Hypocritically, Congress sends our young adults to war yet requires that states enforce the discrimination against them; otherwise it withholds federal funding for the roads. In order to achieve fairness and freedom, much has to be changed.

We are not suggesting a libertarian view that prefers no laws at all. We need laws to avoid chaos, even to guarantee freedom and rights (of life and property), and to promote welfare and fairness.

To avoid chaos, we need rules of the road. Chaos is not conducive to a flourishing economy or a content society. But lawmakers always overstep the basic boundaries of necessity. Laws requiring pedestrians to stop for red pedestrian lights, even if there is an unobstructed view without traffic, lacks common sense and takes away our individual freedom to make personal safety decisions.

If Americans still believe that freedom is important, we should work towards removing thousands of freedom reducing laws on the books, and narrowing necessary laws from detailed uniformity to the simplicity and common sense of Common Law. We need to deregulate the preciseness of laws and regulations. Let's rekindle the spirit of freedom and require that Congress mandate government officials and judges use common sense in law, regulations, and in sentencing verdicts. Common sense requires judgment. Critics say that judgment opens up corruption but the gazillions of regulations on the books haven't prohibited corruption either. Most people are honest. Let's treat them as such and give them the power to use common sense. Common sense will save much money but the most important thing it will save is invaluable: Freedom.

It also means that we become less critical of the choices other people make in their own lives, even if that may make them less healthy. While this may sound textbook libertarianism, we have no choice but to think this way. Otherwise, continuation on our current path of creating more and more laws and regulations year in year out would eventually drown us all or at a minimum puts us all in a bubble.

Only through you, the voter, could this effort be accomplished by forming action committees for freedom, "Americans For Common Sense Laws".

It may be ironic to ask for laws when we just passionately asked to eliminate laws. But Congress should enact into law the following seven proposals that will help reduce the current abuses in the system of justice.

The first law would restore the long lost trait of taking responsibility for one's action. The law we need: To make apologies made to a victim inadmissible in court. This would encourage personal apologies without the fear that the apology could cost our personal fortune in court.

The second law needed is to limit tort charges to those who caused the wrong indirectly through explicit intent or gross negligence, or to those who directly committed the wrong; strict liability as a result of negligence by association should be banned.

The third law needed is to limit the plaintiffs to the victims who were deprived of income or wealth, or suffered emotional distress, and to the dependents of the victim whose standard of living was reduced or eliminated and/or suffered emotional distress.

The fourth law would limit damages awarded to the actual loss of income or wealth while emotional distress would be limited to a lifetime of psychological counseling (in cash or by trust); punitive damages should be unlimited but must be rewarded to the jurisdiction of the court, not to the victim or representing lawyers.

The fifth law would change the incompetent jury system to a professional jury system that will assure true justice instead of the crapshoot it is today.

The sixth new law would provide for national healthcare insurance (at a minimum for catastrophic healthcare). This would remake our unreliable, expensive and dysfunctional healthcare system but above all would reduce significant stress on the American people.

And the final new law would demand that all our laws and regulations are amended to return to common sense and judgment. We could avoid a nightmare in changeover by simply stating that judges and government officials are encouraged to use personal judgment in applying laws and regulations to promote common sense or to prevent undue burden on any party. This will return personal responsibility and accountability on judges and government officials.

All these seven new laws will promote fairness, care, common sense, reduce indifference in attitudes and reduce lawsuits while setting the stage for the return of the famous yet long lost American spirit.

Interest groups, such as the legal profession, and those receiving lobbying money from that profession will cry murder. They will predict a downfall of our nation. They will argue that poor victims will not be able to get fair compensation though the legal system. This is nonsense. It is the lawyers that will loose fat fees, but Americans and America will benefit. It will also restore the ability for counties and cities to return to common sense because it would eliminate the current insanity of frivolous lawsuits against them.

Conclusions

America is a great country. Yet, anything great can be destroyed. Bad attitudes can destroy great things. People with bad attitudes will always exist. But never before did so many terrible attitudes exist among so many groups of Americans as today. Over the last thirty years these wrong attitudes have become so pervasive that America's greatness and prosperity will fall behind other countries unless major and heroic efforts reverse the trend.

Two of the most destructive attitudes that largely developed over the last thirty five years are unhealthy, unconstrained greed and indifference towards the general welfare of America's future and the welfare of Americans. They destroyed something precious that existed in our country just a mere twenty years to thirty ago: Fairness towards other Americans. These terrible attitudes penetrated Wall Street, politicians, talk shows, CEOs, lawyers and others who have taken advantage of every opportunity to get rich regardless of the harm it caused our country or the American middle class.

The indifference on the top rubbed off on Americans with stagnant incomes and without job or retirement security but who noticed with envy the enormous wealth made on the top. Getting rich no matter how has become the rage. Gambling has intensified, Internet scams have blossomed, mortgage brokers sold their soul, and identity thefts turned epidemic to a point that nobody trusts anybody anymore.

Indifference has caused tremendous harm to our country. The resulting consumerism and obsession about materialism replaced the family as the source of happiness. Few stories make that more clear than a recent article by Peter Hong in the LA Times about homeowners in Las Vegas. The following are excerpts:

> Unless homes were constructed in the last two years, properties are outdated and more difficult to sell. One developer recently opened a new neighborhood of homes for $1.7 million to $3 million. Several buyers lived in adjacent neighborhoods where homes were less than five years old; they felt their residence was obsolete. An architect was quoted that some people build houses (to live in) as often as they buy cars.

Many Americans talk with contempt about other countries and show more arrogance towards foreigners than thirty years ago. But our nation has less and less to be proud off. Our economy is permanently on the decline relative to Asian countries and our freedom has been severely curtailed by the most bloated and overregulated bureaucracy in the Western world. Lawmakers have become indifferent to America's original spirit when they promote laws and regulations that cater to powerful lobbyists regardless of the harm it causes America. Our heralded system of justice is no longer designed to serve justice but designed to serve uniformity that by nature is unfair, unjust.

Curing these destructive ills in our society is complicated. These bad attitudes have grown into giant squids that with arms and tentacles have caught all facets of life as their prey. Curing one problem might cause another problem. Therefore, before we attempt to cure the ills, we need to understand all the causes that are for the most part described in this book.

The good news is that most Americans sense that something has gone badly wrong and that we must change. In his recent book <u>Truth and Consequences</u>, Keith Olbermann exposed lies and deceptions of the Bush Administration that make us long for a new person in the White House. Our political candidates for President, campaign on the promise of change. But change from what? Is a change from George Bush all we need? If it were that simple! Merely replacing Bush would ignore the causes that put George Bush in the White House in the first place. Without solving those causes, American voters would repeat the same mistake. We need to understand how it was possible that the American voters elected George Bush, not once but twice.

A quick overview of his accomplishments points to the absence of a repeat of 9/11. Luck or ability? Let's be positive and recognize this as an accomplishment of the Bush Administration. For the rest we can talk all day about his inability to walk the talk and his incompetent leadership. Critics point out that Mr. Bush campaigned on being a "uniter" but in countless speeches by him and the Vice

President, Democrats were purposefully alienated. That's the other half of all Americans. Difficult to recognize that as an effort to unite. Instead it polarized the country in partisanship. After billions of dollars, Mr. Bush lauded Homeland Security into a sure thing for national pride, until hurricane Katrina proved its ineptness. As Jared Diamond pointed out, Mr. Bush seemed unable to think beyond 90 days. Mr. Bush campaigned on huge tax cuts because President Clinton had run a budget surplus. But by the time President Bush submitted his huge tax cuts package to Congress, the economy was faltering and the surplus disappeared. Apparently he couldn't foresee beyond 90 days that the changing economy couldn't afford the huge tax cuts he promised. When oil prices turned excessive, President Bush promoted the use of corn for ethanol but apparently couldn't foresee that this diversion of corn would do great damage to the world food supply and caused subsequent huge price increases that are choking the world's poor. He rightfully decided to punish the Taliban but when he invaded Iraq, there was no evidence of plans beyond 90 days of what to do with Iraq once Iraq's army was defeated. The successes of China's long-term strategies surprised many but the White House offered no plans that would counter China's threat to our economic leadership. We assume that the reason for lack of good plans is that they would have to go well beyond 90 days.

In summary, a guy who lacks the ability to unite the country and lacks leadership ability is not a guy we should have put in the White House. What qualifications attracted voters? Voters apparently chose him over Al Gore because Bush is a guy you could have a beer with and he is very religious, overlooking the nuisance that he could barely construct a proper sentence in English. Of course, in 2000 the electorate didn't know that he wouldn't live up to his promise to unite the country and that he was less than competent but in 2004 the electorate did know his significant failings. Yet, he was re-elected. Many voters said because he favored a constitutional ban on gay marriage, and because his supporters slandered a war hero opponent (John Kerry). That's how shallow America has become. Never mind that Osama bin Laden was still free, al Qaeda was getting stronger, Iraq was a mess, savings rates were negative, oil prices were up, there was a federal borrowing epidemic, China was challenging our prosperity, and we lost vital goodwill in the world.

President George W. Bush' tenure proved that religious leaders, who urge their followers to vote only for the most religious person, contribute to the downfall of America. In Matthew 6:24 Jesus said "No one can serve two masters. Either he will hate the one and love the other, or he will be devoted to the one and despise the other. You cannot serve both God and mammon." Politics is mostly about the mammon. The President of the United States must serve the mammon only. It is not his job to follow the bible. It is his job to improve the economy, to provide fairness to all Americans, to improve job security for American workers, to secure our borders, to abide by the Constitution.

Here we are in 2008. Our country needs change. When we listen to political candidates, the wrong changes are discussed. If the debate isn't about staying in or withdrawing from Iraq, we hear that the new villains are illegal immigrants, globalization and NAFTA. These are not the villains and the tinkering with it that some of our representatives propose will not pull America out of a slowly sinking morass.

The real changes we need are discussed in this book; the major ones are summarized below.

We need a President with strong charisma and leadership to unite the political left and right, and inspire the country, including Congress. We need a President who can think and act beyond 90 days and craft the right vision for America's future. That requires an unusual and smart individual, and is unlikely a person we could have a beer with.

We need a new mindset that all Americans together are America. It is not just the conservatives or the liberals that are the true Americans. We all are. If we continue polarized as we are, we can't keep America great. But united, we can. Just as in business we may have different thoughts about how to achieve our goals, but we agree to work together, united as a team. And so, liberals and conservatives must work in bi-partisanship. My definition of a true patriot is not one who waves the flag and criticizes other Americans:

> Being a true American patriot means that America comes first in everything we do. It's not our personal interests that come first or our party's interest, no, the interest of all Americans and we are willing to sacrifice for it.

Isn't that what our soldiers do? Isn't that what anti-war protesters believe they do? Yes, even anti-war protesters who sacrifice are patriots more so than those highly paid talk-show hosts who pretend to be patriots while basking in luxury, whining about one party or the other, sacrificing nothing.

The change of mindset we need begins with conservatives respecting liberals, and with liberals respecting conservatives. This also means that Congress must begin to care about what really counts. It means that they stop doling out pork such as $400 million bridges to nowhere in Alaska while the levies around New Orleans are still not strong enough to withstand another Katrina. Has Congress no shame?

The President, Congress and action groups must restore fairness for all Americans, the kind of fairness that existed some decades ago but got lost. Most Americans work hard yet for little security and haven't shared for decades in the wealth that our country produces in a global environment. Yet, wealth is piled up on wealth at the top where dynasties are built, and on average are only taxed at 17.5% (federal income taxes) while the middle class pays well over 35% in payroll taxes (including social security taxes). America's income gap and wealth gap is the unhealthiest of any developed country in the world, a sure sign that our country is on a path to misery. It is irrefutable that fairness got lost indeed.

Fairness must be regained. It will take several steps. Congress must first change the tax code by raising the marginal income tax sharply for outrageous incomes from professions, as proposed in this book. This would seriously discourage the current race by CEOs to get the most exorbitant pay package. The main purpose of the change in tax code is to achieve a more normal ratio of average CEO pay to the pay of the average worker, the way it used to be in the nineteen sixties or seventies. This will muzzle the unrestrained, unbridled greed on the top. It will also turn bad attitudes around. Once Americans believe that incomes on the top are becoming reasonable again, relative to the workers' income, the current negative attitude of indifference across the board will begin to disappear.

Further, Wall Street must change its focus from quarterly earnings to long-term earnings. The obsession in public companies to meet Wall Street's quarterly earnings estimates has been counter productive for business and the American worker. Congress and the media should keep the heat on Wall Street to accomplish reform. One suggestion is that Wall Street eliminates the quarterly earnings estimates from its radar screen. Let investors judge the soundness of earnings releases for themselves without comparison to the Street's expectations. If necessary, though undesirable, the SEC could remove the requirements for public companies to release quarterly earnings.

For over 200 years America has been a free country from its oppressor, Great Britain. But for Americans there is more to freedom than being free from foreign oppression. The Bill of Rights spells out guarantees of freedoms against an oppressor, the government. When these rights were crafted there were few laws. They didn't limit the general freedom of Americans. Common Law that America inherited from England is based on common sense and has the capacity to ensure fairness for all Americans. Common Law was the dominating philosophy of our legal system and continued so for the first hundred years. Detailed laws and regulations were anathema to the original American spirit. But over the last fifty years Congress and the Courts decided differently. They succeeded in screwing up the legal system by removing common sense and replacing it with the most detailed regulations anywhere found in the developed world. Not only does legislation limit our freedom, the number of possible situations is infinite and therefore uniform regulations cannot fairly provide justice. Common Law in America now exists only in name. Fairness and common sense no longer exist. We need them back.

The new President and Congress must authorize Government officials to use their judgment of common sense in every situation for the purpose of achieving fairness and efficiency, even if such judgment of common sense "violates" existing laws and regulations. But because the "squid of bad attitudes" has its tentacles in every facet of life, Congress and Supreme Court must instruct judges to throw out lawsuits that would be filed as a result of government officials waiving certain regulations in an attempt to speed up decisions and use judgment of common sense. An example illustrates the point. Suppose a charity wants to upgrade an old building to provide shelter for homeless people, and suppose that local officials issued a common sense waiver from cost prohibitive ADA requirements to install ramps and elevators in old buildings when upgrading. With the present mentality of filing lawsuits at a whim, we can be assured that in such case lawsuits would be filed by some homeless or other individuals, demanding compensation because ADA regulations were violated.

It is as simple as that to help the country regain a sense of fairness and common sense in justice and government services. It also would gain tremendously in the efficiency of our government that seems to be controlled by loggerheads but whose hands instead are in fact tied by regulations.

Next, to secure jobs for Americans in the future, the new President and Congress must accelerate development of new technologies of promising new industries such as renewable energies, green environment, biomedical advances, and groundbreaking automobile technologies. This acceleration of technology development must go hand in hand with the requirement that companies who benefit from these new technologies must produce their products on American soil, thus providing great paying jobs with job security to Americans for as long as these industries have a competitive advantage (usually for the duration of broad world-wide patents).

The President must also tackle our addiction to foreign oil and reduce harmful pollution. More nuclear power plants will do both, and could replace dirty-coal burners to generate electricity. According to environmentalist Laurie David in Discover Magazine, burning coal releases particulates that kill 24,000 Americans annually. Nuclear power plants in America haven't killed anyone and the new designs are safer than ever. For the near term we must drastically increase minimum gas mileage for SUVs and promote European style diesel engines that reduce emissions, and increase mileage. For the long term, the new Chief Executive should decide on standardization of the best renewable energies that will transform our country. Let's avoid another cell-phone or broadband network disaster in America that lacked standards and put America behind most other countries that had a long-term vision. We need a White House and Congress that can think beyond 90 days.

If all these proposals were enacted, the current devastating trend in the widening income and wealth gap in America will be reversed and will restore our sense for social responsibility and accountability in the corporate office, in Congress and in the White House. That alone could avoid an "uprising by Americans" as Alan Greenspan predicted as a possibility.

But to secure our prosperity and cement fairness, more action is needed from Congress and the new President. There is one sickness in our modern culture, the inability of most people in our nation to accept responsibility for their action, and apologize. Instead we have become experts at blaming others. Listen to popular talk shows. Even President Bush doesn't know how to apologize sincerely. He had ample opportunity. Instead he habitually put blame on certain Americans, guess who, and divided America through deceptive speeches. He could have sincerely apologized for the serious mismanagement of Iraq, or for the incredible ineptness of government in the New Orleans disastrous fiasco.

What caused this national trend of replacing personal responsibility with the blaming of others? The main culprit of this attitude is in our system of justice. Admitting guilt through apologies prior to trial is not working to our advantage in a lawsuit and because lawsuits have become commonplace in American society, we have learned that it is far safer to deny responsibility; thus creating a culture of denial. Congress should decide on an easy solution by making apologies, including acts of compassion, inadmissible in court during a trial. Further, after a guilty verdict but prior to sentencing, the court should now admit apologies that were made prior to a trial as a mitigating factor in punishment. In other words, upon an accident or other wrong committed you are better off apologizing than withholding it. This will get Americans in the habit of apologizing and thus taking responsibility instead of playing the blame game. We could now say, without fear for legal repercussion "I am really sorry that this happened because I didn't pay attention; this has taught me a lesson, what can I do to help?"

There is more that needs change in the current system of justice. If we want true justice, and who wouldn't want that, why do we put up with a flawed jury system? Some people consider our current jury system as an untouchable gift from our founders. The jury system wasn't the real gift. The real gift was to provide true justice for all Americans irrespective of their background. If we were to get our day in court, we should all be assured that a competent jury would not be swayed by the well-developed psychology of modern practitioners of the law. We deserve competent jurors and we can change the system to achieve that as outlined in this book.

Our country is the most litigious country in the world. Besides that it has given us a bad reputation, fear for lawsuits dominates many lives. It is unhealthy, expensive, and frankly one of the most deplorable traits of American society that has little to do with justice. Congress and the new President can easily stop this excessive nuisance by removing or drastically capping jury awards for emotional distress and punitive damages, and further by limiting liability of parties that are indirectly responsible. Lawyers (and many representatives in Congress) will fight this proposal but you the voter can demand this action from your representative. Further, there is little justice in most class-action lawsuits. Besides the fact that they hurt American competitiveness in this global world, most of these suits target the innocent party with deep pockets, rather than the truly guilty parties.

We know that we need change in foreign relations. Foreign countries need to accept us as the world leader; otherwise we will not achieve our goals. While our President needs to lead the way, our personal attitude counts too. Arrogant attitudes towards foreigners are not helping us. Turning the world around will be a tough job after seven years of our bewildering foreign policy. Foreign nations just don't trust America anymore. That has hurt America in many ways, not just economically, but for example our ability to hunt down Osama bin Laden and destroy al Qaeda, or to contain nuclear proliferation. Once we have a clear energy policy that will reduce our dependence from foreign countries, we must begin to walk the talk of American values and win over the minds abroad, especially those from Islamic countries. Just a change in their mindset alone could put an end to Islamic terror against America. In the meantime, we could build thousands of Boys & Girls Clubs in Pakistan and Afghanistan for a tiny fraction of the war cost in Iraq, and gain hugely in the mindset of Muslims.

Lastly, we need to address the mystique surrounding the strange decisions that Americans make at the voting booth. Polls show that roughly 70% of Americans speak with contempt about our Congress and President. But who put them in their position of power? The only explanation for this paradox is that Americans are easily misled. Most of us are gullible because as a nation we are politically underdeveloped, a result of our culture that shuns political debate. With our votes we steer America's future, an awful responsibility yet we are not qualified to exercise this responsibility. In business or at home, we are the smart ones. In politics we are not. The proof is in the pudding when we look who is in the White house and in Congress. Let's accept the fact that politicians, advertisements, partisan talk show hosts and other partisan media have misled us and that the only way to exercise our responsibility is to become smarter in politics so that we make the right choices and see through the deception of politicians in whom we believe.

If we truly care about America, and what American doesn't, let's take our responsibility more seriously and become politically savvy. We all agree that it is change that we need. Let's begin with us. We need to change our cultural habit of avoiding political debate.

Let's plan to talk politics as often as we tell jokes or as often we talk about golf or business or children or cooking. It doesn't matter with whom as long as we get into the habit. Of course, discussing politics with people who agree with us will soon become boring. Therefore, we need to seek debate with those with different views. Let's make it fun. Arrange parties for the purpose of talking politics, and require that participants maintain humor, just like the late William F. Buckley Jr. did. Use the time during lunch, dinner or airplanes, and include foreigners. The key is to develop our sense for politics and to know when political ads or smooth talkers on talk shows manipulate us. To jumpstart political knowledge of America's next generation, let's demand non-partisan political debate in elementary school. Once we become politically savvy, we'll get tired of partisan talk shows and smear ads. More importantly, we will choose the politicians that are most qualified to lead us away from a sinking morass to continued prosperity for us and especially for our children.

Our new President will be key in leading the process of change. But he/she alone will be powerless without the help of concerned Americans. What can and will we do to help reverse the trend of America's decline and return America to glory? What will you do? We can't wait until it is too late. Here is an idea. Pick a topic of interest from this book and start, or join, a political action group that will focus on change, the right change. Change begins with us!

978-0-595-52110-4
0-595-52110-X

www.ingramcontent.com/pod-product-compliance
Lightning Source LLC
Chambersburg PA
CBHW022244290526
45785CB00015B/166